Essential
HORSE HEALTH

The most common equine health problems solved

Essential
HORSE HEALTH

The most common equine
health problems solved

Kieran O'Brien MRCVS

David and Charles

Dedication

To my parents Michael and Margaret O'Brien

A DAVID & CHARLES BOOK
Copyright © David & Charles Limited 2007

David & Charles is an F+W Publications Inc. company
4700 East Galbraith Road
Cincinnati, OH 45236

First published in the UK in 2007

Text copyright © Kieran O'Brien 2007
Photographs copyright © Kieran O'Brien except those from sources
cited on page 158 and front cover photograph copyright © Horsepix
Page 6,7 photograph by Matt Roberts copyright © David & Charles
Illustrations on pages 18 (top left, bottom right), 18 (top right), 42 (bottom left),
43, 48, 53, 59, 63, 83, 86, 88, 107, 113, 116, 141 by Maggie Raynor

Kieran O'Brien has asserted his right to be identified as author of
this work in accordance with the Copyright, Designs and Patents Act, 1988.

A catalogue record for this book is available from the British Library.

ISBN-13: 978-0-7153-2542-1 hardback
ISBN-10: 0-7153-2542-6 hardback

Printed in China by Shenzhen Donnelley Printing Co Ltd
for David & Charles
Brunel House   Newton Abbot   Devon

Commissioning Editor Jane Trollope
Editor Jennifer Fox-Proverbs
Editorial Assistant Emily Rae
Designer Jodie Lystor
Production Controller Beverley Richardson

Visit our website at www.davidandcharles.co.uk

David & Charles books are available from all good bookshops; alternatively you
can contact our Orderline on 0870 9908222 or write to us at FREEPOST EX2 110,
D&C Direct, Newton Abbot, TQ12 4ZZ (no stamp required UK only); US customers
call 800-289-0963 and Canadian customers call 800-840-5220.

Contents

FOREWORD

Experience shows that well-informed horse owners and keepers are less likely to delay in seeking veterinary attention for their animals and are more likely to follow any instructions given by their veterinarian.

The purpose of this book to give practical advice on how to proceed in a variety of the most common clinical situations encountered by the average horse owner. I have omitted many of the less common conditions. Every case is different and many problems require trained and experienced clinical judgement. In case of doubt always seek veterinary advice.

THE LAME HORSE – LOCATING THE PROBLEM

Lameness is the commonest veterinary disorder of the horse. This chapter will help you to locate the site of the problem and to decide whether it is something you can deal with yourself or whether you should obtain veterinary assistance to make a final diagnosis and administer treatment. If an obvious external injury is visible or a traumatic event (for example a kick) has been witnessed, then finding the site of lameness is easy. But often there is no such evidence; the horse is merely noticed to be lame when, for example, brought in from a field or being ridden.

LAMENESS – KEY POINTS

- The key to lameness diagnosis is to **first find the site**, and **then find the cause**.
- Horses' legs come in pairs: always compare any suspected abnormalities with the same region on the opposite leg.
- As a general rule 90 per cent of fore limb lamenesses are sited below the knee, whereas in the hind limb the hock or the foot are frequently the source of pain.

Making an initial assessment

Use the following questions to help you to decide what is likely to be wrong:

How long has he been lame?

If there is no evidence of an external injury, the duration of the lameness may give a clue as to its cause. Foot abscesses tend to worsen quickly in that the horse may be a little unsound in the morning but very lame by the evening or the next morning. Long-standing conditions, such as *arthritis* of the limb joints and navicular syndrome, tend to wax and wane, often with periods of virtual soundness interspersed with episodes of lameness or stiffness of varying severity. Sometimes, in the early stages of arthritis, the horse will 'warm out' of the condition when exercised and be virtually sound. However, eventually no improvement in lameness will occur during exercise. Often if the horse is worked hard it will be obviously lame the next day.

Has he been shod recently?

Lameness due to shoeing may occur either immediately afterwards if one or more of the horse's feet have been radically trimmed or if a nail has been driven close to the sensitive laminae, alternatively it may present at any time up to three weeks after shoeing if an abscess develops as a consequence of a misdirected nail (see p.26).

Did lameness occur during or after exercise?

Tendon and suspensory ligament injuries that occur when the horse is exercising tend to cause lameness immediately afterwards. In less severe cases, however, lameness may not be apparent in the horse until several hours after exercise.

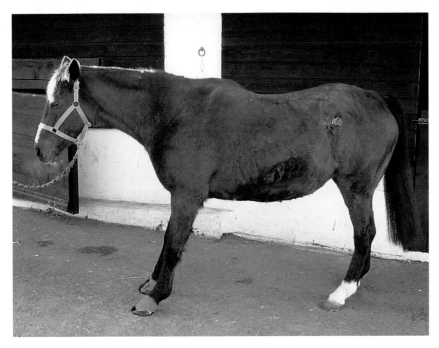

This pony has had laminitis in both fore feet for three weeks and is in moderate pain. It has shifted its weight backwards to off-load the fore feet

How is he standing?

Watch the horse quietly for a few moments – he may lift the lame limb for a few seconds to unload it before replacing it. Conversely horses with mild lameness may stand normally.

Fore limb lameness of moderate severity may cause the horse to stand with the lame limb slightly in front of the opposite sound one (pointing), to reduce the pain by unloading the leg. A horse may attempt to unload a lame hind limb by resting it for an abnormally long time or by bringing it further under the body. A very painful heel region (for example caused by an infected corn or a stone lodged between the frog and the shoe) might cause the horse to stand with the knee or hock slightly flexed when viewed from the side. Horses with chronically painful heels, such as in navicular disease, may stand with bedding stacked under their heels to raise them slightly.

If all four limbs are painful (for example in laminitis) the horse will stand with all of its limbs extended and its bodyweight leaning backwards.

Laminitis cases will regularly shift weight from one leg to another.

Is there any visible evidence of the problem?

With the horse standing square, look at him from in front, from each side and from behind in order to compare the size and shape (the symmetry) of each of the limbs. When viewing from the rear it is helpful to lift the tail to one side.

- **Swollen limb** Inflammation, a wound, bruising or infection may cause a limb to swell. Foot abscesses of more than a few days duration may cause swelling from the coronet up to the knee or hock. Infection spreading from a puncture wound on a limb will cause a painful swelling around the infected area, which expands over a few days up and down the limb if the infection is not treated. Lymphangitis will cause marked and painful swelling of the affected limb from the coronet upwards, initially in the lower limb and later extending upwards to the elbow or stifle (see 'Filled legs', p.10).

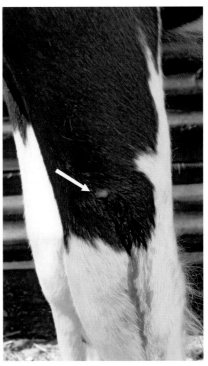

A kick on the left forearm three days ago resulted in a small wound (arrowed) that has become infected, causing a swollen forearm and moderate lameness in walk. Antibiotic treatment resolved the condition

- **Localised swelling** Tendon, check and suspensory ligament injuries will cause swelling behind the cannon bone only. In joint infections or inflammation there may be a enlargement of the fibrous capsule around a joint due to the production of excess joint fluid.

9

FILLED LEGS

Filling (swelling) of one or more legs is an important clinical sign in lame horses. Ask these questions:

- **Is the filled leg(s) painful to touch if gently squeezed with the fingertips?** Filling due to the benign accumulation of lymphatic fluid (oedema) – for example in a box-rested horse's hind legs – is painless. Painful filling suggests inflammation (and often infection) in the affected area.

- **Does the filling disappear completely with exercise?**
  If yes, it indicates that the filling is benign and may be due to immobility.

- **Is more than one limb involved?** If all four limbs are filled it suggest the horse is suffering from some systemic disease (for example, EHV infection, p.72) and the leg filling is a secondary sign.

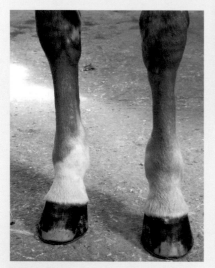

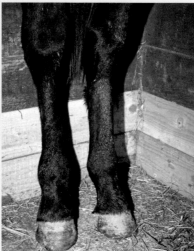

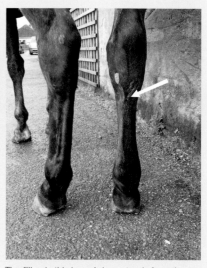

Both hind legs in this horse are filled from the coronet to mid cannon because it has been standing in its stable for 24 hours. The swelling, which is cold and painless to touch (cold oedema), will disappear with exercise. It is likely that the filling is purely due to lack of movement

This horse's right pastern and fetlock are filled in comparison with the opposite leg. The filling is painless on finger pressure. It is likely that there is inflammation in the foot (for example a foot abscess), and the filling reflects an increased blood supply

The filling in this horse's leg extends from the fetlock to the hock. Because the pastern is not swollen, an inflamed foot is not the cause. The swollen area is painful to touch, suggesting that an infection is present there. A small wound was found (arrow)

Are there any clues in his conformation?

If the cannon bones are offset relative to the forearm and the knee (bench knees), the horse will be predisposed to splints (see p.55). Horses that turn their toes inwards (pigeon-toed) or outwards are prone to developing sidebones, lower limb joint arthritis and soft tissue injuries in this region.

Horses with abnormal feet, those with a poor shape and those that are unbalanced may also suffer with problems (see 'The foot and foot balance', and 'Foot balance problems', pp.18–20). Feet with flat, thin soles are more likely to be bruised.

Although poor conformation may predispose a horse to injury, those with perfect conformation can still develop problems due to trauma or wear and tear.

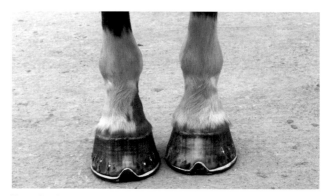

These fore feet are not a matching pair. The horse has been lame in the right limb for several months due to pastern joint arthritis. The reduced loading of this limb has caused the foot to become more upright and narrower

Assessing how the horse moves

The next step is to confirm which leg(s) the horse is lame on. Good control is essential. Use a bridle, Chiffney bit or nose chain if necessary to ensure the horse walks and trots in hand under control and at the speed required. If possible, make the assessment on a level, firm non-slip surface, such as tarmac or concrete.

(consistent with good restraint) so as not to interfere with its free movement (nodding).

If a horse is trotted *too fast* a mild lameness may be masked. Sometimes it is helpful to trot up or down a hill to accentuate a subtle lameness.

Trotting on a *soft surface* may make foot lamenesses disappear or become less obvious, but some lamenesses, for example suspensory problems, may be worse on soft going.

Watch from in front and from the side, to compare the *stride length*, and the *arc of flight* of the limbs. Horses that are lame on both forelimbs tend to have a restricted 'pottery' gait in front when trotted.

In hind limb lameness the stride length is often shorter (the horse doesn't track up) on the lame leg. If the horse is heard to catch its hind toe (due to a reluctance fully to flex the limb joints), careful watching should reveal which leg is involved.

- **Walk the horse quietly on a loose rein**. From the side, watch and compare the stride length of each fore and hind limb.
- **Walk the horse in a small circle**, ideally on a slope, and compare the response in both directions. Watch for the horse lifting its head as it tries to unload the lame leg when it is on the inside. With painful foot conditions, such as laminitis, circling often significantly increases the degree of lameness.
- **Trot the horse on the same firm surface**. Trotting is the best gait for assessing lameness as it is a two-beat movement, i.e. the horse has only one leg supporting the lame leg as that diagonal pair hits the ground. The handler should face forward and not look at the horse. The horse's head should be as loose as possible

Which leg is lame

A horse may be lame on more than one leg, and interpretation of what you see can be very difficult. In mild lameness it takes time and lots of practice to get good at spotting the lame leg, especially if it is a hind limb. Follow this sequence:

- **Walk** Watch the horse being walked in a straight line and in small circles in both directions.
- **Trot away** Have the horse trotted in a straight line away from you, watching (and comparing) first look at the movement of the points of the hips and then the movement of the head.
- **Trot back** Have the horse trotted back towards you, looking at first the head and then the points of the hips.
- **Trot past** Watch the horse trot past in both directions, noting both the stride length (in comparison with the opposite leg) and how much each leg is flexed. Watch for any 'catching' of the hind toes.

Drawing a conclusion

In *fore limb lameness* the head will nod as the horse trots. While watching the head, out of the corner of your eye see which foreleg is out in front when the horse nods. It is the opposite foreleg that is lame.

In *hind limb lameness*, concentrate on the points of the hips, which rock up and down alternately, as the horse trots away. In the sound horse the amount of vertical movement on each side is the same. If the horse is lame behind, the amount of up and down movement on the lame side is greater. This system is in general more reliable than looking for a 'hip hike' or 'dropping of the hip', as both of these phenomena can be very misleading. Sometimes a horse that nods at the trot may be lame behind. More severe hind limb lamenesses may cause a horse to nod its head as the opposite (diagonal) forelimb is extended, because the horse is attempting to throw its weight forward onto this forelimb. It is essential to evaluate the hindquarters carefully every time you look at a lame horse.

And if you are still not sure...?

- Try lungeing the horse on a firm, non-slip surface. This may accentuate the lameness, making it easier to determine the lame leg (but see below).
- You can also repeat the straight-line examination with a rider on board (on a loose rein).

BRIDLE LAMENESS

Sometimes the horse appears to nod its head while being ridden on the bit. If the rider relaxes the contact, the lameness disappears. This is a normal phenomenon seen in some horses and is not true lameness.

EXAMINING THE LAME LEG

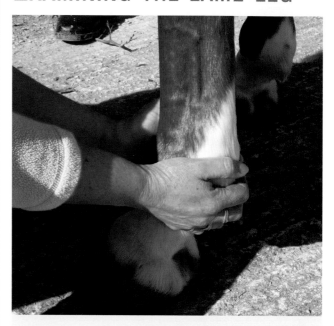

1 Feel the whole limb and foot for heat, swelling or tenderness to touch. Always compare it with the opposite leg. Carefully note if any of the joints are filled.

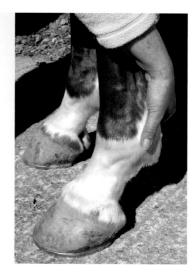

2 Check the strength of the pulse in the digital arteries on each side of the fetlock and compare it with the other three legs. The leg must be weight-bearing. Only light pressure is necessary and you must be patient as a horse's heart rate is quite slow. (See 'Examining the foot', step 2, p.14.)

3 Pick up the foot and squeeze the pastern, then rotate the pastern joints to check for pain ('the doorknob test').

4 Flex the fetlock joint. A horse should not resent this procedure. Compare the response with that in the opposite fetlock.

5 Facing forwards, feel the cannon region carefully with the limb supported, checking for any heat or pain. Feel each of the flexor tendons and the suspensory ligament for swelling, tenderness or abnormal softness. Some normal horses that are working on hard ground, jump frequently or do a lot of fast work may show increased sensitivity to tendon pressure with the fingertips but the response will be the same in both forelimbs. Press the splint region firmly inside and outside to check for pain.

6 Flex the knee to check for resistance to flexion (left). It should be possible to touch the elbow with the heel without any restriction or any resentment from the horse. Press the knee joints with the fingertips to check for pain in that area (right).

EXAMINING THE FOOT

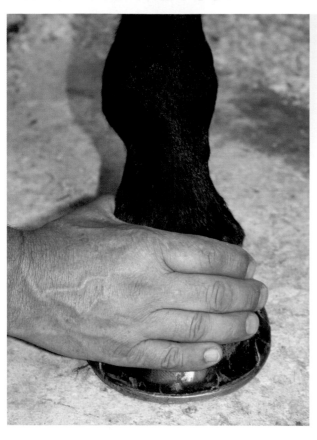

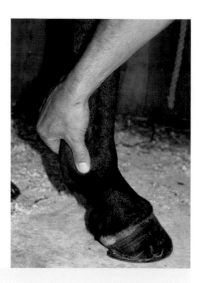

1 Compare the temperature of the hoof with the opposite hoof. Notes: absence of heat does not mean that the foot is not the site of the problem. Some apparently normal horses have fore feet of different temperatures.

2 Feel the strength of the pulse in the digital arteries on each side of the fetlock and compare it with the other three legs. The leg must be weight-bearing and the horse must not be excited or recently exercised. Only light pressure is necessary – be patient as a horse's heart rate is quite slow. In normal horses the pulse is very faint and may be hard to feel. If the foot (or feet) is inflamed, the digital pulse will be stronger and the artery may feel enlarged. A strong digital pulse is common in many foot diseases and is not specific for any of them.

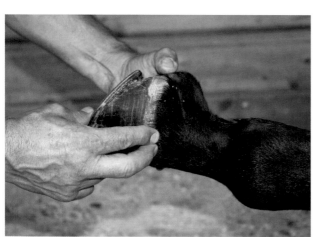

3 Pick up the foot and, using the fingertips, carefully press the coronet all around to find a sore spot, indicating that a foot abscess may be about to burst through.

4 Check the sole carefully for any foreign bodies lodged there. Here a pair of hoof testers is used to locate a painful area for further investigation. Gentle tapping of the sole with a small hammer may also reveal a tender spot.

What the vet will do

As well as making the assessments already described, a vet may also watch the horse being lunged and perform flexion tests.

Lungeing

Lungeing on a firm non-slip surface is very useful because loading on the inside fore and hind limbs is increased, often making subtle lameness more obvious. It is essential to lunge the horse in both directions as many horses are lame on both fore limbs although they may appear lame on a single leg, or not lame at all, when trotted in a straight line.

If lungeing causes the horse to be more lame on the outside leg, conditions affecting the inside of the outside leg, such as corns, or upper suspensory ligament disease, should be considered.

Lungeing on a hard surface is very useful in lameness assessment. The horse should trot slowly, and the surface should be non-slip

Flexion tests

Holding the limb flexed for 30–60 seconds increases pressure within the joints and stretches the structures around them, possibly accentuating a subtle lameness and assisting the location of the site of lameness. Comparing the response of the opposite leg, repeating the flexion test after exercise and with a rider on board, may provide additional information.

Flexion tests are fraught with difficulties in interpretation. The age and previous use of the horse, and the way with which the test is performed (amount of force, duration, consistency in technique), may influence the results especially if performed in sound horses at pre-purchase veterinary examinations. For this reason flexion tests should only be performed by experienced veterinarians.

A flexion test. Any resentment shown by the horse to its limb being held flexed in this way may be significant

FURTHER INVESTIGATION

Often it is not possible to determine the site of pain in a limb without resort to more sophisticated techniques, which range from nerve blocks to x-rays and studying the limbs using various diagnostic imaging systems that have become available to vets through advances in human medicine.

Nerve and joint blocks

Nerve blocks aim to abolish pain in very specific regions. A local anaesthetic is injected around a nerve supplying the region, or into a joint or tendon sheath. The horse is trotted or lunged once the block has taken effect (5–30 minutes). If the horse improves then the cause of lameness can be said, at least in part, to be located in the region or joint blocked.

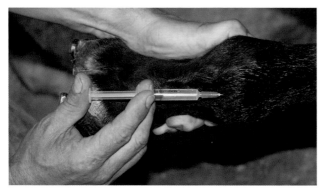

A nerve block. Anaesthetic solution is being injected around the nerves on each side of the fetlock to anaethetise the foot in a case of suspected foot lameness. The horse will be trotted after 10 minutes to see if the lameness has disappeared, confirming that the problem is in the foot

Usually starting at the foot (sometimes each of its three components separately), the clinician moves up the leg selectively anaesthetising different zones until the horse becomes sound. It is then possible to further investigate the region by x-rays, ultrasound, MRI scans, and so on.

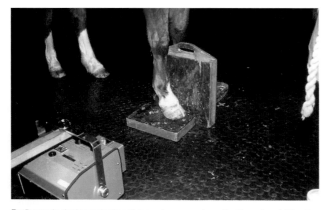

Radiography is the mainstay of many lameness investigations. In addition to fractures, it enables the visualisation of arthritis, bone disease and infections

Ultrasound scanning

Soft (non-bony) tissues will not be visualised on an x-ray and are principally investigated using ultrasound. This technique is especially useful for imaging the tendons and ligaments of the lower limb although it has been used to evaluate joints, suspected fractures, back problems, pregnancy and ovulation, and eye diseases.

A horse receiving an ultrasound examination

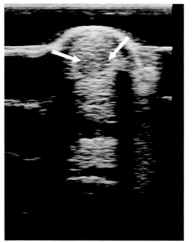

An ultrasound scan of a forelimb of a steeplechaser that pulled up lame after a race. A swelling developed in the superficial flexor tendon of the right forelimb. A large defect in the centre of the tendon (arrowed) indicates breakage of multiple tendon fibres

A very viscous coupling gel is applied to the area. A transducer (a device emitting ultrasound waves) is then placed against the skin. Depending on the density of the structures underneath the transducer, a greater or lesser amount of the waves are reflected back. These reflected waves (echoes) are picked up by the transducer and converted into an image on the screen. Very dense structures, such as bone, reflect a lot of waves, creating a very bright white image on the screen. Fluids (such as blood) reflect no waves and hence blood vessels appear as black 'holes' on the screen.

Bone scanning (nuclear scintigraphy)

In this technique a radioactive isotope is attached to a substance normally incorporated by the body when actively creating bone. The combination is injected intravenously and the isotope accumulates where bone is actively 'turning over', for example at sites of fractures or bone disease, or where there is abnormal activity due, for example, to a ligament becoming partially detached from the bone. The increased radioactivity at these sites is then detected with a bone scanner.

The technique is safe for horses as the radioactive substance that is used emits only a low and short-lived dose of radiation. Bone scanning is especially useful in demonstrating subtle hairline 'stress' fractures, invisible on x-rays, and to investigate other obscure lamenesses where conventional investigations with nerve blocks, ultrasound and other techniques have produced insufficient information to make a diagnosis.

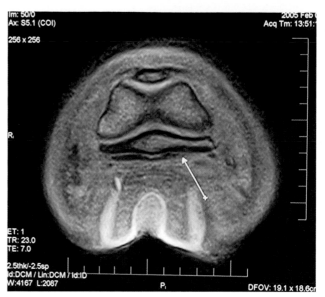

An MRI scan of a foot reveals damage to the ligament attached to the navicular bone (arrow)

Magnetic resonance imaging

The adaptation of human MRI scanners for equine use has resulted in a huge increase in our understanding of complex disorders of equine limbs. Being able to visualise non-bony soft tissue structures has greatly expanded the range of diagnoses now possible, especially in the area of equine foot pain. The site to be examined (usually a limb) is placed in a very strong magnetic field. The effect this has on the existing magnetism within the living tissues is measured to produce an image of the tissues. The procedure is risk-free although currently only the lower limbs of horses can be examined without general anaethesia. The chief drawback with MRI is the huge cost of the equipment.

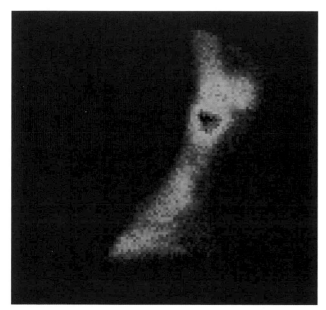

When a two-year-old racehorse presented with lameness after a training gallop, pain was localised to the fetlock region but no abnormalities were seen on x-rays. The bone scan showed an intense accumulation of radioactivity in the long pastern bone. There was a small fracture where this bone joins the fetlock joint

FOOT PROBLEMS

CROSS-SECTION OF A FOOT

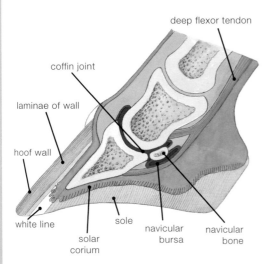

deep flexor tendon

coffin joint

laminae of wall

hoof wall

white line

sole

solar corium

navicular bursa

navicular bone

SOLAR SURFACE OF THE FOOT

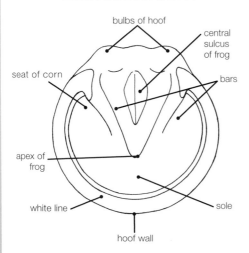

bulbs of hoof

central sulcus of frog

seat of corn

bars

apex of frog

white line

sole

hoof wall

The foot and foot balance

The hoof is a remarkable structure. It has four functions:
- supporting the limb and the weight of the horse
- protecting its internal structures
- pumping blood around the hoof
- providing shock absorption for the whole limb.

KEY FEATURES OF A PERFECTLY BALANCED FOOT

When a foot is 'balanced', its shape and its relationship to the limb ensure, as far as possible, even loading of the structures within the foot. It is a semi-elastic structure that deforms as it is loaded. If the loading is uneven it will deform asymmetrically and over time the deformity becomes permanent. All foals are born with symmetrical (balanced) feet. They start to deform as the foal grows due uneven loading caused by limb conformation, the amount of free exercise the foal is allowed, or inadequate or incorrect hoof trimming.

Perfect limbs are rare and consequently perfectly balanced feet are rare. Foot balance is assessed by looking at the foot and the limb, and by watching the horse walk and trot. The way in which the horse moves each limb and loads each foot when moving provides key information on balance. Because feet are growing all of the time, balance cannot be adequately assessed if it has been a long time since the feet were trimmed. In the balanced foot:
- Viewed from the front a line dropped from the shoulder divides the foot in two, and a horizontal line through the coronet is parallel to the ground.

THE PERFECTLY BALANCED FOOT

A line from the centre of rotation of the coffin joint divides the hoof and the shoe in half, so that distance A is the same as distance B. The bearing surface of the pedal bone is at a 10-degree angle to the ground surface

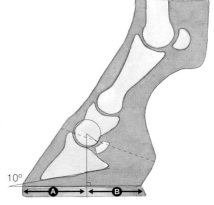

10°

A   B

- Viewed from the side, the front wall of the foot is aligned with a line through the middle of the pastern. This is the known as the *hoof/pastern axis* (HPA).
- Viewed from the side, the wall at the heel is parallel to the wall at the toe.
- When the foot is picked up and allowed to hang free, a line through the middle of the cannon and pastern bisects the hoof. A line across the heels makes a right angle with this line – both heels are of equal height (see illustration, right).
- On the weight-bearing surface of the foot, shoe wear shows first at the centre (toe-clip). The frog divides the hoof into two exactly equal parts. The width of the widest part of the hoof underside is the same as the distance from toe to heel.

SOLE AND HEEL SYMMETRY

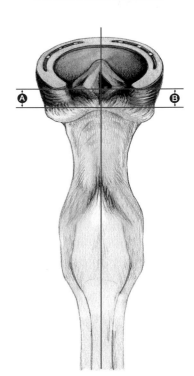

The heel heights A and B should be the same

THE HOOF/PASTERN AXIS

CORRECT   **BROKEN BACK**   **BROKEN FORWARD**

FOOT BALANCE PROBLEMS
The imbalanced foot

Imbalance (asymmetry) is caused by:
- conformational faults – toe-in (pigeon-toed) or toe-out conformation, rotated limbs, long pasterns, narrow chest, or
- poor farriery, usually one of the following:
  - failure to shoe to horse at right angles to the load bearing line of the limb
  - failure to recognise the reason for uneven wear of the shoe and deformity of the hoof
  - failure to observe the basic principles of good shoeing.

The farrier's key skill is in the preparation (trimming and rasping) of the hoof before shoeing. It has been stated that good shoeing is 90 per cent trimming, 10 per cent application of the shoe.

Horses with unbalanced feet will move poorly and develop poor quality feet and may go lame.

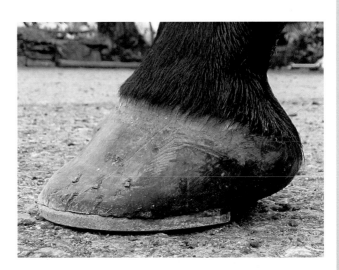

Bad farriery has left the toe too long and the heels completely unsupported by the shoe. There is a high probability this horse will become lame due to the stresses on the structures at the back of the foot

Common foot imbalances

Unequal heel height Where one heel is higher the horse lands on this heel first, and then slams down on the other heel, causing corns and shunting of the entire heel and coronet upwards. Causes of heel imbalance may be base-wide conformation (slight deviation of the cannon outwards from the knee) and failure of the farrier to trim the sole and wall at right angles to a line down though the cannon bone.

In this overgrown foot the outer (right side) heel is higher. The inner heel is collapsed and curving inwards. The shoe has partially come off the wall and is applying pressure to the sole at heel

Long toe/low heels (HPA broken back) If the toe is allowed to grow too long the heels are pulled forward. The long toe causes strain at the front of the hoof (see photo p.19), which pulls the laminae apart at the front

wall causing a mechanical laminitis. Excess strain is also applied to the suspensory apparatus (flexor tendons and suspensory ligament) compressing the navicular bone against the coffin joint and deep flexor tendon, and causing navicular syndrome, arthritis of the coffin and pastern joints, and tendon and ligament injuries.

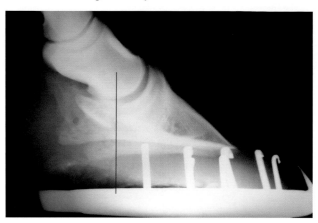

This horse was reluctant to extend its forelimbs in dressage tests. An x-ray of a forefoot shows that the front-to-back balance is very incorrect. The length of hoof on either side of the line dropped from the centre of rotation of the coffin joint should be equal (see 'The foot and foot balance', pp.18–19). Here the ratio is around 75:25. Shortening the toe and shoeing the horse much longer at the heel resolved the problem after six months

Broken forward HPA Overlong heels or a narrow upright 'boxy' foot often cause a broken forward hoof pastern axis. Although not as serious as a broken forward HPA, this can lead to stumbling and excessive landing on the heels.

FOOT ABSCESS (Pus in the foot, gravel)

The commonest cause of lameness in the horse is the development of a foot infection that produces a small pocket of pus within the rigid structure of the hoof. Because the hoof is unable to expand, as the volume of pus increases, the pressure on the sensitive laminae of the hoof wall, or the corium of the sole, also rises rapidly, resulting often in a very lame horse.

   If untreated the abscess will gradually enlarge under the sole. Many will track backwards and eventually will burst out at the coronet of the heel. Although the foot may look normal, invariably there is a tender spot on the coronet for a day or two before pus breaks out. If the pus is released, either by being drained through the sole or wall, or by bursting out at the coronet, the lameness very quickly decreases, unless there is associated damage to the soft tissues of the foot.

Clinical signs

- Lameness takes about 24–48 hours to develop. Some horses may be so lame they refuse to move, sweat and are in obvious distress.
- There will be an increased digital pulse, which can only be assessed if the horse can be induced to bear some weight on the leg. Very often the affected foot is much warmer than the opposite one, although very small abscesses can have little or no effect on foot temperature. A tender area will be found with hoof testers.

The infection enters the foot:

- most commonly via dirt trapped in the *white line*, the junction between the sole and the wall (covered by the shoe). Laminitis can make the white line wider than normal, resulting in an increased susceptibility to abscesses. Widening of the white line may also occur in horses with excessively long toes.
- via foreign bodies (including shoeing nails, splinters of wood, thorns from recent hedge trimming, sharp stones) penetrating the sole and frog.
- via cracks in the sole or hoof wall.

Abscesses may develop spontaneously in bruised feet, for example in corns.

What to do next

- Ask your vet to check the horse.
- If you find a foreign body lodged in the sole, if possible, remove it to prevent it being driven deeper into the foot. **Note carefully the exact site, depth and angle of penetration. Sometimes the vet will arrange for an x-ray with the foreign body in place to determine the depth of penetration.**
- If there is no sign of pain, sensitivity or swelling elsewhere in the limb, the vet will check the hoof with hoof testers. The shoe may be removed to allow closer examination of the white line.
- An area of discolouration in the sole overlying the painful spot, or the site of penetration, will be pared out with a sharp hoof knife to allow the pus – either thick and black, or green and runny – to drain. A bandage is then used to protect the opening (see 'Bandaging a sole abscess', p.22). If an extensive area of sole has been removed a disposable baby's nappy (newborn size) with duct tape on top makes an excellent foot bandage.
- Wall abscesses are especially painful and may not drain adequately unless a notch of hoof wall is removed.
- If a tender spot is found on the coronet, a poultice may be applied for a day or two to the painful area to encourage the pus to break out there.
- In general, 'tubbing', in which the foot is periodically immersed in a bucket containing warm water and a handful of Epsom Salts (magnesium sulphate), and polticing are not necessary once the pus is draining (see 'When to use a poultice', p.23).
- **Tetanus antitoxin** is given to unvaccinated horses or to those whose vaccination status cannot be confirmed.
- **Antibiotics** are not normally used unless (in addition to drainage) the sensitive sole or wall has been breached (but see 'Deep foot penetrations')
- Once the hole ceases to drain the shoe is replaced. The opening in the white line can first be filled with medicated wax (Keratex Hoof Putty) or cotton wool and Stockholm tar. A large hole in the sole, may require a pad under the shoe for a few weeks. Hoof wall notches can be repaired with flexible synthetic hoof material.

DEEP FOOT PENETRATIONS

Deep penetration, for example by a nail, through the middle third of the frog (usually through the grooves in the centre or at either side) can cause serious lameness as this part overlies two very important structures in the horse's hoof, the navicular bursa (blue arrow) and the coffin joint (red arrow). Infection in these sites causes severe lameness and is exceptionally difficult to control, often requiring flushing of these structures under general anaesthesia and extensive antibiotic treatment. **Seek urgent veterinary attention if a penetration is found in this region.**

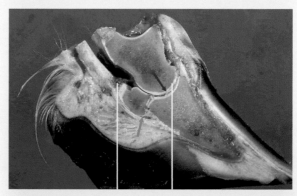

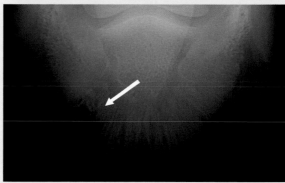

This horse went suddenly lame on a hind leg when jumping a cross-country fence. Blood was flowing from a puncture in the sole. After a few days an abscess developed, which despite adequate drainage did not resolve. An x-ray showed that the penetrating foreign body (probably a sharp stone) had fractured the rim of the pedal bone

FOOT ABSCESSES

This lame horse had a nail lodged in the sole just behind the shoe (arrowed). When removed the entry site was explored, revealing an abscess

This horse was very lame with a white line abscess that had a large accumulation of black pus under the sole. When an opening in the white line was created with a hoof knife the pus flowed out. In 24 hours the lameness was much reduced

An abscess in this horse's left forefoot has made the foot much warmer than the right, resulting in the mud drying more quickly

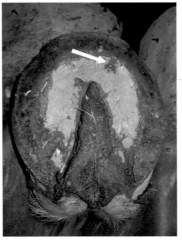

This horse had been lame for 24 hours. An area of tenderness was identified with hoof testers. When the shoe was removed a small amount of pus was visible on the surface of the sole (arrow). When explored with a hoof knife, a crack was found. It extended through the full thickness of the sole and had a small abscess underneath

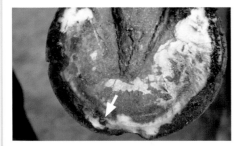

A little bead of pus (arrowed) draining from a small abscess exposed at the white line following removal of the shoe. The horse was slightly lame

This horse was very lame and the limb was swollen from the coronet to the knee. After a week the lameness suddenly improved. A sole abscess had tracked backwards towards the heel and burst out at the coronet of the heel, causing a wide area of separation (arrowed).

Bandaging a sole abscess

Before applying a bandage, pack the abscess cavity with a paste made by mixing granulated sugar and povidone iodine (Betadine Antiseptic Solution). This will not impede drainage as pus will dissolve it.

1 Fix a cohesive bandage (Vetrap, Equiwrap, Wrapz) directly on top of the abscess opening and over the whole sole.

2 Wrap duct tape over the entire hoof and slightly up on to the pastern, sticking it to the coat. Use two thicknesses over the sole.

This horse has been wearing a foot bandage for 24 hours. The duct tape is worn through to the wall around the rim, highlighting the need to ensure that extra layers are applied there.

3 Pay special attention to the rim of the hoof as this is where the bandage will wear through. Apply about six turns of tape here. To prevent wear the horse should be stabled on rubber mats or on a generous bed right up to the door. Change the bandage daily.

When to use a poultice

Commercial gauze poultices have largely superseded traditional poultices made, for example, from kaolin or bran. Modern poultices (for example, Animalintex) are pads impregnated with chemicals, which when moistened with warm water form a gel that attracts water. When applied to skin overlying an abscess, the poultice draws water through the tissues, softening the skin and helping infection to break through to the surface. Because the coronary band is the junction between the hoof and the skin, applying a poultice here is effective. It is arguable whether the traditional practice of applying a poultice to the sole promotes

drainage because hoof is not skin. However the poultice will clean the sole effectively allowing the vet to visualise better any potential entry points for infection. It addition, poulticing may soften the sole and wall a little, making exploration with a hoof knife easier.

Once the pus has been found and a drainage hole created, there is no logical reason to continue poulticing. (Note: overnight a poultice forms a discoloured gel, which is easily confused with pus.)

CORNS

A corn is a painful bruise in the sole at a specific site, known as the 'seat of corn' (see photo).

Corns are a common reason for slight to moderate lameness. They are caused by:

- Long intervals between shoeing. The hoof wall overgrows until it overlaps the shoe at the heels. The inner branch of the shoe (towards the heel) then comes to rest on a focal area of the sole between the bars and the wall (usually on the inside heels) causing bruising. The condition is rare in unshod horses.
- Poor foot trimming and shoeing, poor foot conformation with low collapsed heels. Badly fitted shoes that are too short in the heels will overload this region.
- Hoof imbalance especially where either the outer or inner heel is higher than each other, causing overloading of the lower heel. Horses with weak low heels may have persistent problems with corns.

Usually there is gradual or sudden onset of mild lameness, worse on hard ground especially on turning. One or both fore feet may be affected. There might be a slight increase in the strength of the digital pulse especially on the affected side. Hoof testers applied to the heel may cause pain. If the shoe is removed and the heel pared out, streaks of blood and obvious bruising is seen in the 'seat of corn'.

Preventing foot abscesses

- Regular hoof trimming (especially of unshod horses) to prevent cracking and splitting of the hoof wall.
- Careful sole preparation during trimming and shoeing to remove any pockets of dirt.
- Avoidance of sharp, flinty ground.
- Application of hoof disinfectant to the wall and sole.
- Correction of any nutritional deficiencies affecting hoof horn quality.

What to do next

Remove the shoe and stable the horse for 48 hours. Specific treatment of the bruised area is not necessary. The horse can then be re-shod after the feet have been trimmed correctly. The branches of the shoe should be sufficiently long and placed over the hoof wall only, so that no further pressure occurs on the seat of corn.

To relieve pressure on the corn, the farrier may fit either a 'seated out' shoe, where the solar surface close to the seat of corn is slightly hollowed to make it concave, or a bar shoe, to disperse the load over a wide area.

Preventing corns

Ensure the interval between shoeing is never more than six weeks. Horses that suffer repeatedly from corns may benefit from shoeing even more frequently and may need surgical shoeing with, for example, a bar shoe or egg-bar shoe. Ensure the hoof balance is checked.

This horse was mildly lame and the lameness was accentuated when lunged. A small corn (top right) had developed on the inside of the forefoot under the shoe at the *seat of corn* (see illustration, p.18). Streaks of blood were visible when the sole was pared away. The affected area was sensitive to hoof testers

BRUISED SOLES

The sole in most riding horses is naturally concave, about 1cm (½in) thick and remarkably resistant to pressure from uneven or stony ground. The domed shape imparts additional structural strength. In some horses, especially the finer breeds such as Thoroughbreds, the sole is unusually thin and flat. Flat soles may also be a result of hoof imbalance. Horses with thin or flat soles are susceptible to sole (and pedal bone in some cases) bruising especially if ridden on stony or hard ground.

One or more feet may be bruised. Hoof testers if applied to the bruised area will cause pain. If the sole is non-pigmented (white foot) and is pared with a hoof knife, streaks of blood may be seen. These are not visible in pigmented (dark) feet unless the bruising is severe.

A small slightly pink area of discoloration was revealed when the sole was cleaned (arrow). This is a mild bruise

More extensive areas of bruising are visible in this sole. This horse will need to be kept indoors on a soft bed for several weeks

What to do next

The horse should be box rested for 2–3 days on a deep bed to allow the feet to recover. It may be necessary to re-shoe, adding a protective pad. Thin-soled horses that suffer from repeated bruising or are simply reluctant to stride out and jump on hard ground might benefit from long-term protection with pads. Pads do have disadvantages however:

- They increase the rate of shoe loss as compression of the pad by the horse's weight causes the nail clenches to rise.
- They interfere with the normal function of the frog in absorbing concussion, stimulating hoof growth and acting a sensor for limb position.
- Dirt and small stones can become trapped under the pad causing lameness. It is best if the space between the rear part of the pad and the heels is sealed by silicone gel after the shoe has been nailed on.

- They neutralise the concavity of the sole and cover the frog, so there is a significant loss of grip when the horse is working on firm ground, for example in summer jumping. Pads are available with a ridge overlying the frog to provide additional grip.

An alternative, and better, form of long-term protection is a liquid rubber polymer (for example Equithane Hoofpak) that bonds to the sole, eliminating the dirt-trapping space and forming a perfect custom-made protective layer. To assist retention a plastic mesh may first be fitted across the sole and under the shoe (see photograph, p.36).

LAMENESS CAUSED BY RECENT SHOEING

Many horses are slightly tender on their feet for a day or two after shoeing. It is best to wait for 24–48 hours before notifying the farrier as the horse may move normally once it has become accustomed to its newly trimmed feet and new shoes.

Recent shoeing may induce lameness if:

- One or more the feet have been radically trimmed. Depending on the degree of trimming some horses may be reluctant to walk over stony ground but will often move normally on a soft surface. If the horse is left unshod the effects of trimming are more severe.
- A nail has been driven close to the sensitive laminae (a nail bind). The farrier may remove it immediately if he is aware of it, but if not the nail may inadvertently be left in place. Correct placement of the nails can be very difficult in thin-walled feet or unco-operative horses.
- A misdirected nail enters the sensitive laminae (a prick) and causes an abscess to develop in the hoof wall. This may occur at any time up to three weeks after shoeing. The nail may have been left in place or removed and re-directed by the farrier.
- After dressing the hoof, trimming the wall and fitting the shoe, the shoe may press on the sole, especially at the toe if the wall has been excessively lowered.

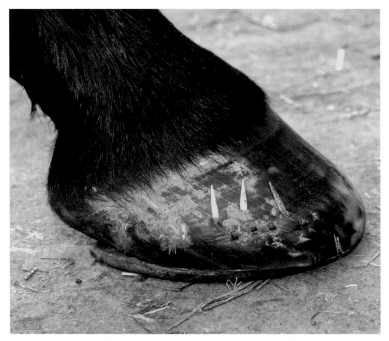

A partially shod foot. Unlike here, the nails should emerge in a straight line angled downwards to the heel. The higher the nail emerges, the closer it is to the sensitive structures in the hoof. The wall is thinner towards the heel so it is desirable that the heel nails are not too high. Conversely, if the nail emerges too low, there may be cracking around it because it has not been driven thrrough a sufficient thickness of wall

 What to do next

- Check the sole. If over-trimmed it will give on moderate finger pressure. Ideally there should be no reaction from the horse to anything other than very firm finger pressure on the sole unless the horse (for example, in Thoroughbreds) naturally has thin soles.
- Horses suffering from nail bind (usually the nails towards the heels) may resent tapping of the relevant nail clench with a hammer when the foot is weight bearing. Nails that emerge unusually high in the hoof wall are especially suspicious. If an abscess develops due to a 'prick' the horse may be very lame.
- Ask the farrier to re-visit. Each nail will be removed individually and the response of the horse checked. In a pricked horse pus may be seen flowing from the nail hole if the shoe is removed. The hole can be flushed with antiseptic solution and the shoe re-applied after a few days. Tetanus antitoxin is given to unvaccinated horses.
- Lameness caused by radical trimming may be relieved by rest and confinement on a deep bed, and possibly by a course of phenylbutazone until further hoof growth has taken place. If unshod it might be helpful to shoe the horse. Your vet will liaise with your farrier to determine the best course of action. Occasionally fitting of remedial shoes or protection of the sole with a pad may be necessary.

Preventing shoeing lamenesses

- Poor hoof quality with brittle fragmented walls may leave the farrier with very limited space in which to insert nails. Fundamental issues of foot balance and hoof horn quality may need to be addressed.
- Horses that are difficult to shoe because of fear or restlessness are more likely to suffer from nail bind or pricks because of their reluctance to keep the foot still when the shoe is being nailed on. Between shoeings, work on accustoming the horse to the sound and feel of the hammer, preferably every day.

LAMENESS CAUSED BY LOST SHOES

Shoes are lost because:

- The horse is overdue for shoeing and the shoes have become loose. The nail heads may have become worn, and the clenches may have risen, allowing them to be opened and the shoe to be pulled off.
- The hind foot treads on heel of the corresponding front shoe. The following makes this more likely: where the ends of the front shoes extend beyond the heels (for example in some surgical shoes such as egg-bars); where the toes of the fore feet are overlong and hence break-over is delayed and in heavy going where the fore feet cannot be lifted by the horse to get out of the way of the hind feet quickly enough.
- The hoof walls are brittle, of poor quality or undermined by white line disease (p.29).
- The nails have been emerged too low in the wall, i.e. they have been driven through the wall outside of the white line and are not supported by sufficient thickness of wall.

Losing a shoe can cause *lameness* in several ways:

- Some horses, especially those with thin soles, which have been accustomed to being shod all of their lives may remain footsore until the missing shoe is replaced. Without the shoe they will often move normally on soft ground but appear lame on hard. Replacement of the missing shoe will usually result in an instant 'cure'.
- If the shoe is lost while the horse is being worked but the rider continues to ride the horse without a shoe (especially on roads or stony ground), excessive wear of the wall and bruising of the sole may occur.
- The shoe may be pulled off by the horse turning or jumping in heavy ground and the nails may rip portions of the wall away resulting in a painful foot.
- The shoe may become twisted under the hoof resulting in the horse treading on a broken nail, or on the toe- or quarter-clips, causing a sole penetration.

❓ What to do next

- The farrier will attempt to fit a new shoe. Most horses will quickly become sound. If the sole has been bruised adjacent to the wall it might be necessary to fit a wide-webbed shoe that has been seated out to prevent sole pressure.
- If the wall has been badly damaged so that insufficient nails can be used, it might be necessary to use glue-on shoes or to repair the wall with synthetic hoof material. Alternatively, it may be necessary to wait for further wall growth to occur before the horse can be re-shod.

THRUSH

Thrush is a bacterial infection of the frog and frog grooves. The causal bacteria thrive in the deep, warm recesses of the hoof, especially if the frog is overgrown or the heels have been allowed to overgrow, deepening the clefts. It is a disease almost exclusively of stabled horses, especially if kept on deep litter, with warm, urine-soiled damp bedding and without frequent picking out of the feet. Horses with naturally deep frog clefts (especially Warmbloods) are especially susceptible to this disease.

Thrush has a characteristic unpleasant smell. If the frog is examined dark, thick, liquid matter (hoof material dissolved by the bacteria) can be seen usually in the central cleft but also in the side clefts if the frog has overgrown. The horse is not usually lame unless the infection has eroded through to the sensitive layer underneath the (usually central) cleft. In these cases the horse will flinch if a hoof pick is pressed into the bottom of the cleft.

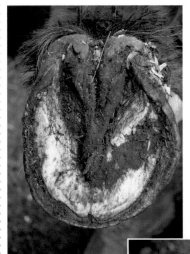

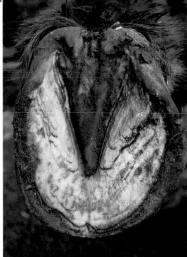

Thrush infection is present in the grooves in this overgrown frog (left). The farrier has trimmed away all of the diseased hoof (below)

What to do next

- By far the most effective treatment is for the farrier or vet to cut away all of the overgrown frog and abnormal hoof. If the horse is subsequently kept on dry bedding and the hoof regularly picked out, this treatment alone may suffice. Although foot antiseptics are useful for this condition they will never result in a total cure unless combined with trimming of the diseased foot. Suitable antiseptics are iodine, hydrogen peroxide or Hoof Disinfectant (Life Data Labs), applied with a toothbrush and scrubbed in.

- Deep central frog clefts that are covered by heel bulbs in their upper reaches cannot be pared out without entering living tissue on each side. In these cases a large cotton bud, made from an artery forceps (available from your vet) and a piece of cotton wool, is moistened with water and forced from the rear into the depth of the clef until it emerges in the middle of the frog (see photo below). This is repeated several times with clean cotton wool. A fresh bud is then dipped in disinfectant and pushed through.

Preventing thrush

Thrush is prevented by:

- Regular trimming of the frog at shoeing to remove any overhanging portions and any areas where bedding can become trapped. Although current farriery practice favours very limited routine trimming of the frog, the farrier should check carefully for thrush at every visit and trim the affected areas if necessary.
- Daily picking out of the feet of stabled horses, paying particular attention to the central frog cleft.
- Regular application of a hoof disinfectant in persistent cases.
- Keeping the horse on clean dry bedding.

A strong cotton bud made from cotton wool and artery forceps is used to clean the very deep central frog cleft in this warmblood

WHITE LINE DISEASE (Seedy toe)

Bacteria and fungi may invade the white line and cause degeneration of the hoof wall. This infection if uncontrolled will track upwards and outwards from the point of entry, undermining and weakening the hoof wall. Horses with poor quality hoof structure, horses that have previously had laminitis and those with unbalanced feet, kept in damp environments and irregularly or insufficiently trimmed (especially if the toes are allowed to grow too long) are all susceptible to white line disease. The effect of over-long toes, and pedal bone rotation in laminitis, is to stretch the white line at the toe, thereby making it wider and more easily invaded by hoof-destroying microbes.

One or more feet may be affected. The infection is usually detected by the farrier when dressing the wall prior to fitting the shoe. It causes a cavity containing a powdery, flaky grey-white material that may extend up the wall from anywhere along the white line. If extensive, a hollow sound may be heard if the wall is tapped with a hammer while weight bearing. Weakening of the wall may cause cracking and difficulty in retaining shoes. Most affected horses are not lame unless the infection has sufficiently weakened the attachment between the hoof wall and the pedal bone, allowing the pedal bone to rotate.

Many horses have mild, localised areas of white line disease without any lameness. These may be unnoticed by the owner and are (usually only partially) trimmed by the farrier at each shoeing. If infection spreads and causes extensive under running of the wall, healthy areas of wall may have to carry a disproportionate amount of the horse's weight, possibly causing lameness.

Preventing white line disease

White line disease can be prevented by:
- Regular trimming and balancing of the feet.
- Using hoof disinfectant. This can be applied to the sole at trimming and shoeing. All old nail holes and cracks can be flooded with disinfectant.
- Correcting any nutritional deficiencies leading to poor hoof quality (see p.31).

What to do next

- The farrier or vet will pare away all of the underrun wall with a sharp knife or electric burr, and then remove all of the powdery material with a wire brush. It is essential that every last bit of underrun wall is removed.
- A hoof disinfectant (for example Life Data Labs) is painted onto the exposed area every few days until new wall grows down to cover the defect (about 1cm/½in a month). The horse must be kept in a clean dry environment during treatment. A seated out, flat broad-webbed (wide) shoe, sometimes a bar shoe, is fitted to support the foot while new wall grows. Glue-on shoes, such as the Sigafoos, below, may be used if there is insufficient wall to hold enough nails. If it is necessary to remove a large portion of wall the horse may become unavoidably lame and may need to be unshod for several months while new wall grows. The wall can be repaired with synthetic hoof material but only after it has been confirmed that no further diseased wall is present. This may take several weeks and a number of treatments.

  All predisposing causes, for example overgrown or unbalanced feet, must be corrected at the same time. It may be necessary to shoe the horse with surgical shoes to correct hoof imbalance or lack of support.

The Sigafoos shoe incorporates a strip of Kevlar fabric bonded to the shoe. It is ideal for horses that have had large wall resections as part of white line disease treatment. When bonded to the hoof wall with an acrylic adhesive, the fabric secures the shoe and provides additional structural strength to the hoof. No nails are used

HOOF CRACKS

Hoof cracks are common, especially where the feet have been allowed to overgrow. They are commonest at the toe in the forelimb and to the side in the hindlimb. There are several types: vertical cracks starting at the coronet (sandcracks); vertical cracks starting at the ground surface (grass cracks); horizontal cracks. Those cracks that are only partially through the thickness of the wall are usually painless, while those of full thickness can be painful – causing lameness – and may become infected.

These shallow cracks are present on all four feet and may reflect poor hoof quality, or excessive drying of the feet in hot, dry weather

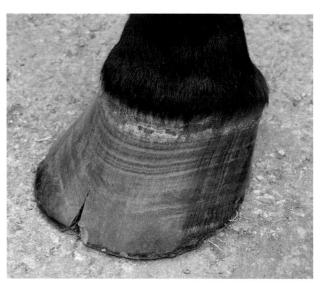

This brood mare's feet are trimmed very infrequently, resulting in overgrowth of the hoof wall and splitting at the toe. If left untreated, the split may extend through the white line resulting in a hoof abscess

WHAT CAUSES CRACKS?

- Overgrowth of the feet.
- Hoof imbalance increasing overall stresses on the hoof or concentrating stresses in one place, for example overlong toes or inner to outer imbalance.
- Major trauma to the coronet may result in permanent interference to hoof production at the site of the injury. A deep irregular fissure (a false quarter) may develop in the wall below the damaged coronet and is usually incurable.
- Poor hoof quality (p.31).
- Excessively dry or moist conditions.
- Poor foot care (prolonged intervals between trimming).
- Previous trauma or infection.
- Horizontal cracks may reflect an interruption in hoof growth, for example, where an abscess has broken out at the coronet, or, in the heel region, abnormal stresses, usually due to collapsed or weak heels.
- **Farriery** Long-term bad farriery may lead to:
  - vertical wall cracks due to excessively long toes
  - poor support of the heels (shod with the shoe too short) resulting in horizontal cracks at the heels
  - failure to correct inside/outside hoof imbalance resulting in abnormal stresses on one heel and consequent crushing and cracking of the wall
  - fine nailing', where the nails emerge too low, may cause the wall to crack and split.

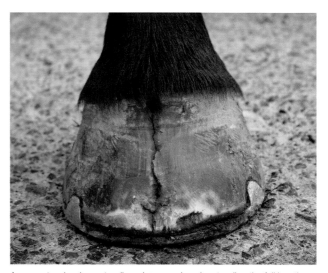

A very extensive, long-standing, deep sandcrack extending the full length of the wall and almost through its full thickness. It was repaired by enlarging the crack with a burr and filling it with hoof repair material. This procedure bonded the two sides together and allowed new growth from the coronet to continue down the wall without splitting

What can be done

- Superficial cracks may cause minimal problems and, as treatment is prolonged and expensive, it may not be justified.
- Full thickness vertical cracks should be treated. Traditionally farriers have grooved the crack transversely at its upper limit to prevent it propagating. This has been proved to be of limited efficacy. *It is essential that the fundamental reason for the crack is addressed first,* by trimming and balancing the foot (see pp.18–19), and dealing with adverse environmental effects on the feet or nutritional deficiencies in the horse's diet (see 'Causes of poor hoof quality', below).

- The hoof wall must then be stabilised by one of the following techniques:
  - Fitting a bar shoe with quarter clips to limit expansion of the hoof when weight bearing. In the case of cracks towards the heel, the wall below the crack can be lowered to prevent weight bearing at that site. A heart-bar shoe is then fitted to spread the load onto the frog.
  - Bridging the crack with metal clips, plates or wire.
  - The most effective technique is to widen and deepen the crack with a motorised burr. The enlarged crack is then filled and stabilised with synthetic hoof repair material.

CAUSES OF POOR HOOF QUALITY

- **Ill-health** Horses that are generally unhealthy due to some disease may have unhealthy feet also.
- **White line disease**.
- **Dietary deficiencies** Studies have shown improvement in hoof quality following long-term supplementation with calcium (1kg/2lb 3oz dried alfalfa per 200kg/440lb bodyweight daily) and biotin (25mg daily). Additional dietary sulphur, methionine and zinc may also be beneficial. Supplementation may need to continue for 6–18 months before an improvement is seen. Broad-spectrum hoof supplements, such as Farriers' Formula, may also be helpful.

- **Environment** Constant wetting of the feet and immersion in urine-soaked bedding weakens hoof horn. Bedding should be kept as dry as possible. A thin layer of clean woodshavings, frequently replaced, on rubber stable mats is ideal.
- **Excessive use of hoof greases, oils and tars** These are not beneficial to hoof quality because they inhibit the natural loss of moisture from the hoof wall. Conversely, excessive rasping of the protective layer on the surface of the hoof may result in undue moisture-loss causing brittle hooves.

STUMBLING

Stumbling may reflect foot problems, weakness or a more complex *neurological problem* that affects placement of the feet (see pp.148–152). *Fatigue* may cause stumbling and injury, especially in horses that are forced to continue over uneven or soft ground (for example in a cross-country competition) when tired.

Foot problems include:

- Overlong toes, either because of poor foot balance (long toes and low heels) or a long period since the feet were last trimmed.
- Overlong feet with relative 'shrinking' of the frog so that frog pressure does not occur. The frog has an important role in 'position sensing' by the horse and lack of frog pressure deprives the horse of important input information.
- Stumbling may occur after recent shortening of long feet,

until the horse becomes accustomed to the new toe length (2–3 days).
- Heel pain (for example navicular syndrome) causing a shortened stride and toe-first landing. Upper limb pain may also cause a shortened stride.

What to do next

Stumbling related to foot problems can be helped by:
- treating any primary lameness
- shortening the toe and balancing the foot
- trimming to allow more frog contact with the ground
- rolling the toe of the shoe or setting it further back under the wall
- providing additional length of the shoe at the heels.

NAVICULAR SYNDROME

Rare in ponies, navicular syndrome is a common condition in Warmblood horses, Thoroughbreds, Irish Draught crosses and Quarter horses. A hereditary tendency to develop the disease has been found in Dutch and Hanoverian warmbloods. Although poor foot balance may be an important inciting cause, some affected horses have well balanced feet. As knowledge of the diseases of the horse's foot increases through the use of new techniques such as MRI, theories about navicular syndrome are constantly being revised. Because of the complexity of the disease, the term *caudal* [rear] *third* [of the hoof] *syndrome* is now also used. It is currently thought that the disease involves the navicular bone, its supporting ligaments and the deep flexor tendon. Anything that accentuates the pressure of the tendon against the navicular bone, for example a long toe or unsupported collapsed heels will cause disease in any or all of these structures.

Clinical signs and diagnosis

- Stiffness, especially when first coming out of the stable, initially disappearing as the horse warms up.
- An increased tendency to stumble
- Decreased stride length and a reluctance to go forward, especially downhill.
- Reluctance to jump and unexplained refusing in a hitherto willing jumper.
- Intermittent forelimb lameness, varying in severity from day-to-day and often affecting more than one limb. The lameness may initially improve with work.
- Lameness that is worse on turning, when lunged (the inside leg is lame) or when worked on hard ground.
- There is often no reaction to hoof testers.
- When viewed from the side at the walk, some horses land toe-first.

Diagnosis

- Confirmation that the pain is located in the navicular area is obtained by selectively anaesthetising the heel region (palmar digital nerve block) or the navicular bursa in the lame leg. Because of the interactions between the different structures in this disease, sometimes interpretation of nerve blocks can be difficult.
- Some horses have characteristic x-ray changes. In other cases x-rays may be normal and the diagnosis may require the use of MRI or nuclear scintigraphy. X-rays also provide important further information on foot balance.

Local anaesthetic is injected into the navicular bursa in this lame horse, suspected of suffering from navicular syndrome. After five minutes the horse will be re-examined to determine whether the lameness has improved or disappeared

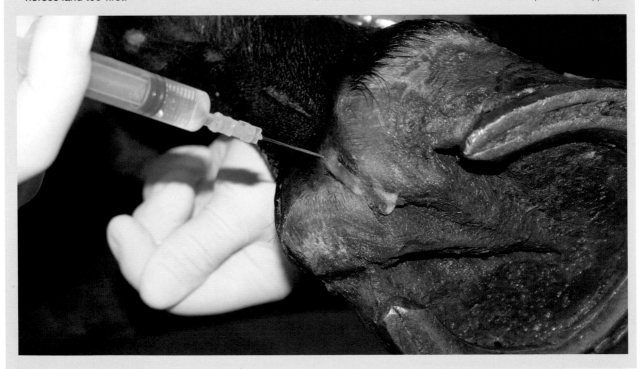

What to do next

- It is critical that the feet are *carefully balanced* using x-rays as a guide.
- *Remedial shoeing* to bring the point of break-over (the point at which the toe rotates as the horse advances the limb) backwards, to support the heels and to restore the hoof-pastern axis to normal, may help. Re-balancing the feet may take as long as 12–18 months to have a fully beneficial effect. During this time it may be possible for the horse to remain in light work. In some horses correction of foot balance alone, without any other treatment, may cause the disease to resolve, although it may take a long time.
- The *specialised farriery* demanded may require the assistance of an experienced remedial farrier recommended by your vet.

- *Surgical treatment,* involving cutting of the ligaments that suspend the navicular bone on each side (navicular suspensory desmotomy) in order to reduce the mechanical stress on the bone and tendon helps some horses in the short-term but the long-term response has been poor.
- Long-standing cases with extensive changes in the navicular region may respond poorly to treatment. In these cases the horse may be worked while receiving phenylbutazone in the feed. Over time the dose of the drug may have to be increased to unacceptable levels. Most equestrian disciplines will not permit horses receiving any medication to compete.
- *As a last resort* when other methods have failed, and only if the response to nerve-blocking the heel nerves is good, surgical severing of these nerves (de-nerving) is possible. There are, however, long-term complications with this treatment, including the development of painful swellings (called neuromas) on the ends of the severed nerves.

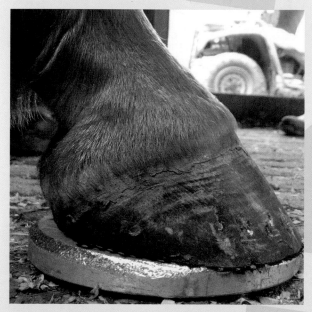

This horse has been fitted with an egg-bar shoe, which extends beyond the collapsed heels to provide support. In addition the shoe is thicker at the heel, thereby helping to restore the hoof-pastern axis to near normal by slightly raising the heels

- *Drug treatment* with isoxsuprine given by mouth helps some horses but not all. Recently intravenous tiludronate has been shown to be effective in some cases. Warfarin is no longer used.
- Some horses also have coffin joint or navicular bursal disease and these must be treated too.

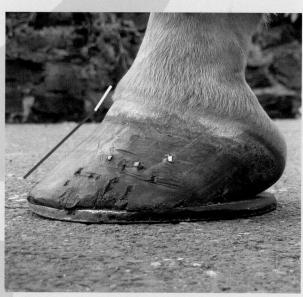

The farrier has attempted to support the heels of this horse, which is lame with navicular syndrome, with an egg-bar shoe but has not addressed the fundamental problems in the horse's foot. The hoof/pastern axis remains broken back (p.20), the toe is overlong and the front wall of the hoof starts growing at a normal angle (yellow line) but as it lengthens it is pulled forward (blue line)

LAMINITIS

Laminitis is a very common and painful disease, especially of ponies. It may occur a single acute episode and commonly re-occurs due to inadequate dietary control. *Obesity is a major risk factor* in predisposing horses to laminitis. Obese horses have large fat deposits on the neck (resulting in a thick crest under the mane) over the ribs (which may be hard to feel) and over the rump. The size and hardness of the neck fat are sometimes taken as an indicator of susceptibility, but this is a myth.

How does diet-induced laminitis occur?

There are two principal theories as to the mechanism whereby diet-induced laminitis occurs:

- **The vascular theory** The abnormal bacterial activity in the horse's large intestine caused by the intake of high-sugar feed results in the uptake of large amounts of *amines*, which cause the blood vessels in the feet to constrict, thereby depriving the laminae of their blood supply and causing them to degenerate.
- **The enzyme theory** It is proposed that the abnormal activity in the intestine causes the absorption of an unknown substance that causes excessive activity of the enzymes (matrix metalloproteinases) that normally break down the bonds between the sensitive and

CAUSES OF LAMINITIS

- Excess intake of lush grass high in soluble sugars (fructans) usually in spring and autumn. High starch diets (usually from cereal grains) in sport or show horses may have the same effect.
- A severe toxaemia, arising for example, from a severe infection in the uterus (womb) after foaling or from colic.
- Long-standing non-weight bearing lameness in one limb, which may cause laminitis in the opposite limb due to overloading.
- Excess concussion, for example in a horse being driven or ridden fast on asphalt roads.
- Equine Cushing's disease (p.140).
- Rarely, as a side effect of corticosteroid (cortisone) medication.
- Metabolic syndrome, suffered by excessively obese horses, in which the large fat stores may produce corticosteroid-like hormones.

The classical stance of a severe laminitis case. Frequent shifting of weight by alternately resting different limbs every few minutes also occurs

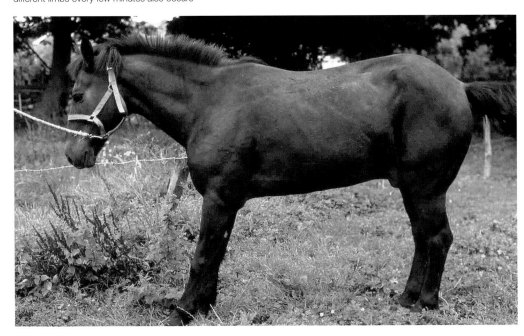

insensitive laminae allowing the foot to grow. (Toxins absorbed from an infected uterus may have the same effect.)

The effect of these changes in the feet is that the bonds between the sensitive laminae on the surface of the pedal bone and the insensitive laminae in the inside of the hoof wall (a Velcro-like attachment) become weakened, resulting in some cases in rotation or sinking of the pedal bone. In severe cases the pedal bone may rotate until the tip penetrates the sole, or sinks to such a degree that the entire pedal bone is in danger of coming through the sole (a sinker).

 ## Clinical signs

- Initially the horse shows a reluctance to walk quickly and may favour walking on softer ground when led. If asked to turn in hand there is obvious pain in the inside leg. There is an increased strength of the digital pulse in the affected feet. Foot temperature is variable and an unreliable guide to diagnosis.
- The horse is otherwise bright and eats normally. If kept on the same field, after a few days it becomes reluctant to move, shifts its weight from foot to foot and adopts the classic laminitic stance, leaning backwards with the fore feet extended to reduce the weight they bear. If hoof testers are applied to the sole in front of the apex of the frog the horse will flinch.
- Severe cases may spend a lot of time lying down, may sweat and be in great discomfort.
- Recovered cases may show evidence of a previous bout. Rings in the hoof wall (which do *not* in themselves indicate that the horse has had laminitis before) will *diverge at the heel*, unlike in the normal horse where the rings are *parallel*. The sole may be flat or convex, and the white line at the toe is much wider than normal.

Left: This horse is a severe 'sinker'. The pedal bone laminae have separated from the laminae on the inside of the hoof wall almost the whole way around the hoof, resulting in loss of support for the horse's weight, and sinking of the pedal bone. Instead of a straight line from the front of the pastern onto the hoof, there is a obvious depression where the bone has sunk

Laminitis – the effect of season		
% soluble sugars in grass	morning	afternoon
After overnight at 16°C (61°F)	14	23
After overnight frost	24	28

If the night is warm, the sugar (fructan) made by the grass during the day is partially consumed by the plant during the night. But if the weather overnight is cold (for example in May or September), the sugar level does not fall. Further sugar is added each day, causing the level in the grass to rise steeply. This explains why laminitis is more common when the daytime weather is warm but the nights are cold and why the safest time for grazing is in the morning.

THE LAMINITIC FOOT

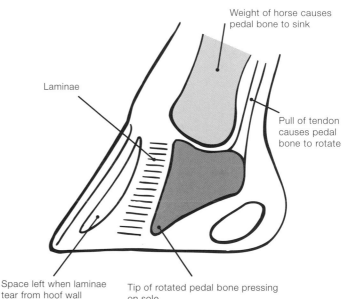

Weight of horse causes pedal bone to sink

Laminae

Pull of tendon causes pedal bone to rotate

Space left when laminae tear from hoof wall

Tip of rotated pedal bone pressing on sole

Why does treatment of laminitis fail?

It is not unusual for laminitis cases to be very difficult to treat and eventually the horse will have to be put down.

The reasons for treatment failure are:

- Failure to recognise the disease and take aggressive treatment action early enough
- Failure to fit frog supports
- Failure to confine the horse to a stable all of the time
- Failure to feed an appropriate diet once the diagnosis has been made
- Inability to control the pain in severe cases
- Lack of skill and experience in the vet and farrier

What is the prognosis?

If detected early the horse may recover in less than a month, sometimes in not much more than a week. It is essential however that even rapidly recovering cases are box rested for *six weeks* for full mechanical strength to recover in the foot. Over time, with the aid of x-rays, may be able to trim the feet to restore the pedal bones to their correct position. More advanced cases may take *2–12 months* to recover and some will remain 'footy' for life. Sinkers require specialised treatment by a remedial farrier over many months and many do not respond.

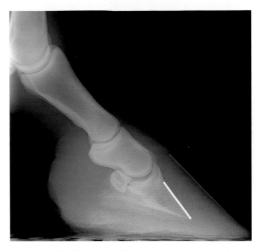

In a normal foot the front of the pedal bone (yellow line) should be parallel to the front of the hoof (red line). In this x-ray the two lines are diverging, indicating that the pedal bone has rotated

What to do next

Laminitis is an emergency. The way the horse is treated in the first 24 hours critically affects the outcome of the case and time taken to recover. If in doubt it is always best to proceed as though the horse has laminitis.

- Remove the horse from pasture immediately and put it in a stable with a deep bed of woodshavings or sand. Fit a plank across the doorway at floor level so that a deep bed can be provided right up to the door. The horse must remain in the stable until fully recovered. If sand is used, forage should not be fed from the stable floor as an excessive intake of sand may occur, resulting in colic.
- Summon veterinary help. If likely to be delayed, fit temporary frog supports (see below).

- Contrary to traditional advice, *do not walk the horse*. This will further disrupt the Velcro-like attachment of the pedal bone to the inside of the hoof (see photo p.35, bottom right).
- Withhold all concentrate feeds and instead feed a chaff product recommended for laminitics, along with a limited amount of high fibre coarse hay or haylage. Hay or haylage should be soaked by immersion for 8 hours before feeding, to leach out the soluble sugars.
- Do not starve the horse. Starvation will have little or no effect on its weight in the short term, is inhumane and will deprive it of essential nutrients to repair the damaged feet. Conversely, because the horse will be stabled for a long time before it recovers, it will readily

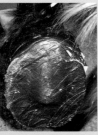

Far left: A crepe bandage makes an excellent temporary frog support. The bandage must be shortened with a knife so that none protrudes beyond the apex of the frog. A cohesive bandage holds it in place, then duct tape is wrapped over the top (left). With weight bearing, the crepe bandage will crush to the shape of the frog. If the horse is obviously more uncomfortable with the supports, they are probably too thick. Unroll part of the bandage and re-position it. Right: these commercially available frog supports offer no significant advantages over a crepe bandage

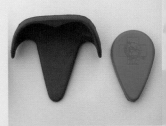

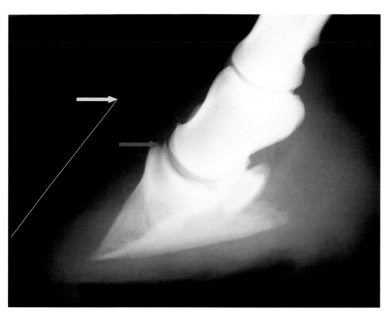

This horse has had severe laminitis for four weeks. A metallic marker (white line) has been placed on the front of the hoof. The top of the marker (yellow arrow) is positioned to show the position of the coronet. The distance between the coronet and the top of the pedal bone (red arrow) – the founder distance – is about twice the normal amount, indicating that the pedal bone has sunk in the foot (a sinker), because of the loss of attachment of the laminae in a significant part of the hoof. This horse will be lame for many months until new hoof growing down from the coronet re-establishes the laminal attachment

The pedal bone has rotated in this Arabian stallion, resulting in a line of bleeding in the sole where the rim of the rotated bone is pressing on it

gain weight due to its inactivity and become over-fat. For these reasons, it should only be fed just enough. Inevitably there will be times in the day when the horse has nothing to eat.

- Feed a dedicated hoof supplement unless the essential nutrients are already present in the chaff product.
- The vet may administer an anti-inflammatory injection (usually phenylbutazone) and possibly other drugs to improve the blood supply to the feet. If the laminitis has been caused by toxaemia, this will also be treated aggressively.
- Frog supports will be fitted to support the pedal bone and prevent rotation or sinking. These may be temporary supports, for example rolled crepe bandages taped to the feet. Later on more permanent support is provided

in the form of rubber polymer infill or plastic or steel heart-bar (heart-shaped) shoes.

- The vet may obtain x-rays of the feet to establish the position of the pedal bone (see photo). These are best taken 3–4 weeks after the onset when the pedal bone has settled in its final position and can used as a guide to prognosis for long-term use, and as a guide for the farrier when trimming or remedially shoeing the feet.
- The feet must be trimmed every four weeks.

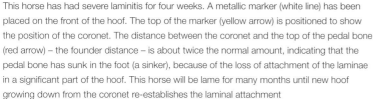

Permanent support has been provided using a rubber polymer. Polymer is not applied in front of the frog, to avoid pressure on the rim of the pedal bone

A plastic 'Imprint' heart-bar shoe, which can be glued to the foot

Preventing laminitis

Restrict grass intake

Because it is very difficult to establish how much grass horses are eating, a 'boom and bust' approach is best. Allow the horse to graze a normal paddock (non-fertilised, and not pure ryegrass) for a maximum of four hours per day (two hours if the horse has suffered from laminitis before). Fructan levels in grass are lowest from late at night to early in the morning. Turnout should be as early as possible with the horse removed from grass by mid-morning. The 'down time' can be spent in a loose box or wandering in a pen, with access to some hay and low-sugar high-fibre feed. The aim is to ensure that the periods of disruption of the gut bacteria by grass intake are short, and are 'settled' by an extended period of hay feeding. The frequent practice of allowing animals to graze, say, only at night or only during the day, that is for 12–18 hours, is just too long a period for safety. Alternatively the area of grass available can be restricted using an electric fence. The area of the pen must be so small that the grass is tightly grazed. Remember grass grows surprisingly quickly and an apparently bare patch may still generate sufficient grass to trigger laminitis. If necessary, supplementary feed, such as hay and or straw can be provided daily. If the horse isn't eating the hay, then the pen may be too large.

Where a pony is kept as a companion for a bigger horse, a pen can be made in the field for the pony, while the horse has unrestricted access to the whole field.

Use an electric fence tester regularly to check the output of the fence battery or whether the charge is present in the entire fence (wires commonly fail). Hungry horses will soon discover if the fence is 'live' or not. Consider fitting a small mains fencer unit, which may be more reliable and cheaper in the long-term.

Determining the correct size of a 'starvation' paddock is difficult. It should provide sufficient grass for one day's grazing, and be used for two to three days

Use of a grazing muzzle is an attractive option in that the available grazing area or grazing time can be greater. Muzzles are a far from perfect solution. Apart from the fact that some ponies seem to be able to remove them in spite of exhaustive efforts to keep them in place, they can cause rubs and skin irritation from prolonged wear. They should therefore only be used intermittently.

Tethering the pony on a long lead can be extremely effective if done with care by ensuring gradual introduction, close supervision, a quick-release system, careful selection of the site to avoid hazards and the provision of water and shade. Unfortunately and unjustifiably this method has largely fallen out of use.

Provide exercise

Laminitis is rare in fit animals (unless they are rested due to injury and the feeding rate is not reduced). Provide as much *exercise* as possible to keep the bodyweight down. If a child rider is not available, ponies can be lunged or led from a horse (or bicycle) while exercising. It can be almost impossible to reduce the weight of a fat native pony without exercising it.

Feed with care

If supplementary feed must be provided then use *high-fibre low-starch* feeds for example coarse hay or haylage (avoid soft haylage), straw, high-fibre cubes, *unmolassed* sugar beet and high-fibre chaff products (such as Dengie 'HiFi', Dodson & Horrell 'Safe and Sound' and

Spillers 'Happy Hoof'). Do not feed conventional horse and pony nuts, coarse mixes and other starchy feeds or nuts.

High-fibre chaff products, especially those fortified with vitamins and minerals required for hoof growth, are ideal for laminitics

Founderguard, an antibiotic feed supplement from Australia, claims to prevent laminitis by controlling the abnormal chemical activity in the large intestine. It is only available on veterinary prescription. Experience suggests that it is of very limited value in grass laminitis control and is more appropriate for concentrate (starch)-induced laminitis.

Be vigilant

Look for the early signs The onset of the disease is slow and often missed. If your pony normally trots to the gate for a titbit and all of a sudden merely walks, but seems otherwise 'normal', it may well be in the early stages. When led or ridden a tendency to favour grass verges rather over hard tarmac, or walking with a stilted 'straight-legged' gait may be warning signs. **If in any doubt, get the pony off the pasture immediately and don't wait for the full-blown signs to appear.**

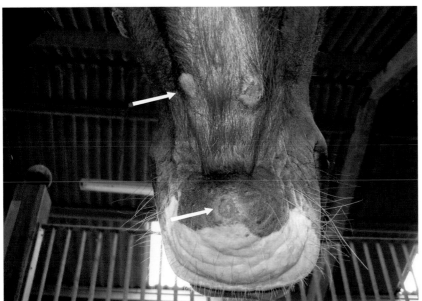

Grazing muzzles severely limit grass intake, but they must be used only for short periods or skin rubs will develop (arrows)

Dealing with other causes

Laminitis due to toxaemia is usually very severe and difficult to treat. Mares with severe womb infections will be treated with frog supports, intensive antibiotics, and drugs that minimise the effects of the toxins. The uterus will be flushed to remove bacteria and toxins, and intravenous fluids will be given in large quantities. Severe colic cases will receive surgery to correct the surgical problem.

Concussive laminitis in addition is treated with rest on soft bedding and remedial foot care as already outlined.

Cushing's Disease cases require drug treatment (see p.140) in addition to dietary control.

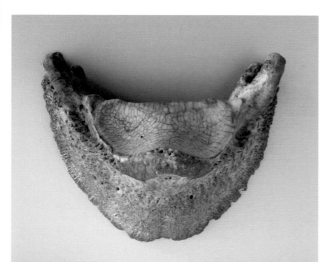

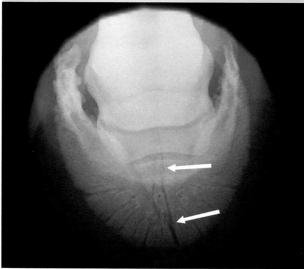

A normal pedal bone (top). A fracture through the centre of the pedal bone into the coffin joint (above). Even if the fracture heals, this horse is likely to remain lame

FRACTURED PEDAL BONE

Along with splint bone fractures, pedal bone fractures are the commonest limb bone fractures seen in horses. The injury is usually due to trauma to the bone while being exercised on a hard surface, often while turning.

Clinical signs

- Sudden onset of severe lameness, usually while being worked.
- Increased digital pulse in the affected limb.
- There may be diffuse pain in the foot, revealed with hoof testers, and the horse will especially resent percussion of the sole with a hammer. The appearance is similar to that of a sole abscess and cases are often initially thought to be an abscess but no pus is found on investigation.
- The diagnosis is confirmed by x-raying the foot, although the plane of the fracture may be such that multiple views are required to detect it. Sometimes very subtle fractures will only be found if the foot is x-rayed several times over the first 2–4 weeks.

Treatment

Treatment involves complete box rest with immobilisation of the foot. This is achieved by applying a bar shoe with quarter clips to restrict expansion of the foot. Other treatment techniques include encasing the foot in casting material, or fitting a shoe with a steel rim overlapping the hoof wall and filling the gap between the wall and the shoe with a rubber polymer. Occasionally the bone fragments are surgically screwed together.

The fracture usually responds very well to treatment with most horses returning to soundness in 6–12 months. However, if the fracture line extends into the coffin joint there may be residual arthritis of the joint resulting in permanent lameness.

COFFIN JOINT DISEASE

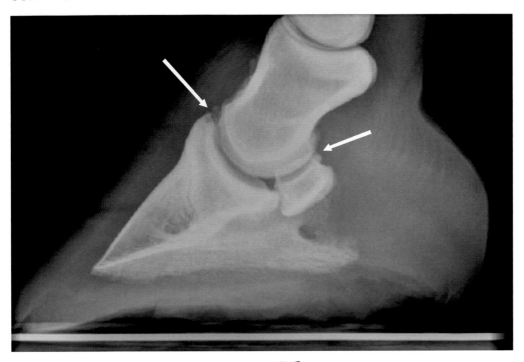

There is extensive new bone (arrows) laid down in the joint in this case of coffin osteoarthritis

The coffin joint is a high motion joint and is subject to trauma resulting from poor foot balance, uneven ground, heavy loading and rotational and sliding forces due to jumping and sharp turning. Arthritis (see p.43) in one or both forelimb coffin joints is common. Hindlimb coffin joint disease is much less common. Damage may occur to the joint surfaces, the joint capsule and its supporting ligaments (collateral ligaments).

Treatment

Acute cases with no x-ray changes may respond well to rest, medication of the joint (p.45) and, critically, correcting any foot imbalances that may have caused the problem. Horses showing extensive x-ray abnormalities indicating the presence of osteoarthritis respond much less well to treatment. Injuries to the collateral ligaments require box rest for two months followed by four months walking exercise, combined with remedial shoeing.

Clinical signs and diagnosis

Lameness is the main sign, sometimes associated with filling of the joint (there may be a small fluctuating swelling just above the coronet in front). The lameness may be sudden in onset or more insidious. If affected in both forelimbs the horse may not be overtly lame but may show poor performance, reluctance to jump or a shortened stride at the trot. Often lameness is increased when the horse is lunged on a hard surface.

Diagnosis

- Flexion of the lower limb may cause increased lameness in some but not all cases.
- The vet may anaesthetise the joint by injecting local anaesthetic into it and then checking for any improvement in lameness. However this may also anaesthetise other regions in the foot, complicating the diagnosis.
- Some horses show typical x-ray changes. In those that don't, an MRI scan of the foot may be helpful. Coffin joint disease may occur in association with other foot problems, such as navicular syndrome (p.32).

LEG PROBLEMS

In this section

Joint problems • Osteoarthritis • Windgalls • Sprained fetlock • Swellings in the cannon region • Strained tendons • Check ligament injury • Suspensory ligament injury • Splints The enlarged hock • Stifle problems • Exertional rhabdomyolysis

How joints work

A joint is the place where two bones meet. Normal joints ensure smooth, pain-free movement. To protect against wear the ends of the bone are covered with cartilage, a firm, springy, rubber-like substance with high resistance to wear. The cartilage:

• absorbs impact by compressing when loaded
• protects the bones underneath.

Joint fluid (synovial fluid) is a pale yellow highly viscous fluid present in the joint (see photo, p.107, bottom left). It is produced by the lining of the joint capsule, a tough membrane that surrounds every joint. Loading of the joint squeezes joint fluid in and out of the cartilage. Joint fluid:

• lubricates the joint to keep friction on the surface of the joint to a minimum
• provides nutrition to the joint cartilage.

The joint capsule holds the fluid in the joint and supports it during movement.

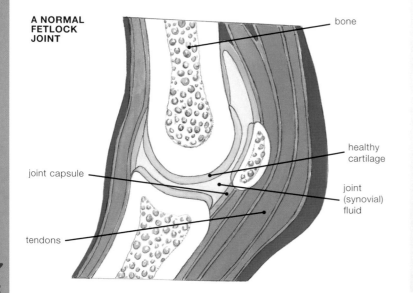

A NORMAL FETLOCK JOINT

bone

joint capsule

healthy cartilage

joint (synovial) fluid

tendons

JOINT PROBLEMS – KEY POINTS

Joint inflammation (arthritis) occurs when a joint is traumatised. This may occur because:

• The joint suffers *repetitive low-grade trauma* – the commonest reason by far. This occurs in the athletic horse as a consequence of the work it does. Factors that increase the amount of trauma are:
  ▪ **Age** The older the horse the greater the cumulative stresses on the joint will be.
  ▪ **Conformation and shoeing** Bad conformation and unbalanced feet result in uneven loading of the joints.
    Horses with poor conformation – for example, sickle hocks, toe-in or toe-out forelimbs, or base narrow/base wide (the forelimbs are not parallel) – are much more likely to develop arthritis, and will do so at an earlier age if they live an active life.
  ▪ **Work** Horses that jump, race and are ridden over long distances are more likely to develop wear and tear on their joints than horses that lead a more sedentary life.
• The joint is forced into an *abnormal position* or over-flexed/over-extended – a joint sprain.
• The internal structures of the joint are damaged, for example a 'chip' fracture of one of the bones in the joint.
• The joint has become *infected*, either by invasion of the joint by bacteria from the circulation (a common condition in young foals) or more commonly an external injury results in penetration of the joint.
    Joint infections are very destructive of the joint cartilage and must always be treated as an emergency.

THE IMPORTANCE OF GOOD HOCK CONFORMATION

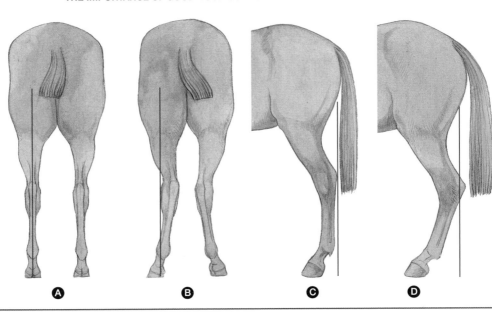

In good hock conformation (A) a line dropped from the point of the buttock goes through the middle of the hock, the middle of the fetlock and the middle of the back of the hoof. The horse in B has cow hocks. When trotting the limbs will not move straight (the horse will plait) and there will be uneven loading of the hock joints, predisposing to bone spavin. Viewed from the side (C), the line from the buttock should touch the back of the hock and the fetlock. Sickle hocks (D) predisposes hock joint disease and curb formation

Consequences of arthritis

Lameness.
Pain if the joint is manually flexed (sometimes).
Enlargement of the joint due to:

- Increased fluid – the inflamed joint capsule responds by producing more fluid, resulting in a 'puffy' joint. Increased fluid production is very variable and in low motion joints such as the small hock joints there may be no perceptible enlargement.

- Localised enlargement (for example, around the pastern joint – high ringbone) – due to the laying down of extra bone around the joint as part of the disease process.
- Erosion of the joint cartilage, which may eventually wear down to bone.
- The synovial fluid may become thinner and its constituents become abnormal.

OSTEOARTHRITIS (formerly Degenerative joint disease or DJD)

Osteoarthritis (OA) is a specific type of arthritis that is extremely common in the horse and, after sole abscesses, is the second most common cause of lameness.
The joints most commonly involved are the:

- coffin joint (see p.41)
- pastern joint in both fore and hind legs
- fetlock joint, principally in the forelimbs
- knee joints
- lower hock joints.

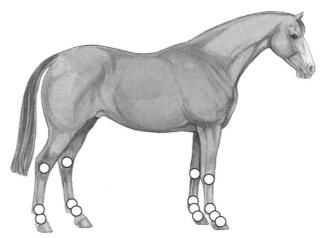

COMMON SITES OF OSTEOARTHRITIS (DJD) IN THE HORSE

Clinical signs

The lameness in osteoarthritis is usually mild to moderate and only rarely severe. It may start simply as 'stiffness' the day after exercise, especially if the horse been box-rested overnight. Often the stiffness will improve as the horse warms up. Eventually obvious lameness appears, although it may vary in severity from day to day. The disease often affects the same joint in both limbs.

Affected horses may show a restricted range of motion when the joint is flexed, and if a flexion test is performed the lameness is usually increased. The response to flexion must be interpreted with care as false-positive tests (i.e. no disease in the joint) are common.

Pastern joint OA (High ringbone)

Usually there is no increased joint fluid but, in long-standing cases, new bone may be laid down, resulting in an obvious hard swelling around the joint (ringbone, see photo, p.46). This must not be confused with thickening of the ligaments on one or both sides of the joint, which is common in otherwise healthy horses with toe-in or toe-out conformation.

Fetlock joint OA

One or both fore fetlocks may be involved and there is usually increased fluid in the joint (windgalls, p.46). If the horse is lunged the lameness is usually worse on the inside leg.

Knee OA

Knee (carpal) OA is mostly seen as a secondary complication of a fracture of one of the small bones in the knee or a sprain of one of the ligaments between the bones. It occurs mainly in Thoroughbred racehorses.

Hock OA (Bone spavin)

The hock is the commonest site of OA in the horse. The disease usually occurs in the middle-aged to older horse, particularly in those that have had an active working life and poor hock conformation (see illustration, p.43). Often the signs are subtle initially and may include stiffness, an apparent back problem or poor engagement of the hindlimbs when being schooled. Lameness eventually becomes obvious but it is usually mild to moderate. Frequently both hocks are affected.

When trotted there is poor hock flexion, sometimes with the toe catching; viewed from behind often the hind leg is brought inwards and the horse lands on the outside of the hoof first. There may be increased tension or resentment of pressure on the back muscles behind the saddle. This is often incorrectly diagnosed as a primary back problem. Only rarely are there visible external signs. A few cases develop a bony swelling on the inside of the hock level with the ergot.

Diagnosis of osteoarthritis

The diagnosis of osteoarthritis is straightforward if an injection of a local anaesthetic into the joint or region quickly abolishes the lameness. However in some parts of the limb, due to the proximity of other structures (for example the suspensory ligament in the hindleg), the result may be misleading as diffusion of the anaesthetic may anaesthetise adjacent structures.

Typical x-ray findings include narrowing of the joint spaces, the formation of 'new' bone around the edges of the joint and thickening of the bone immediately under the joint cartilage. Arthritic joints accumulate the radioactive isotope that is seen during bone scanning (p.17).

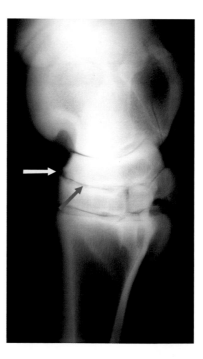

An x-ray confirms that this 10-year-old horse has bone spavin in both hocks. There is narrowing of the joint space due to cartilage breakdown (blue arrow) and new bone has formed on the front of a joint (yellow arrow)

What to do next

Only in early cases where there are minimal or no x-ray changes is a complete cure possible. In the majority of cases treatment is only palliative. The arthritis is not cured but is suppressed.

- **Management changes** The horse should spend as much time at pasture as possible to encourage gentle use of the affected joint(s). A reduction in the amount of work is advised, although regular gentle exercise is beneficial. Often the condition will recur if the original amount of exercise is resumed. Although on the one hand continued use of the joint will cause progression of the disease, on the other hand some joint loading is necessary for the health of joint cartilage, and movement helps to prevent a restricting fibrous reaction from forming around the joint. In addition a small percentage of spavin cases will self-cure because continued exercise causes the affected joints to fuse.
- **Correction of obvious predisposing factors** Horses with unbalanced feet will need remedial trimming and shoeing (see right). Obvious predisposing factors in the joint are treated surgically (for example a chip fracture can be removed arthroscopically).
- **Drug treatment** Drugs used to treat OA can be divided into:
  - **Drugs that give symptomatic relief**, such as phenylbutazone. This is very effective, at least in the initial stages, although the dose often has to be increased over time as the disease progresses. The horse receives an initial high dose that is then reduced to the lowest possible dose sufficient to keep the horse sound. Long-term low-dose treatment with phenylbutazone appears to be generally safe in the horse.
  - **Drugs that modify the disease**, such as corticosteroids, hyaluronan and PSGAGS (polysulphated glycosaminoglycons, such as 'Adequan'). These are often administered directly into the affected joints or given systemically. Recently the drug tiludronate has shown some promise in the treatment of bone spavin.
  - **Nutraceuticals** These drugs are added to feed and are sold through feed stores and other outlets without veterinary prescription. They are often based around glucosamine and chondroitin, which are the building blocks of joint cartilage. Experimentally both have been shown to inhibit cartilage damage in the horse. However, there are a number of concerns about these products. The optimal dose the optimal dose of glucosamine for a 500kg horse is 10g (10,000mg) per day, which is often well above the dose rate stated by the manufacturers of over-the-counter products. The concentration of glucosamine in some products is very low; because the products are unlicensed and unregulated, big variations in the actual level of the drugs (in comparison with the claimed levels) have been found. Although in principle these drugs can be recommended for treatment and prevention, veterinary advice should be sought.
- **Surgical treatment** It is possible surgically (or chemically) to destroy the joint cartilages resulting in fusion of the adjacent bones. This is an option in hock OA and may result in soundness. It is also used in pastern joint OA with more limited success.
- **Remedial shoeing (spavin only)** Improvement may occur with these surgical shoeing techniques:

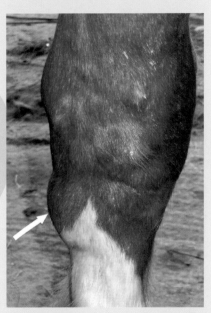

Unusually in spavin, this mare's hock has a large bony swelling (arrow) on the inside. She has advanced spavin but the bony reaction has caused the affected hock joints to fuse. Consequently the mare is not lame

  - rolling and squaring off the toe allows easier break-over.
  - raising the heel using a graduated shoe will help horses with a broken back hoof/pastern axis (p.20).
  - shoeing the affected leg with a shoe that has a wide outside branch (that overlaps the edge of the hoof) helps to stop the pronounced inward swing of the limb when trotting.

WINDGALLS

This is a general term given to fluid swellings just above the fetlock. Articular windgalls refers to excessive fluid in the fetlock joint, causing a soft swelling just above the joint on each side. Filling of the tendon sheath (tendinous windgalls) causes a swelling at the back of the fetlock extending one third of the way up the cannon.

Windgalls (windpuffs) are common in young horses, especially after breaking when first required to work hard. They often disappear without treatment. In some horses they are permanent and some windgalls (especially tendinous windgalls in the hindlimbs) become quite hard. Usually no treatment is required.

There is usually no lameness and opposite limbs are the same. However, a single-leg windgall, especially if associated with lameness, should be investigated by the vet.

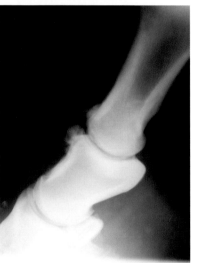

Above: This 18-year-old Thoroughbred was lame on both forelimbs. There is an obvious firm enlargement around the front of the pastern joints (arrows). An x-ray showed advanced signs of arthritis in both pastern joints (left). The horse has been receiving low-dose phenylbutazone for a year and has remained sound and in light work

Pre-purchase examinations and osteoarthritis

It is not uncommon for positive flexion tests to occur in non-lame horses being examined for a prospective purchaser. Because OA slowly progresses over time, it is possible that some of these horses are suffering from early OA that has genuinely not been noticed by the seller. In the absence of more information, vets often take a cautious approach and advise against purchase, especially if the horse has poor limb conformation or when only one limb produces a positive flexion test. In addition, a positive flexion test will usually exclude the entire limb from veterinary insurance cover.

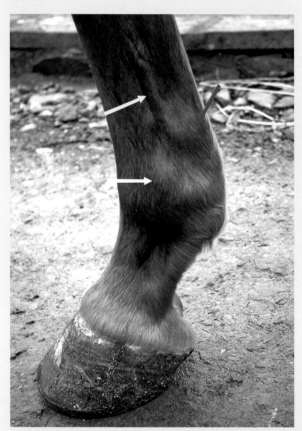

A filled fetlock joint (articular windgall – white arrow) anatomically separated from a filled tendon sheath (tendinous windgall – blue arrow) by the suspensory ligament (yellow arrow)

SPRAINED FETLOCK

This uncommon problem occurs in horses that lead active lives, especially those that jump.

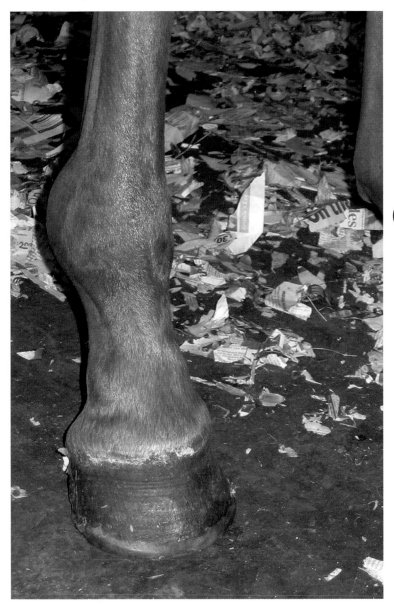

This sprained fetlock was hot and swollen. It was painful for the horse if manually flexed

Clinical signs

There is a sudden onset of moderate, usually forelimb, lameness. The fetlock joint capsule becomes distended (articular windgall). Often in addition there is diffuse heat and swelling around the fetlock joint. If the joint is manually flexed the horse resents it (compare both sides).

What to do next

If the horse is very lame, radiographic examination (p.16) is desirable to check for chip fractures within the joint, and certainly should be performed if the horse fails to respond to treatment within seven days, or if the lameness recurs when work is resumed. These treatments are used:

- Box rest (p.118) until all swelling around the joint is resolved
- Cold hosing of the joint (p.51)
- A pad and a stretchable pressure bandage is applied firmly from the coronet to just below the knee. This should be changed three times a day.
- Anti-inflammatory drugs are given
- Hand walking may start once the acute inflammation has subsided
- Mild cases will improve quickly and can resume work after 10–14 days
- In some cases medication of the joint with hyaluronan is beneficial, especially in cases that have failed to respond to the above regime

Swellings in the cannon region

There are number of structures in the cannon region that can become injured. Sometimes even localised injuries can result in diffuse swelling making identification of the injured structure difficult. Pressure bandaging to limit the swelling, careful localisation of the pain, and ultrasound scanning may provide help in identification.

Principal structures that become injured:
- flexor tendons at the back
- inferior check ligament roughly in the middle
- suspensory ligament just behind the cannon bone.

With the leg both raised and weight-bearing, each structure should be carefully felt for heat, pain and swelling (see pp.12–13).

THE ANATOMY OF THE CANNON REGION

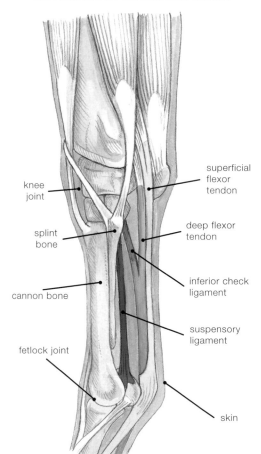

knee joint

splint bone

cannon bone

fetlock joint

superficial flexor tendon

deep flexor tendon

inferior check ligament

suspensory ligament

skin

CANNON REGION SWELLING
The key questions to answer are:

- **Has the horse recently been exercised?** Tendon and ligament injuries are usually caused by over-extension during fast work or jumping.

- **Does the swelling extend to the coronet?** Usually injuries to these structures will not cause swelling in the pastern although suspensory branch injuries may cause the fetlock on the side of the injured branch to appear swollen.

- **Is the area diffusely painful to touch?** If it is, then a localised infection or lymphangitis is likely.

- **Is the opposite limb the same?** It is rare for tendon and ligament injuries to affect both limbs at once.

STRAINED TENDONS
Injuries to the superficial flexor tendons (breaking down) commonly occur in horses that jump or work at speed. They are unusual in low speed disciplines, such as endurance riding, except where the horses are working in sand. Tendon injuries are rare in ponies.

Racing Thoroughbreds, especially steeplechasers and hurdlers, have a high incidence of tendon injuries, especially when the going is fast and the distance of the race is long. Recent research found that 43 per cent of a sample of apparently normal steeplechasers in training had evidence of early tendon breakdown on ultrasound scanning, and problems were more common the older the horse.

This photograph of a steeplechaser landing after a jump shows the extreme stretching force placed on the tendons and suspensory ligament of the leading leg of a horse jumping at speed (arrow)

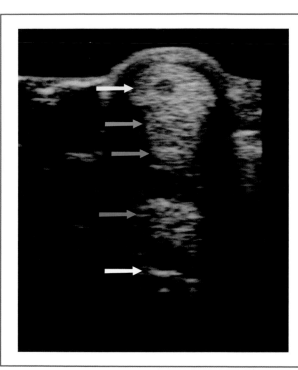

An ultrasound scan of the cannon region of a steeplechaser, which was swollen the day after a race.

Yellow - The superficial digital flexor tendon. A dark hole is present, a 'core lesion' – an area of ruptured tendon fibres

Green - Deep digital flexor tendon

Orange - Inferior check ligament

Pink - Suspensory ligament

White - Cannon bone

Tendons are composed of millions of tiny 'crimped' fibres running along their length. The crimping allows the fibres to stretch making the tendons very elastic. In a galloping horse they are stretched close to their limit of stretch at every stride. As the horse ages and the workload accumulates, the tendon becomes less well able to cope with this huge stress. Tendon breakdown involves rupture of the fibres. The greater the number of fibres that break, the more severe the injury.

 Clinical signs

- Heat in the tendon region is a frequent early sign.
- Swelling of the tendon. The edges feel round rather than sharp when felt with the limb unloaded. The tendon may feel softer, and be painful to touch (compare both sides).
- Lameness – variable in severity. Some horses may pull up lame at the end of a race and the tendon on the affected limb may feel completely normal. It may take several hours for swelling to appear.
- Mild cases, when healed, may leave no residual signs in the tendon. More serious cases will result in a 'bowed' tendon (convex when viewed form the side), which is detectable for the remainder of the horse's life.

Confirming the diagnosis

Ultrasound scanning allows the vet to examine the tendon structure in detail and confirm the diagnosis. It will also allow him or her to determine the severity of the injury, advise on the appropriate treatment and the length of the rest period and monitor healing by sequentially scanning the tendon at intervals during the recovery period (see 'What to do next', p.51).

This racehorse sustained a tendon breakdown 12 months before. The tendon region is now convex (bowed) rather than straight. This appearance will remain for the horse's life

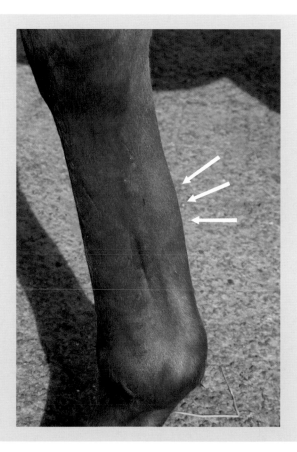

Key facts in tendon injuries

Heat in the tendon is an important sign that should not be ignored. The tendons of exercising horses should be regularly felt to detect heat, either first thing in the morning or in the late afternoon. Bandages should not be worn when stabled (unless strictly necessary) as they will inhibit the detection of heat.

The *degree of lameness* bears little relation to the severity of the tendon injury. A horse that has heat in a tendon but is not lame cannot be assumed to have only a very slight injury. Some horses with obvious core lesions on an ultrasound scan may not be visibly lame, but a severe injury will result if the horse is galloped or raced.

Healing occurs very slowly. Even a mild injury may take 12 months to heal fully before the horse can resume fast work. Uncontrolled turnout during the healing phase can significantly damage the tendon. The aim of treatment is to restore the original structure of the tendon as far as possible to reduce the risk of re-injury.

The broken tendon fibres are replaced by *scar tissue,* which after 12–18 months matches or even exceeds the pre-injury tendon strength. However, scar tissue, unlike normal tendon tissue, is not elastic and will not stretch when the tendon is loaded. For this reason re-injury is very common if the horse resumes the original level and type of work. *Controlled loading* of the tendon during the healing phase (as distinct from complete box rest) aids in limiting

A longitudinal scan of a team chaser's tendon shows disruption of the tendon fibres (arrows). The second scan taken 6 months later shows that the damaged area has been partially replaced with reasonably normal tendon

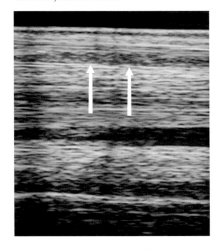
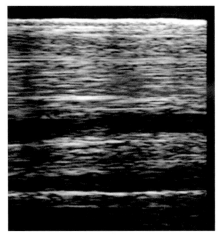

Various treatments

Over the years, myriad treatments have been used for tendons. Few have stood the test of time.

- **Tendon injections** A variety of drugs including hyaluronan, enzymes and PSGAGS ('Adequan') have been injected into tendons. Current evidence suggests they are of limited value. However new therapies are being developed all of the time.

- **Tendon splitting** A fine sharp blade is introduced into the damaged part of the tendon and an incision made which connects the core lesion to the outside of the tendon. There is evidence that core lesions fill in more quickly if splitting is done in the first week or so.

- **Shockwave therapy and therapeutic ultrasound** The latest research suggests that these therapies do not have a major effect on tendon healing.

Stems cells being injected into a tendon using ultrasound to guide the needle into the core lesion

These sequential ultrasound pictures show how stem cell injection of the core lesion (left) resulted in remarkable healing at one (middle) and two (right) months later

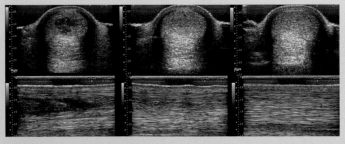

What to do next

- Frequent cold hosing limits inflammation and is more effective than applying ice. Cooling lotions, gels and clays have a very transient effect.
- Box rest the horse and apply a substantial support bandage from the coronet to just below the knee.
- The leg should be scanned around days 7–10. Scanning before this can underestimate the degree of damage present.
- The vet may give anti-inflammatory drugs either systemically or directly into the tendon.
- After about a week, if the horse is comfortable, short periods of very gentle hand walking can start, on level ground, followed by cold hosing and bandaging.

A controlled exercise programme then starts.

- **The horse is not turned out until it resumes full work.**
  - For the next eight weeks hand walking continues, building up to 45 minutes daily. Towards the end of this period the horse can be ridden at walk. It is then rescanned and the healing evaluated.
  - From nine weeks, add gentle trotting, starting at five minutes daily and building up to 30 minutes at eight months post-injury. Scanning should be done to monitor healing as each increment of work is increased.
  - Introduce gentle cantering, building to short periods of galloping after 10–11 months. Assuming a satisfactory appearance on scanning, full training can be resumed at 12 months.

Clay tendon-cooling products work by acting as carriers for volatile substances that have a cooling effect through evaporation. The clay is inert and has no therapeutic properties. Contrary to traditional practice, these products should never be covered with a bandage as this prevents evaporation

- **Stem cell treatment** Stem cells are harvested from the horse's bone marrow, grown in the laboratory and then injected into the core lesion 4–6 weeks after the injury occurred. The aim is to stimulate the production of normal tendon tissue rather than scar tissue in the damaged area. Early results from this technique suggest that it may work very well.

- **Firing** Burning of the skin and tendon with hot needles (pin firing) or rods (bar firing) has been practised for centuries. Studies have shown no beneficial effect other than enforced rest.

- **Blistering** – the application of a highly irritant material to the skin – has no effect on the tendons and should not be done.

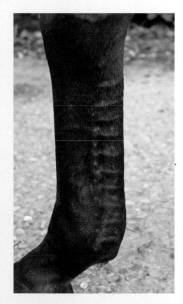

The parallel scars on this horse's leg indicate that it has been bar-fired. This outmoded treatment is no longer recommended

Swellings in the canon region

CHECK LIGAMENT INJURY

The check ligament is a band of fibrous tissue that extends from back of the knee to the middle of the deep flexor tendon (see illustration, p.48). It is only about one third as strong as the deep flexor tendon and is especially susceptible to injury in jumping horses. The ligament becomes more fragile with age. Forelimb check ligament injuries are common, especially in older (greater than 8 years) ponies, cobs, warmbloods and cross-breeds.

Clinical signs

The horse suddenly becomes moderately or severely lame. There is an area of swelling on the inside and outside of the mid cannon region but not at the back (which distinguishes the injury from a tendon injury). An ultrasound scan shows the disruption of the ligament.

What to do next

- Box rest the horse and once comfortable, gently walk it in hand.
- Cold hosing several times a day, support bandaging and anti-inflammatory drugs are helpful.
- Start a gradually ascending programme of walking exercise with serial monitoring by ultrasound.

Injuries of the check ligament tend to heal much quicker than tendon injuries and most horses can resume work 3–6 months afterwards. There is usually a detectable swelling in the region for the rest of the horse's life. However premature return to work or turning the horse out in the early stages of the injury results in greater risk of failure of healing.

Occasionally horses with a recurrence of the injury, or those managed inappropriately initially, show persistent lameness because the ligament fails to heal. Injection of the ligament or in some cases surgical severing of the ligament may be necessary.

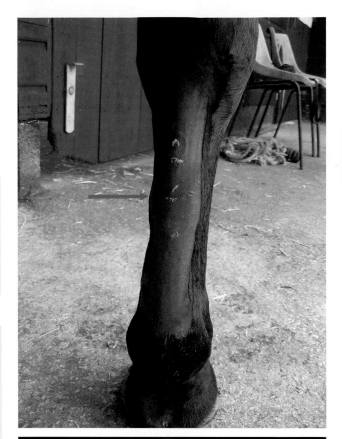

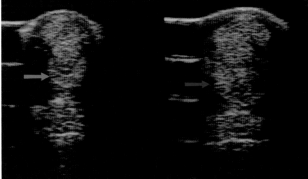

The firm swelling (arrow) in the mid cannon region of this horse (top) resulted from an inferior check ligament injury sustained three months before. An ultrasound scan of both forelegs of the horse (above) shows that the normal check ligament (green arrow) on the left foreleg is much smaller and more distinct than the damaged one on the right foreleg (red arrow)

SUSPENSORY LIGAMENT INJURY

The suspensory ligament supports the fetlock joint. It originates at the back of the knee and runs immediately behind the cannon bone. Two thirds of the way down, the body of the ligament divides into an inner and outer branch, which in turn attach to the sesamoid bones on each side. With the limb weight-bearing the ligament appears as a tight bone-like structure just behind the cannon bone. Injury to the suspensory ligament is becoming more common, especially in the hind legs.

Suspensory injuries occur:

- At the top of the ligament just below the knee – *proximal suspensory desmitis (PSD)* – in the fore and hind limbs. Horses of all ages and types are susceptible but the condition is especially common in dressage horses and older high-level competition horses. Foot imbalance (fore and hind) and straight hock conformation predispose to PSD.

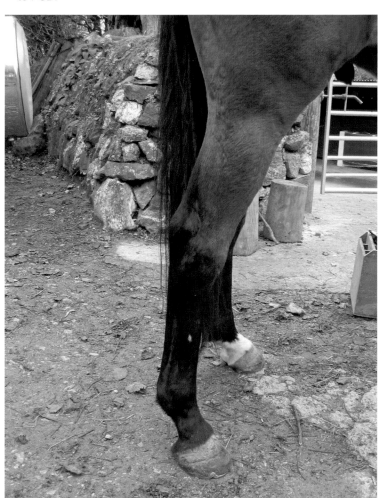

Abnormally straight hock conformation predisposes to hindlimb proximal suspensory desmitis

- In the *body (middle part)* of the ligament, especially in Thoroughbred racehorses.
- In *one (occasionally both) branch.* Branch injuries are common in all types of performance horses. Poor foot balance is an important predisposing factor.

THE SUSPENSORY LIGAMENT VIEWED FROM THE BACK (WITH THE TENDONS REMOVED)

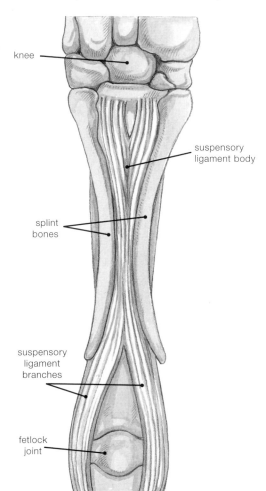

knee

suspensory ligament body

splint bones

suspensory ligament branches

fetlock joint

The suspensory ligament divides into two branches in the lower third of the cannon area. The splint bones lie next to it on each side

Clinical signs

- **PSD** Transient heat and pain may be found at the top of the suspensory ligament but this is often missed. Variable degrees of lameness occur. Sometimes there is no overt lameness just subtle signs such as stiffness, a reluctance to go forward, lack of power when jumping or unexpected refusing, and difficulties in performing certain dressage movements (such as canter pirouette). Abnormalities when ridden (and the response to nerve blocks) may only be appreciated by the rider.
- **Body injuries** Lameness (which often resolves quickly) and swelling in the middle of the ligament. There may be pain if the ligament is squeezed with the limb supported (compare both sides).
- **Branch injuries** One (or both) branches swell and are painful in the early stages. Lameness is variable and may be absent. There may be an associated fracture of the end of the nearby splint bone.

Confirming the diagnosis

PSD can be difficult to diagnose and may require a combination of selective nerve blocks, ultrasound scanning, x-ray, bone scanning and MRI (pp.16–17). Body and branch injuries are usually reasonably obvious and can be confirmed using ultrasound.

What to do next

- Box rest with anti-inflammatory and cold therapy (cold hosing, ice packs) are used at first. Thereafter controlled exercise is a key component of treatment.
- Shockwave therapy is reported to be helpful in forelimb proximal suspensory ligament disease.
- Recently a surgical procedure in hindlimb PSD (in which the nerve that supplies the area is severed and adjacent nerves are released from compression by the enlarged ligament) has produced good results, significantly better than shockwave or a rest/controlled exercise regime.
- Stem cell therapy has been used in suspensory body injury.

Shock wave therapy is administered to a case of proximal suspensory desmitis. The probe delivers pulsed acoustic pressure waves, generating high-stress forces on the area. A pain-killing effect has been demonstrated. The mechanism by which this therapy appears to improve healing is at present uncertain

SPLINTS

The two splint bones lie one on each side of the cannon bone. They are connected to the cannon by a dense ligament. A 'splint' is caused either by a sprain of this ligament or by direct external trauma to it. The horse's body responds by laying down bone in the ligament to stabilise it. Splints most commonly develop in 2–4 year old horses, and usually affect the inside of the forelegs, occasionally the outside of the hindlimbs. Predisposing causes are direct trauma to the ligament (for example being knocked by the opposite hoof in toe-out horses), or overloading from above due to conformation or excessive exercise (especially lungeing).

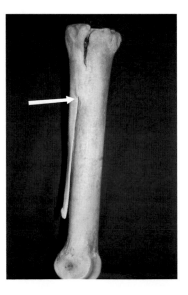

A view of the inside of the cannon bone. A splint is present (arrow), joining the splint bone to the cannon via a bony junction

Clinical signs

When the splint is actively forming the horse may be lame at trot. Heat, swelling and pain on finger pressure occur in the splint region. Most of the swelling is soft tissue inflammation. As this resolves, the ligament turns to bone, leaving a smaller, permanent, hard swelling. The lameness then disappears. Some splints form with little or no lameness or inflammation.

The condition may be confused with a fractured splint bone (the commonest fracture in the horse) or a fracture may occur as part of the splint process. Fracture cases are invariably lame, for a longer period, and the swelling extends over a larger area. Large splints may impinge on the adjacent suspensory ligament causing lameness, often some time after the splint has formed.

Treatment

Box rest for 4–6 weeks is desirable and in principle will result in a smaller splint. The time taken for the splint to resolve is very variable, ranging from 2–3 weeks to 2–3 months. Cold hosing, ice packs, topical application or injection of anti-inflammatory drugs or shockwave therapy may help. Work should not resume until there is no pain reaction to firm finger pressure on the splint. Before this time some fitness may be maintained by swimming exercise. If the final splint is large, protective boots should be worn at exercise.

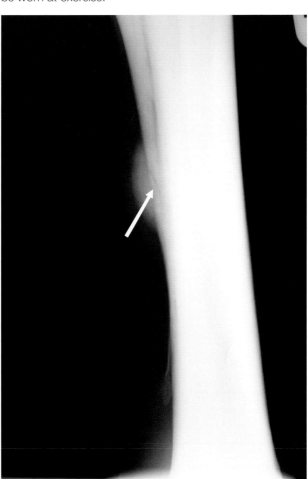

An x-ray of a splint that failed to resolve in the usual period of time. A faint fracture line (arrow) is visible in the middle of it

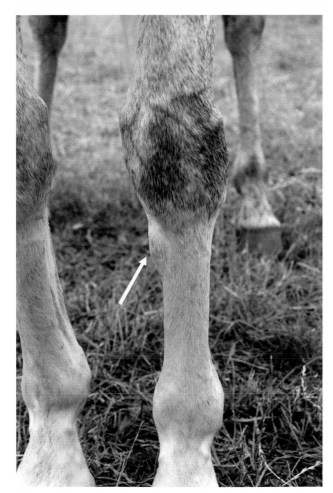

A large splint (arrow) has developed on the inside of this Arabian horse's foreleg. The cannon bone is quite offset in relation to the forearm (bench knees), causing excessive loading of the inside splint bone and consequent splint formation

The enlarged hock

Diffuse or localised enlargement of the hock is a common phenomenon, and there are a large number of causes.

DIFFUSE ENLARGEMENT

Filling of the large hock joint – bog spavin

The large joint at the junction of the tibia and the hock (the tarso-crural or TC joint) will fill with excess joint fluid in many diseases of the hock. Bog spavin is a general term for this filling. There are many causes including:

- **Sprain of the hock**, caused by quick turning or stopping. This will injure the joint capsule and the supporting ligaments.

- **Poor conformation** such as straight hocks, sickle or cow hocks, predisposing to abnormal stresses on the TC joint.

- **A joint cartilage development problem** in young horses (less than 2 years old) called osteochondrosis (OCD). Occurring in many joints, the hock is a particular predilection site in Shires and warmbloods. Disruption and fragmentation of the cartilage surface causes inflammation within the joint. Lameness is variable in severity (often mild), changing from day to day. Some cases do not become lame and many self-cure without treatment. If the horse is lame surgical treatment is necessary to remove the abnormal cartilage.

- **Fractures** in or close to the joint.

Many young horses (1–2 years old) develop bog spavins and the problem often disappears without treatment (assuming the horse is not lame) as the horse becomes older. It is advisable to x-ray these cases if there is any lameness or if treatment is attempted. Draining the fluid tends to produce a transient improvement in that the joint re-fills fairly quickly, especially if the horse has poor conformation. Pressure bandaging to prevent re-filling and injection of the joint with corticosteroids or hyaluronan following drainage can be done but the joint must always be x-rayed to first in order to rule out OCD or other damage to the joints.

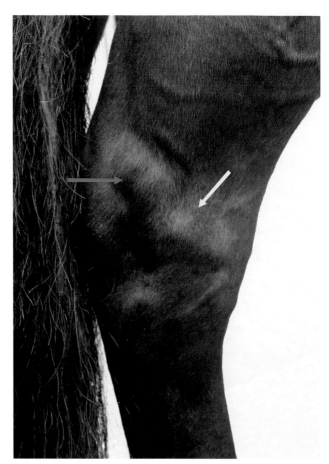

In this hock there is a slight filling of the TC joint – a small bog spavin (yellow arrow) – and the tarsal sheath – a thoroughpin (green arrow), see p.58

Infection

Infection under the skin (cellulitis) can cause marked swelling of the hock and lameness. Occasionally the swelling will be on one side only. Lameness is often severe but may improve with walking. The area will be painful on finger pressure. The horse may have a raised temperature and close inspection often reveals a wound or a small area of skin penetration. The vet will check for joint infection also. Treatment is with antibiotics and, if a joint is infected, copious flushing of the joint, which may have to be done under general anaesthesia.

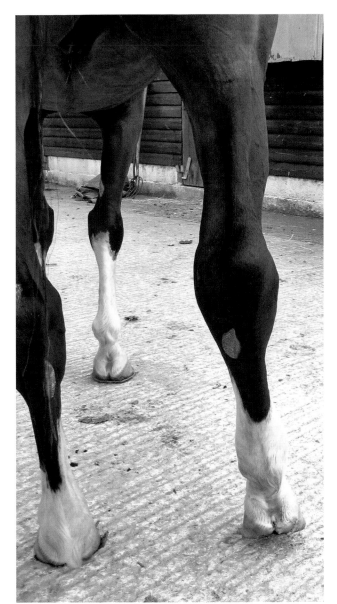

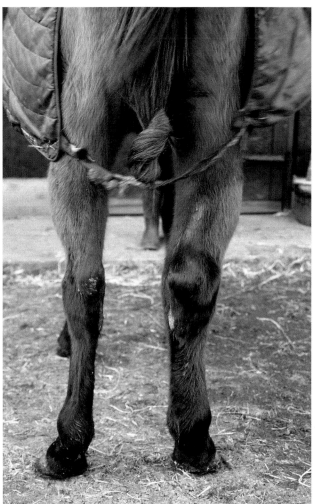

Lymphangitis can cause severe lameness. In this case (above), the entire right hindlimb is swollen and painful to touch

The right hock is quite swollen in this lame eventer (left). A small wound on the inside caused both a joint infection and infection under the skin around the hock

Lymphangitis

This is a common condition that is not very well understood. It is most frequently seen in stabled horses and has a tendency to recur, sometimes eventually causing a permanently enlarged leg. It appears to be caused by infection gaining entry to the lymphatic system of the leg. Often a small wound or an area of 'cracked heel' infection is found.

There is marked swelling of the leg (usually the hindleg) often starting from the pastern or fetlock region and gradually extending upwards over 1–2 days. If the horse is box-rested the swelling may eventually extend from the lower leg to the stifle. The horse is very lame although the lameness will ease if the horse is hand-walked. Squeezing the swollen area with the fingers will cause the horse to snatch its leg upwards and outwards. The swollen area 'pits' on finger pressure. Occasionally, in more long-standing cases, serum may weep through the skin.

Prompt administration of antibiotics, corticosteroids and possibly phenylbutazone will cure the condition, but is essential that the horse is hand-walked several times a day and if possible, also turned out all of the time so that it can move around. To prevent recurrence, the affected leg should be bandaged if the horse is stabled for more than 12 hours.

LOCALISED SWELLINGS

Thoroughpin

A tendon sheath surrounds the deep flexor tendon as it passes over the hock. A thoroughpin is a filling of this sheath, resulting in an ill-defined fluid swelling just above the point of the hock, in front of the Achilles tendon. There is no heat or lameness. The cause is assumed to be repeated low-grade trauma, perhaps aggravated by poor hock conformation.

Mild to moderate thoroughpins are common in young horses and often resolve without treatment. However, the fluid can be drained, followed by injection and pressure bandaging to prevent re-filling (as in bog spavin). Some cases have damage to adjacent structures and may require more investigation.

Capped hock

Repeated trauma to the point of the hock, often caused by the horse lying on insufficient bedding will eventually result in a permanent thickening. In a few cases, a fluid-filled structure (a bursa) also develops and can be quite large. There is no lameness but the appearance is unsightly.

Treatment includes provision of a deep bed (preferably woodshavings or paper) and topical application of a corticosteroid/DMSO solution. Drainage and injection may be attempted as in bog spavin.

A similar bursa may develop at the point of the elbow, a capped elbow or shoe boil, due to repeated trauma from the heel of the shoe when the horse lies down. A sausage boot applied around the pastern will protect the elbow.

Curb

The plantar ligament is a thin band of tissue that extends from the point of the hock to the top of the cannon bone. A curb is a sprain of this ligament and can be felt as a small hard bump at the back of the leg level with top of the cannon. Poor hock conformation, especially sickle hocks, predisposes to this condition. Some curbs are caused by direct trauma to the ligament, even when the hock conformation is good.

In some, but not all, horses in the acute stage there is heat, swelling and slight lameness present. Often the acute stage is unnoticed but it may be treated by rest, cold application and anti-inflammatory drugs given both topically and systemically.

The curb swelling is permanent. Because curbs are a significant blemish in the show ring, attempts are made to treat them by blistering and firing, but with limited success.

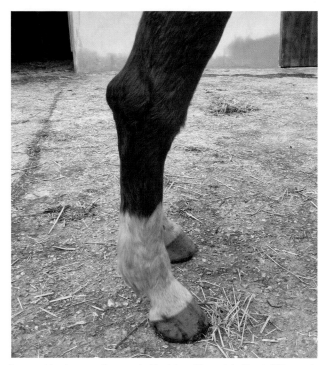

A capped hock caused by repeated bruising of the point of hock. This mare's bed was a thin layer of straw placed on concrete

FALSE CURBS

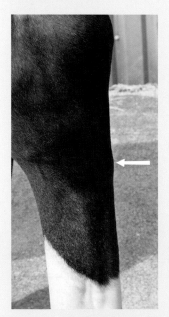

False curbs, where a large head of the splint bone protrudes behind the leg, are very common and can be distinguished from true curbs by careful palpation. Closer examination of this suspected curb revealed that the head of the outside splint bone was naturally quite large but the plantar ligament was flat, indicating this was a false curb and of no significance.

Stifle problems

UPWARD FIXATION OF THE PATELLA

This is the commonest stifle problem. The patella (kneecap bone) gets 'trapped' in an upwardly displaced position because one of its ligaments (the medial patellar ligament – on the inside) becomes hooked over the inside end of the femur.

The disease affects young horses (1–4 years) mostly, and all breeds and types. It is particularly common in Shetlands (often affecting both hindlegs). Horses that are underweight, poorly muscled behind or unfit are especially susceptible. Most commonly, the condition is intermittent.

**RIGHT STIFLE JOINT
VIEWED FROM THE INSIDE**

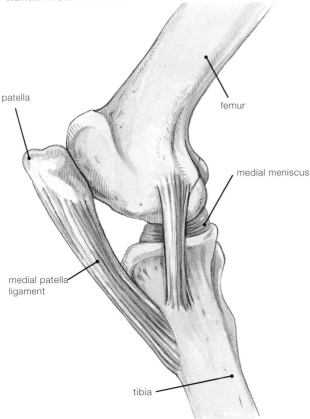

patella

femur

medial meniscus

medial patella ligament

tibia

In upward fixation, the medial patellar ligament gets hooked over the end of the femur

Clinical signs

- The patella briefly 'catches' as the horse walks.
- If circled on the lunge at the walk and watched carefully the horse is seen to briefly abnormally extend the hock and then release it. The stifle can be seen to 'pop' as the patella frees itself.
- Walking up and down hill can cause the patella to catch briefly.
- Sometimes the patella becomes locked in the abnormal position. The hock and stifle are held rigidly extended and cannot be flexed. In this case, the locked patella can be freed by backing the horse or, if that fails, by manually pushing the patella downwards and inwards in the direction of the opposite elbow.
- Some long-standing cases develop an inflamed stifle joint and become lame. These must be carefully investigated, including x-raying the stifle.

What to do next

- Many horses will outgrow this condition if they are broken in and ridden. However, they may suffer from it again if they have to be box-rested, as the hindlimb muscles become slack.
- Build up the hindquarter (quadriceps) muscles by frequent straight line work (avoid lungeing) – uphill and downhill trotting is often effective. If stabled, simply turning out the horse to pasture is often effective.
- If the horse is underweight improving the overall body condition by worming and increased feeding is necessary.
- If conservative treatment fails other options include:
  - Fitting a raised heel shoe on the affected side may help mild cases.
  - Injecting or longitudinally splitting the medial patellar ligament to provoke a fibrous reaction in it. The thickened ligament is less likely to become hooked over the femur.
  - Surgically severing the ligament. This is very effective but some cases (18% in a recent survey) may develop patellar fragmentation and other stifle problems afterwards. To help prevent these, the horse must be box-rested for at least three months afterwards with an ascending programme of exercise.

OTHER STIFLE PROBLEMS

Fracture of the patella is a common fracture in event horses colliding with a fence. Usually the inner side of the patella is fractured and pulled away by the medial patellar ligament. Resting the horse combined with cutting the ligament may be curative.

Osteochondrosis is a problem of joint cartilage development that commonly occurs in the stifle joint in Thoroughbred horses. Signs can be seen from four months of age. There is usually excess fluid in the joint. Lameness is very variable although some have a sudden onset of severe lameness. Often both stifles are affected. If the horse is less than eight months old many will self-cure (unless very lame) if box-rested. If it is older than eight months then surgical treatment is necessary. This allows removal of cartilage fragments free in the joint and loosely attached to the joint surface, and scraping away unhealthy cartilage. (See also 'Filling of the large hock joint', p.57.)

Meniscal damage The menisci are two thick pads of cartilage that cushion the two points of contact between the end of the femur and the top of the tibia (see illustration, p.59. Damage to these is an infrequent but serious cause of stifle lameness. Some cases respond to box rest and graded exercise while others need stifle surgery. The prognosis of mild injuries is good but more severe injuries often do not recover.

Other leg problems

EQUINE RHABDOMYOLYIS SYNDROME (ERS, Azoturia, Monday morning disease)

Traditionally, this cramp-like condition was believed to be caused by exercising a horse after a short period of rest on high level feeding (hence 'Monday morning', after a rest on Sunday). However the clinical picture seen in ERS is now thought to reflect multiple causes but with a broadly similar set of clinical signs. A UK survey of racing Thoroughbreds found that around 6 per cent of horses in training were affected each year. All breeds and types of horse are affected.

Key facts in ERS

- Contrary to traditional belief, there is no association between ERS and lactic acid production in muscles. Consequently supplements that aim to control acidosis, such as sodium bicarbonate and di-methyl glycine (DMG) are ineffective.
- Female horses are on average about twice as likely to suffer as males.
- The full clinical syndrome is not universal. Some cases just show poor performance or a mild transient lameness or stiffness after exercise.
- Some horses develop a single episode of ERS because they are exercised beyond their level of fitness especially after a rest period. Sometimes a concurrent respiratory infection can increase the risk.
- Other horses suffer repeatedly from the disease. These cases may be suffering from polysaccharide storage myopathy (PSSM – mostly Quarter horses, draught breeds, Appaloosas, Warmbloods) or recurrent exertional rhabdomyolysis (RER – mostly Thoroughbreds and

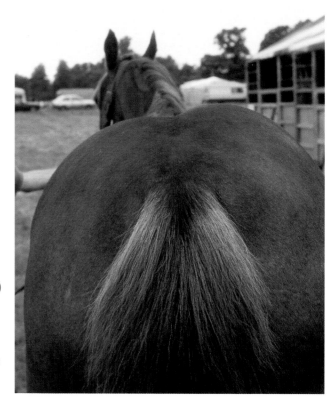

This endurance horse developed ERS at the end of an 80km (50 mile) race. The right gluteal (rump) area was hard and painful to touch. Occasionally, as in this case, the affected muscle visibly swells

Arabians). These are complex metabolic disorders that may be genetic in origin.
- Recurrent cases should receive a detailed investigation to determine whether they have PSSM or RER.

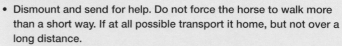

✓ Clinical signs

- A muscular cramp-like syndrome appears when the horse is exercised. Typically it appears shortly after exercise starts, often as the horse is asked to quicken from a trot to a canter or asked to go up a hill.
- Often the horse slows down and unexpectedly is reluctant to go forward.
- Eventually it is obvious to the rider that something is wrong with the horse.
- The horse sweats disproportionately in relation to the amount of work it has done. The rider may think the horse has developed colic.
- If asked to walk forward the horse walks with a stiff, stilted hindlimb gait.
- The muscles of the rump (gluteals) or loins may feel tense and hard, on one or both sides.
- In some cases no abnormal muscles can be found but the horse is clearly in pain.
- After a few hours the horse may produce dark purple urine, due to muscle pigments from damaged muscles getting into the circulation and from there into the urine via the kidneys. In mild cases the urine may not be discoloured.

Atypical cases

Some cases do not occur as described above. The condition may appear:

- Ten to 15 minutes after the horse is returned to its stable or asked to stand still after a normal bout of exercise.
- In endurance horses in the 'vet gates' during the rest period between phases of the competition. Fluid and electrolyte deficiencies (due to losses in sweat) may predispose horses.
- In grazing horses in some countries where a rare syndrome of rhabdomyolysis has been found.

? What to do next

- Dismount and send for help. Do not force the horse to walk more than a short way. If at all possible transport it home, but not over a long distance.
- Although it is traditional to keep the hindquarters warm by rugging, it is not known if this is of benefit.
- The vet will administer a pain-killing anti-inflammatory drug. If the horse is severely affected, sweating profusely or if it is an endurance horse in mid-race, intravenous fluids will be given. A horse in severe pain may need to be sedated.
- A blood sample may be taken to confirm the diagnosis. High levels of muscle enzymes, released from damaged muscle cells, are found in the blood.
- Box rest the horse overnight. The next day the majority of cases will be clinically normal and may be turned out. If still abnormal, box rest should continue until the horse is moving freely, does not resent muscle pressure and has normal-coloured urine.
- Initial turnout in a small paddock with minimal hard feed is ideal. The horse should not resume work until a blood sample confirms the muscles have recovered. Short periods of work are re-introduced and care is taken to ensure the horse is properly warmed up.

Recurrent cases

Horses that repeatedly suffer from the disease should be investigated for obvious predisposing factors. A muscle biopsy from the muscles at the root of the tail will help to diagnose PSSM. There is currently no available test for RER.

The typical 'port wine'-coloured urine passed by the more severe cases of ERS

Preventing ERS

Irrespective of the cause, the current state of knowledge suggests the following will help to prevent further attacks.

- Keep the horse in the pasture for a large part of the day. Use a turnout rug if the weather is cold. If possible provide 24-hour turnout. While at grass, manage as a potential laminitic – avoid lush, especially ryegrass, paddocks. A sparse paddock is ideal.
- Exercise regularly and try to avoid rest days. If the horse is rested, drastically reduce the amount of additional feed and ensure it is turned out.
- Modify the diet:
  - Ensure as much of the food requirements as possible come from forage. Alfalfa chaff is a good feed to use.
  - If the calorie needs of the horse cannot be met by forage alone, to provide additional calories with a low-starch high-oil feed designed for ERS cases – these are available commercially. Calories can also be provided in the form of vegetable oil.
  - Ensure the vitamin and mineral profile of the diet is correct. Additional electrolytes (principally salt) must be provided. Consult a nutritionist.
  - Although anecdotally additional vitamin E and selenium have been beneficial, most affected horses are not deficient.

ERS is common in endurance horses and can occur at any stage of the race, but mainly shortly after the start (in the first 10km) or much later. The clinical signs vary considerably, ranging from an acute severe hindlimb lameness in one or both hindlegs, to a milder form without firmness or swelling in the affected muscles. Horses that suffer from exhaustion later in the race may also develop ERS

RESPIRATORY PROBLEMS

In this section

Assessing the respiratory system • Nasal discharge • Nosebleeds • Coughing • Strangles • Reccurrent airway obstruction • Abnormal breathing sounds at exercise

How respiration works

In the lungs, oxygen is transferred from the air into the bloodstream and then delivered to all the tissues of the body. Oxygen uptake in the lungs is a key factor in performance.

During inspiration, air enters the nasal passages and is warmed and humidified in the head before passing through the larynx into the windpipe *(trachea)*. The trachea divides into two main *bronchi*, which in turn divide many times to form progressively smaller bronchioles. Finally, the smallest bronchioles connect to many millions of tiny air sacs, *alveoli*, where *gas exchange* (oxygen in, carbon dioxide out) takes place. Although some filtration of larger dust particles in inspired air occurs in the nose, most of the smaller dust particles enter the lungs.

THE RESPIRATORY SYSTEM

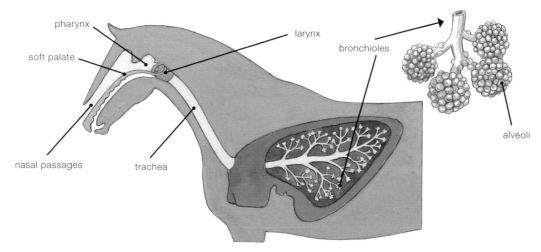

Oxygen delivery to the bloodstream can be impaired by:
- obstruction to the airflow in the upper airways, for example in the nasal passages, throat or larynx
- obstruction to airflow in the lower airways, caused principally by the presence of excess mucus or spasm of the bronchi
- inflammation of the lining of the smallest airways causing thickening of their walls and preventing diffusion of oxygen through them into the bloodstream. The main causes are infection or an inflammatory response to stable dust.

ASSESSING THE RESPIRATORY SYSTEM

You can assess the general condition of a horse's respiratory system by:

- **Taking its rectal temperature** (p.154).
- **Observing its respiratory rate** Watch the horse breathe while standing quietly. The respiratory rate (normally 8–16 breaths per minute) may be increased because of:
  - respiratory disease causing poor uptake of oxygen from the lungs – the breathing rate increases in an attempt to compensate
  - fear – a frightened horse breathes more deeply and rapidly
  - excitement
  - recent exertion
  - elevated body temperature – a small increase in respiratory rate is sometimes present
  - anaemia or another disorder of the circulatory system.
- **Noting the respiratory effort** During quiet breathing, movement of the chest should be barely visible. In some normal horses, at expiration the floor of the abdomen may lift slightly. If it lifts appreciably with each expiration the horse is forcing air out of the lungs, which means expiration has become active rather than passive, usually this is because of spasm of the bronchi and/or obstruction of the small airways by mucus.

- **Checking nostril movement** during breathing – normally there is no perceptible movement during quiet breathing. Flaring of the nostrils in a non-nervous horse suggests laboured breathing.
- **Checking for a nasal discharge** If there is a discharge, is it from one or both nostrils, and is the discharge mucus,

A respiratory infection in this horse has resulted in a thick yellow discharge from both nostrils

pus or blood, or a mixture of these? Does the discharge smell? (Upper molar teeth infections that have extended into the sinuses usually cause a very smelly discharge.) Is there food material present in the discharge? (This indicates a swallowing problem.)

- **Looking at the eyes** Some sinus disorders may cause obstruction of the tear duct as it crosses the wall of the sinus. There may be excess overflow of tears from one eye or a discharge. Some respiratory infections (for example EHV and EVA viruses) may cause a discharge from both eyes.

This horse has severe lung disease. The nostrils flare (open) noticeably at every breath

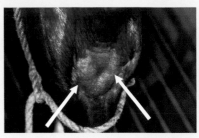

A view of the underside of a horse's head. The hair has been clipped to reveal the enlarged submandibular lymph glands (arrows)

- **Feeling the lymph glands** in the angle of the jawbone. They enlarge and become tender to touch in response to infection and inflammation in the head and throat regions. In strangles infection (see p.72) the enlarged glands may eventually burst releasing yellow pus.
- **Squeezing the trachea** where it joins the larynx and hold the pressure for a few seconds. If the horse has a cough, this action will often provoke a fit of coughing. A single cough is probably not a significant reaction.

A blob of mucus coughed up by a horse and deposited on the ground outside the stable door

- Note whether there are discharges anywhere else. Horses with recurrent airway obstruction (RAO or COPD, see p.75) will often deposit lumps of grey-yellow discharge on the stable floor, in the water bucket or especially on the ground outside the stable.
- **Is the horse otherwise well?** Horses with RAO are often bright and eating normally whereas horses with respiratory infections, especially in the early stages, may have an elevated body (rectal) temperature and may be a bit depressed with a reduced appetite.

What will the vet do

In addition to making the assessments on p.64, a vet will listen to the trachea and chest with a **stethoscope** to detect abnormal sounds as the horse breathes, indicating excess fluid (mucus) in the airways, narrowing of the airways, or the presence of inflammatory debris in them. A diminution or complete absence of the normal breathing sounds in a part of the lung might indicate pneumonia or the accumulation of fluid in the space between the lung and the chest wall (pleurisy).

Re-breathing To amplify the sounds the vet may make the horse breathe more deeply by temporarily closing off the nostrils or getting the horse to breathe for a while into a plastic bag. This deep breathing may provoke a fit of coughing if the horse has inflamed airways.

A fibre-optic endoscope has been inserted into this horse's trachea via its nose and pharynx

Endoscopic examination
A flexible fibre-optic (or video-) endoscope is introduced through a nostril and slowly passed through the upper airway. The nasal passages, pharynx, soft palate and throat are visualised first. The movements of the larynx during breathing are carefully assessed to detect any paralysis on the left side. The endoscope is then passed through the larynx and on down into the trachea until the division of the trachea is seen.

During the endoscopic examination the vet may perform a *tracheal wash* to assist with the diagnosis. A sample of the fluid in the trachea is obtained by passing a sterile tube through the endoscope. Sterile saline is then injected through the tube. The saline washes some secretion from the tracheal wall and then runs backwards into the tracheal 'sump'. The tube is withdrawn to the sump and the fluid collected using a syringe.

Tracheal washes are especially useful in detecting mild inapparent respiratory infections of performance horses, in investigating horses with long-standing coughs, and in monitoring the response to treatment.

A tracheal wash is obtained via a catheter passed through the endoscope

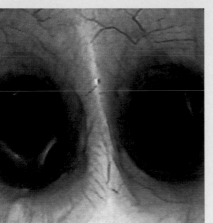

A view through the endoscope of the carina, the point at which the trachea divides into two main bronchi

In this typical tracheal wash sample small flecks of mucus are visible floating in the liquid

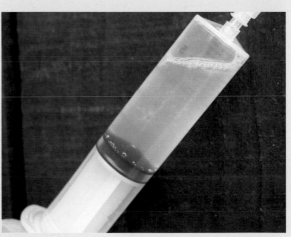

Nasal discharge

Discharges from the nose are a common symptom of respiratory disease. In most cases a discharge from one nostril only indicates the problem is in the head region (i.e. forward of the larynx) but a discharge from both nostrils suggests the problem may be in the head or in the lungs.

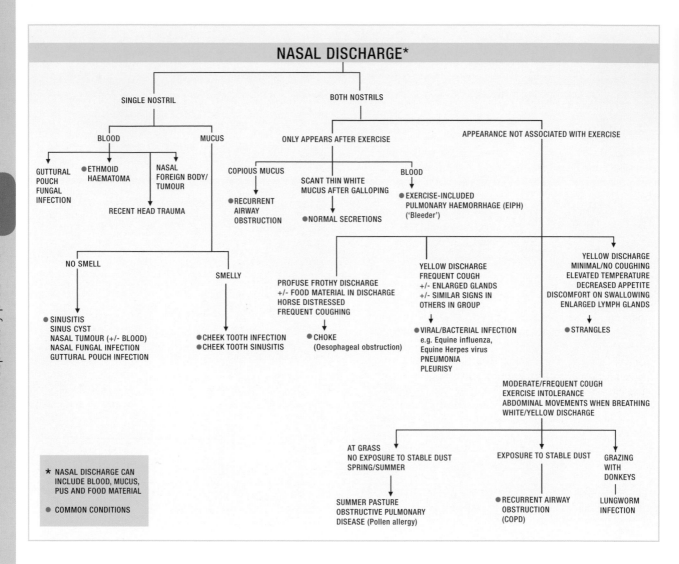

SINUS INFECTIONS

The sinuses are large air-filled cavities in the horse's skull. Their function is to warm and humidify inspired air. They are lined with a layer of mucus-secreting glands. The mucus is continuously produced and exits the sinus through small openings into the nasal passages.

- Primary sinusitis results when an upper respiratory infection, which involves the sinuses, results in excess mucus production and swelling of the lining of the sinus.

The swelling and excess mucus will impede drainage from the sinus. Eventually the sinus becomes filled with pus, which results in a permanent discharge from one of the horse's nostrils.

- Secondary sinusitis results from the extension of a cheek (premolar or molar) tooth root infection into the sinus overlying the tooth. The presence of a tumour or cyst in the sinus of the horse may also be the cause of secondary sinusitis.

POSITION OF THE SINUSES

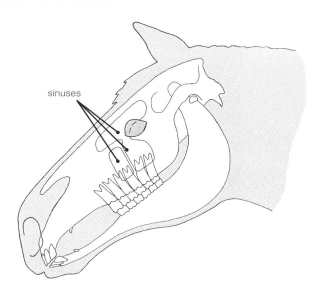

sinuses

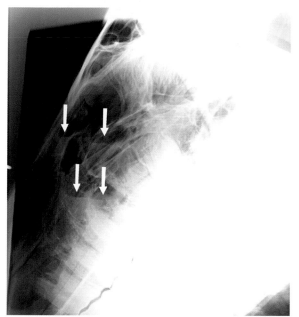

There is fluid in this horse's sinuses, shown by horizontal lines (arrows)

What are the signs

Almost always only a single side of the head, involving one or more sinus compartments, is affected. There is nasal discharge of pus (sometimes blood-stained) from one nostril. In primary sinus infections the discharge is usually odourless but in tooth root infection there is usually a foetid smell.

Confirming the diagnosis

Endoscopic examination (p.65) Pus can be seen flowing from the region of the sinus drainage opening.
X-ray of the head Fluid rather than air can been seen in the sinuses, and a cyst, tumour or a diseased tooth root may also be seen.

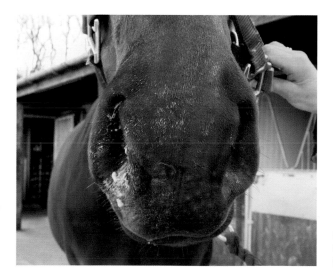

Treatment

Primary sinusitus is treated with antibiotics. If it does not respond a small opening is made in the side of the face immediately overlying the sinus cavity in order to allow a flexible tube to be inserted. The tube is kept in place by a balloon inflated at its end. The sinus can be flushed for several weeks through the tube and into the nose. The success rate of treatment is good.

In sinusitis that is secondary to a tooth root infection, extraction of the diseased tooth is an essential first step, followed by flushing of the sinus.

A fractured upper right cheek tooth in this horse has resulted in infection of the underlying sinus. The discharge has a noticeably unpleasant smell

Nosebleeds

Nosebleeds are common in horses but they are rarely severe. The bleeding will usually stop if the horse is left quietly alone in a stable. Attempts to stop the bleeding by packing a nostril or applying ice packs to the head are both unsuccessful and counterproductive as the resultant resentment by the horse will raise its blood pressure and accentuate the bleeding.

FINDING THE CAUSE

The key questions to answer are:

- **Is the horse bleeding from one or both nostrils?** If from one nostril the source of the bleeding is likely to be in the head. If from both, the horse is in most cases bleeding from the lungs.
- **Does the bleeding occur only when the horse is worked?** If yes, then exercise-induced pulmonary haemorrhage (EIPH) is the likely cause.

- **Are there any other nasal discharges in addition to blood?** The presence of mucus in the discharge, either mixed with blood, or on its own when the horse is not bleeding, suggests that the bleeding is part of a more complex disorder in the head.
- **Has there been a recent traumatic event**? (A fall for example.)

Bleeding after exercise (both nostrils)	No exercise association (one or both nostrils) (p.70)
EIPH	Trauma to the head
	Ethmoid haematoma
	Guttural pouch mycosis
	Nasal tumour
	Nasal foreign body

EXERCISE-INDUCED PULMONARY HAEMORRHAGE
(EIPH, bleeders, breaking a blood vessel)

Bleeding from both nostrils is a common condition in horses performing fast work. Many types of horses are affected, including flat racers and steeplechasers, polo ponies, eventers and trotters. The incidence is higher the faster the work, the older the horse and the longer its racing career. Endoscopic examinations of horses immediately after racing has shown that bleeding from the nostrils represents the tip of the iceberg in that a high percentage of horses show traces of blood in the trachea after racing. Only when this bleeding is severe (in less than 3% of cases) is blood seen at the nostrils. Studies have shown that mild bleeds into the lung have little or no effect on racing performance but more serious bleeds do reduce performance. Recurrent mild bleeds in the lungs may cause damage over time.

Much research has focused on determining the causes. Currently there are three main theories:

- The impact of the forelimbs hitting the ground at the gallop transmits pressure waves through the chest causing damage to the small blood vessels (capillaries) in the lung, resulting in bleeding.
- Due to the huge increase in output of the heart at the gallop, very high blood pressures develop in the blood vessels of the lungs. These pressures may exceed the capacity of the capillaries to withstand them.
- The presence of disease in the small airways, especially when caused by dusty stable environments makes the capillaries more fragile.

 Confirming the diagnosis

The horse is examined with an endoscope 30–40 minutes after strenuous exercise to check for blood in the trachea. If possible the examination should be done after racing as the effort on the racecourse is likely to exceed that expended on the gallops and consequently the risk of bleeding is greater.

? What to do next

EIPH is one of the most difficult conditions to control. Most 'nutritional aids' are ineffective. A reduction in the frequency of bleeding in training will help to allow the blood vessels to repair. Here are some suggestions to alleviate the problem:

- limit strong exercise gallops to once a week
- nasal dilator strips ('Flair') have been shown to reduce the incidence of EIPH. They reduce airway resistance to airflow thereby reducing airway pressure changes in the lung. In turn the stress on the lung blood vessels is reduced. Nasal strips can be used in training or in competition but are not permitted in Thoroughbred racing in the UK, Europe and some states of America.
- ensure the stable environment is as dust-free as possible (see pp.76–77). Ideally, train the horse from grass without any stabling. Sometimes corticosteroids are giving by inhalation but a withdrawal time before racing must be observed
- arrange for a post-exercise (30–60 minutes) endoscopic examination and tracheal wash to check for any concurrent airway infections or other disease, so these can be treated
- avoid training and racing on hard ground
- give the diuretic drug frusemide ('Lasix') by intravenous injection two hours before galloping. This drug is not permitted under the rules of racing in some countries

Horses suffering repeated attacks may have to be retired from fast work.

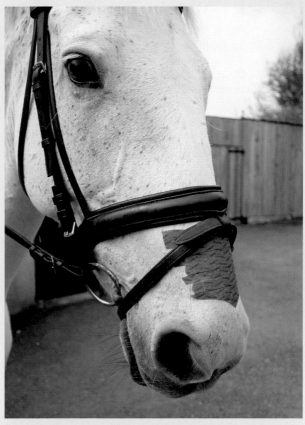

The 'Flair' nasal strip decreases the negative pressure in the airway at inspiration, and has been shown to reduce the incidence of EIPH

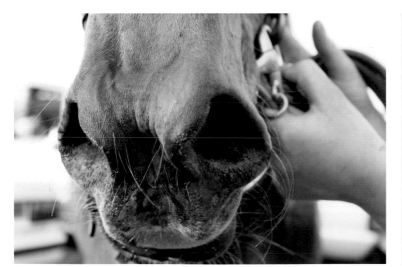

Blood was visible at the nostrils of this racehorse immediately at the end of a race

How common is EIPH?	
Prevalence of EIPH in 270 flat racehorses endoscoped immediately after racing	
Overall prevalence	55%
Two year olds	40%
Three year olds	64%
Older horses	81%
Note: only a small percentage of horses had visible blood at the nostrils	

NOSEBLEEDS NOT ASSOCIATED WITH EXERCISE

Trauma to the head

Falls, kicks to the head, rearing over backwards or other head trauma can result in bleeding from one or both nostrils. If bleeding occurs into the sinuses the blood may pool there and gradually escape into the nostril over several days, often turning brown. Treatment is not usually necessary. For other head wounds see Wounds, p.104.

Progressive ethmoid haematoma

This is the commonest cause of recurrent single-sided nosebleeds in the horse. Dark green, red or purple benign tumour-like structures develop in the back of the nasal passages or in the sinuses. They can be visualised using an endoscope and sometimes by x-ray.

Typically, slight nosebleeds occur and resolve spontaneously in a few hours, only to occur repeatedly over the next few weeks. Treatment is by surgical removal or more commonly by injection with a chemical agent via the endoscope.

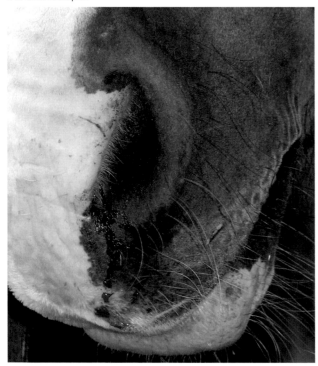

This horse suffered from four slight nosebleeds over a two-week period. It had an ethmoid haematoma,

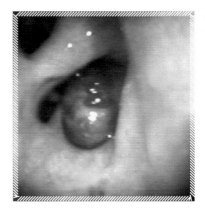

An endoscopic view of an ethmoid haematoma at the back of one nostril

Guttural pouch mycosis

The gutteral pouch is unique to the horse. It is a large cavity lined with blood vessels and nerves that runs the length of the tubes that connect the back of the throat with each ear. Gutteral pouch mycosis is a rare but potentially fatal condition in which a localised fungal infection occurs on the surface of a large artery in the wall of the guttural pouch. Extension of the infection through the wall of the artery may result in bleeding into the pouch and from there through the nostril. Sudden very severe haemorrhage may occur and the period from the first appearance of slight one-sided nosebleeds to a severe bleed can be less than three weeks. For this reason any horse that suffers more than one nosebleed over a period of a week must have an urgent endoscopic examination. Symptoms may include discharge of muco-pus from a single nostril or damage to the nerves controlling the swallowing muscles.

Treatment involves surgically tying off (occluding) the affected artery and spraying the infected area with an anti-fungal drug via the endoscope.

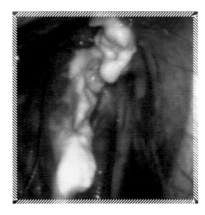

This fungal plaque was growing in one guttural pouch on top of a large blood vessel

Coughing

Coughing is the most common symptom of respiratory disease but it may occur in situations where the respiratory system is healthy, for example if the pharynx is stimulated by the presence of a foreign body (usually a twig). The cough reflex is triggered by stimulation of the receptors in the wall of the pharynx and bronchi by debris and fluid. Coughing is a protective response in which the horse tries to expel the irritating material and consequently suppression of coughing may not always be desirable.

FINDING THE CAUSE

The key questions to answer are:

- **Is one horse or a group involved?** Infectious causes usually affect more than one horse.
- **Is the temperature elevated and/or the horse depressed?** These symptoms are usually seen in infectious causes in the early stages.
- **How long has the horse been coughing for?** If for more than two months, the cause is likely to be RAO.
- **What is the horse's environment?** If it is bedded on straw and fed dry hay, it may have RAO.
- **What is the nature of the cough?** Harsh, dry hacking coughs tend to occur in upper respiratory tract infections. Productive coughs usually indicate the presence of lower respiratory system disease.
- **Does the horse cough while eating?** If yes it usually means the horse has an inflamed throat (for example, in strangles).
- **What is the nature of the nasal discharge, if present?** If food material is present it suggests the horse has a swallowing problem (for example, choke, strangles or paralysis of the pharynx).
- **Does the horse have laboured breathing?** In mild respiratory infections the breathing is normal, whereas in RAO and more serious respiratory infections the breathing is laboured and breathing movements are obvious.

Infectious (groups of horses)	Non-infectious (single horses)
Equine influenza (p.72)	Recurrent airway obstruction (RAO) (p.75)
Equine herpes virus (EHV) (p.72)	Summer pasture-associated obstructive pulmonary disease (p.78)
Strangles (coughing not a major symptom) (p.72)	Post-viral respiratory disease (p.79)
Bacterial lower respiratory tract infection (p.73)	Lungworms (p.79)
Equine viral arteritis (p.73)	Less common (p.79): Food/saliva inhalation (pharyngeal paralysis, choke, strangles) Pneumonia and pleurisy Foreign body in airways Tracheal collapse Tumour in the chest

INFECTIOUS COUGHING

Equine influenza

The virus always originates from a recently infected horse, often a new arrival on the yard. The infection spreads rapidly through a group of horses. Spread occurs by direct contact and by the airborne route as coughing propels an aerosol of infected droplets into the environment.

The infection starts with an elevated temperature (up to 40°C) and the horse is depressed. Then a harsh dry cough develops, followed by the appearance of an initial watery and later grey-yellow mucoid discharge from both nostrils. Foals are more severely affected. Horses partially protected by vaccination will show milder signs. Affected horses are infectious for others for about 10 days then clear themselves completely of the disease (no long-term symptom-less carriers occur).

Equine herpes virus (EHV)

This is an extremely common infection as the virus persists for years in the body once a horse becomes infected. Up to 75–90 per cent of normal adult horses carry this virus, usually without showing any signs. The virus lies dormant until some stress (for example a long journey) stimulates the horse to shed the virus in its nasal secretions and infect other horses.

There are two main strains, EHV-1 and EHV-4. Both cause respiratory disease but in addition EHV-1 causes abortion in mares and paralysis in older horses. Outbreaks occur in weanlings and yearlings, with elevated temperatures, nasal discharge and coughing. Milder infections occur in older horses. These mild infections may be unnoticed by the owner or trainer but may cause loss of performance. Very severe and potentially fatal infections may occur in newborn foals. Following recovery, immunity lasts for only 3–6 months so repeated infections may occur.

Strangles

The source of an outbreak is either a clinically affected horse or more commonly a symptomless carrier animal introduced to the group. This is usually a recovered case. Although most recovered cases are no longer infectious after a month, some may carry the bacteria for years and thereby spread infection from yard to yard.

Strangles is a bacterial infection of the throat and associated lymph glands caused by *Streptococcus equi.* Affected horses are depressed, off their food and have a high temperature (up to 41°C/105.8°F). The lymph nodes under the jaw and elsewhere on the head enlarge and become tender to the touch. The horse may swallow with difficulty and stand with its head and neck extended because of pain. The horse may cough especially while eating. After 7–10 days the lymph glands may rupture releasing thick yellow pus. The lymph glands at the back of the throat (retropharyngeal nodes) may burst into the guttural pouches or though the skin over the parotid salivary gland. Outbreaks caused by a milder strain of the organism, with no obvious lymph gland enlargement just slight nasal discharge and some coughing, are increasingly being recognised.

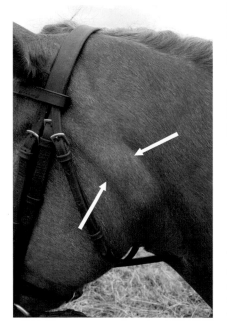

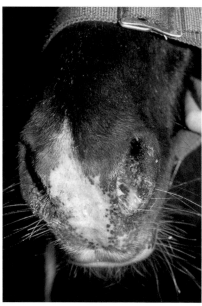

A case of strangles, with a thick yellow nasal discharge

The parotid salivary gland (arrowed) is often mistaken for a lymph gland. It will sometimes spontaneously (and harmlessly) enlarge when a horse is moved to a new paddock, especially in the spring

Bacterial lower respiratory tract infection

Bacterial infections of the lower airways are common in young (2–4 years old) racehorses in training. It is believed that infections spread from horse to horse by close contact. Clinical signs vary greatly from slightly reduced exercise tolerance without any other signs, to mild overt disease with coughing, elevated temperature, nasal discharge and enlargement of the submandibular lymph nodes. Examination of the trachea with an endoscope reveals excess mucus, and large numbers of bacteria can be cultured from a tracheal wash.

Equine viral arteritis

This virus is common in continental Europe and North America but absent from the UK, although the increasing trade in horses from the Europe to the UK makes its spread more likely. The source of infection is usually either a carrier stallion (the virus persists in the genital tract and is transmitted via semen) or a clinical case. Affected horses have an elevated temperature, swelling (oedema) of the legs and scrotum, swelling of the conjunctiva of the eye ('pinkeye'), discharges from the eye and nose, coughing and diarrhoea. Pregnant mares may abort.

If the virus is suspected the vet must be immediately notified. If the vet confirms the infection, the government veterinary authorities will be notified.

Confirming the diagnosis

The precise cause of respiratory infections can be diagnosed by blood tests (EHV), swabs from the nasal passages and throat (EHV, influenza and strangles), and tracheal washes (bacterial lower respiratory infections). Recently, rapid identification of the infecting organism has become possible using DNA detection techniques.

What to do next

Quarantine Where possible, isolate affected cases, preferably in a distant field with no nose-to-nose contact with other horses. Isolation is of limited value in respiratory virus infections because often considerable spread has occurred before the first case is recognised. However in dealing with *strangles* isolation is *critical*. The disease spreads slowly and requires close contact (see 'Combating strangles').

COMBATING STRANGLES

Divide the yard into three groups of horses:

- **Group 1, strangles-affected horses**
  Keep these well away from the others, and give them separate feed bowls, water supplies, and so on. Anyone handling them should wear separate outer clothing and disposable gloves. Feed the horses easily swallowed soft food (for example, soaked cubes).

  Although 90 per cent of horses completely rid themselves of the infection after a month, 10 per cent will remain carriers. Therefore, four weeks after the end of clinical signs in each individual, it is essential that every recovered case should have throat swabs taken (three swabs over a two-week period) to confirm they are no longer infectious before they are removed from isolation.

- **Group 2, currently healthy horses that have been in close contact with affected horses**
  These may be incubating the disease. Take their temperature daily for 15 days (the maximum incubation period) and if any develop a fever (>39°C) they should be assumed to be early clinical cases. The original source of the infection may be a carrier animal in groups 2 and 3. It may be necessary to obtain swabs or guttural pouch washes through the endoscope to find it.

- **Group 3, currently healthy horses that have not been in contact with affected horses**
  Carefully monitor this group.

Close contact facilitates the spread of respiratory infections

Treatment of infectious respiratory diseases

Treatment comprises rest, prevention of spread and elimination of secondary infections with antibiotics.

Experience shows that horses which are not rested while suffering from a respiratory infection are more likely to remain chronically infected and, subsequently, to develop RAO (see opposite). Other than gentle walking exercise, coughing horses should not be worked.

Antibiotics Mild respiratory infections with minimal discharge and coughing may resolve without treatment other than rest and keeping the horse in a dust-free environment. Young horses and those with prolonged coughing and a heavy nasal discharge may require antibiotic treatment. It is generally accepted that treatment of clinical strangles cases with antibiotics may impair the development of their immunity. However in-contact horses possibly incubating strangles or very early cases (elevated temperature only) may be treated with penicillin as a precaution. A prolonged course is required.

Other drugs Sometimes drugs (such as phenylbutazone) are given to reduce the temperature and make the horse feel more comfortable, to open the small airways (bronchodilators) and to thin the abnormal amount of mucus (mucolytics) and assist its clearance.

Air hygiene Keeping affected horses in the cleanest air possible greatly aids their recovery (see RAO, opposite).

PREVENTING INFECTIOUS RESPIRATORY DISEASE

Prevention aims to avoid introduction of the disease by quarantine, and to increase resistance by vaccination.
Quarantine Keep new arrivals at a yard away from resident horses for three weeks, ideally in a stable block or field well away from the main yard.

Vaccination

• **Equine influenza** Vaccination is by intramuscular injection. The primary course comprises two injections 4–6 weeks apart, followed by a first booster at six months. Thereafter booster injections are given annually. Recent evidence suggests that for effective immunity more frequent boosters may be required. Under International Equestrian Federation (FEI) rules boosters must be given every six months. In some countries an intranasal vaccine is available.

• **Equine herpes virus** An intramuscular vaccine is available, given initially at a 4–6 week interval, followed by six monthly boosters. The vaccine is only of limited efficacy and its main role is in reducing outbreaks of EHV-1 abortion in pregnant mares.

• **Strangles** The currently available vaccine is given by injection into the inside of the upper lip.

Strangles vaccine is injected into the upper lip using a special short needle on the syringe

NON-INFECTIOUS COUGHING

Recurrent airway obstruction (RAO)

Formerly known as chronic obstructive pulmonary disease (COPD), RAO is a very common condition but when mild it often goes unnoticed. A disease of stabled horses, it is caused by an allergic response to small particles in the stable air. These particles comprise fungal spores from mouldy hay and bedding, fragments of forage mites and their faeces, fragments of plant material and dust from the animal's coat. Poor ventilation increases the concentration of these particles in stable air and compounds the problem.

What to look for

Horses with RAO will be exposed to stable dust, if only for a short period each day; for example the horse may be brought inside for tacking up, or given a haynet briefly after exercise. Some or all of these signs will be seen:

- normal rectal temperature
- coughing occurs at rest and at exercise (some horses have minimal coughing). Lumps of coughed-up mucus may be seen on the ground in front of the stable door
- greyish-yellow nasal discharge, especially when the head is lowered after exercise. However, many cases have no discharge
- increased respiratory rate (often 16–25 per minute)
- increased respiratory effort. The horse may have bi-phasic (double) breathing at expiration. The chest collapses as normal but in addition the horse then contracts its abdominal muscles to help expel air from the lung. An obvious 'lift' of the floor of the abdomen is seen with each expiration
- there may be audible wheezing and crackling if you listen to the horse breathe by holding your ear close to a nostril
- reduced tolerance of exercise with early fatigue. This may be the only sign that there is a problem in some cases with RAO
- some cases develop a sudden onset acute form with marked breathing difficulty and frequent coughing. The horse may be in distress and the signs may be mistaken for colic.

Confirming the diagnosis

Endoscopy of the trachea will show copious mucus present. In contrast to bacterial respiratory infections, no or very few bacteria will be cultured from the tracheal wash.

(Continued on p.78)

Conventional straw bedding (usually deep-littered around the edges) combined with poor ventilation, results in high levels of breathable dust in the stable air

Coughing – non-infectious

PREVENTING RECURRENT AIRWAY OBSTRUCTION (RAO)

The key to eliminating RAO is air hygiene. The cleanest air is in the middle of a field. It follows that horses on dust-free management should spend as much time as possible out of the stable. Ensure that muckheaps and barns containing hay and straw are not close by.

Woodshavings readily support fungal multiplication if they are undisturbed and there is faecal contamination

Once opened, haylage must be used quickly. Re-covering will not adequately exclude oxygen, and promotes heating and secondary fermentation

Bedding

- Straw, irrespective of quality, must not be used. Dust-extracted woodshavings (not sawdust), shredded paper or cardboard are good but they must be managed correctly. If allowed to become very dirty or if deep-littered, they are worse than straw. Other organic bedding, for example, chopped hemp, flax or dust-extracted straw, decompose and eventually encourage fungal multiplication, and therefore are unsuitable unless a thin layer is used and replaced frequently.
- Don't have the bed too deep. It is essential that the entire bed (right to the edges) is turned over every day to ensure that it is as clean and as dry as possible.
- Rubber mats with 10cm (4in) of bedding on top makes the bed easier to keep fresh than a deep one.
- Do not bank up the sides of the bed to prevent casting. Undisturbed banking encourages fungi to multiply. To prevent the horse becoming cast, fix a 5 x 3cm (2 x 1½in) batten, 1m (3ft) from the ground right around the stable.
- Do not deep-litter. Keep the bedding scrupulously clean.
- Always muck out with the horse out of the stable and allow dust levels to fall before restabling.

Feeding

- Dampen all hard feed, and feed at floor level to encourage drainage of secretions from the horse's airways.
- Consider feeding haylage.
- If feeding hay, soak it beforehand. The soaking time depends on the volume of hay and how tightly it is packed. Soaking leaches soluble sugars from hay, making it less nutritious than unsoaked hay, so soaking should be just sufficiently long such that the last piece the horse eats is still wet.

The water in soaked hay turns brown due to leaching of soluble sugars

Leave the stable door open most of the time to improve airflow

The stable

- Most stables are poorly ventilated, especially those with low roofs and no air inlets other than the upper half of the door. It is essential that another inlet, for example on the rear wall, be provided. A simple way is to drill 4–5cm (1½–2in) holes all along the top of the back wall.

- If the stable has windows leave them open all of the time or better still remove one or all panes of glass.
- Groom the horse out of doors.
- An ideal system is to allow the horse to wander around a small yard in front of the stable. The haylage can be fed there to encourage the horse to spend a lot of time out of doors.

Troubleshooting

If your dust-free environment doesn't seem to be working consider the following possibilities:

- Bedding and feeding routines are being followed, but a thick layer of stable dust and cobwebs remain on the window ledges, roof trusses, etc.
- The horse is being briefly exposed to stable dust, for example at tacking up. A very short exposure is sufficient to trigger RAO.
- 'Contaminated' air is gaining access to the stable from somewhere else. Dust-free techniques will not work unless all the horses in the same building are managed similarly.
- Your lorry or trailer is dusty. Ideally use rubber mats with a thin layer of fresh shavings only at the rear. Muck out the vehicle as soon as you can. Never travel a horse with a haynet in its breathing zone. Feed only haylage or soaked hay to horses while travelling. Leave the air vents fully open and unload the horse as soon as you arrive.
- Remember that if the horse stays overnight elsewhere, e.g. at a show, you must apply the same rigorous approach to dust-free management.

Space boarding is an excellent way to provide draught-free ventilation. The size of the gaps should be the same as the thickness of the boards

Due to the small airspace, airborne dust levels during travelling can be significant

Treatment

Often the best thing to do is to turn the horse out to grass while the adverse stable environment is sorted out (see pp.76–77). The horse should not be ridden until the respiratory rate and effort has returned to normal.

The inhaler is applied to one nostril while the other is held closed. The corticosteroid medication is released into the inhaler by pressing the aerosol puffer. The horse is allowed to take two breaths per puffer actuation

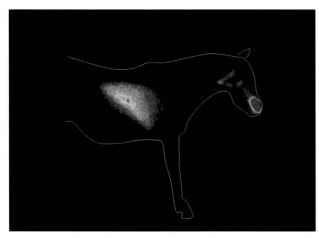

Inhaled corticosteroid medication has been given a harmless radioactive label to demonstrate that it reaches the lung

- Corticosteroid drugs very efficiently suppress the allergic reaction in the lungs. Although the drug can be given by mouth or by injection, the inhalation route is preferred as high doses can be delivered directly to the lungs with a reduced risk of side effects. Unfortunately many horses will not accept the inhaler.

- Drugs are given to relieve the spasm of the bronchi and aid clearance of the excess mucus. These treatments are only palliative and will work poorly if a dust-free environment is not also provided.

The long-term outlook

Except for very longstanding cases where there are permanent structural changes in the lungs, most cases of RAO are fully reversible, although the horse retains the sensitivity to hay and straw for life and will relapse if kept in a dusty environment at a later stage.

Summer pasture-associated obstructive pulmonary disease (SPAOPD)

This uncommon condition is caused by an allergic reaction to inhaled pollens and outdoor moulds and is seen from spring to autumn in grazing horses without access to hay and straw. The appearance is identical to RAO but the onset is often sudden, the signs are frequently severe and they occur in horses that are at grass

Some horses are allergic to pollens produced by plants and grasses in their pasture

Treatment

SPAOPD is a difficult condition to control because of the difficulty of preventing access to the inhaled allergens. The horse needs to be stabled for most if not all of the day and may require administration of corticosteroids by mouth or by inhalation throughout the pollen season. The condition self-cures in the autumn but will return again in the spring. Moving the horse to a different geographical area has cured some cases, presumably because the allergens were not present in the new location.

Post-viral respiratory disease

Although the majority of horses will fully recover from a respiratory virus infection in 2–3 weeks, a small percentage continues coughing for several months. The cause may be virus-induced damage to the respiratory system which may take a long time to resolve, or it maybe because the virus has induced a state of 'hyper-reactivity' in the airways which manifests it self as coughing in response to exercise, cold air and stable dust.

Treatment includes a prolonged rest and provision of a dust-free environment, ideally 24-hour turn out to grass.

Lungworms

Lungworms cause mild, infrequent coughing in horses. Because modern worming drugs are extremely efficient, lungworm infection is now very rare. Donkeys are the natural host of the parasite but they show no signs of infestation. When horses graze fields that have been occupied by donkeys they may develop a cough.

Unlike donkeys, horses do not shed eggs or larvae in their faeces so faecal analysis is of no value in diagnosis. Characteristic changes are seen in a tracheal wash. Treatment with wormers that contain ivermectin or moxidectin is very effective.

Less common causes of single horse coughing

Food/saliva inhalation

The most important of these is oesophageal obstruction (choke, see p.89). Swallowing difficulty and inadvertent inhalation of food material may occur:

- after laryngeal tie-back surgery (see p.81)
- due to abscesses in the pharyngeal wall in strangles
- because of paralysis of the pharynx in a fungal infection of the guttural pouch. The fungal plaque grows on and damages the nerves supplying the swallowing muscles as they traverse the wall of the pouch.

Pneumonia and pleurisy

Rare in Europe and the UK, but slightly more common in the USA, these conditions usually arise either because of food inhalation into the airways (for example, choke) or because the horse has been stressed and immuno-suppressed through long-distance travel (shipping fever). The horse appears very ill, has an elevated temperature, increased respiratory rate, a nasal discharge, and a painful chest. Intensive treatment is necessary and the mortality rate from these conditions is high.

Foreign body in airways

Foreign bodies (usually brambles) can become lodged in the nose, pharynx or trachea. There is very frequent coughing and the horse shows obvious distress. The foreign body can be seen via the endoscope and removal may require a general anaesthetic.

Tracheal collapse

This is a rare condition of small ponies, usually in old age. They cough and may make an abnormal 'honking' noise at exercise. Endoscopic examination confirms the diagnosis but there is no effective treatment.

Tumour in the chest

Chest tumours (usually lymphosarcoma) are rare in horses. There is weight loss, occasional coughing, and sometimes fluid accumulation both in the chest and under the skin. There is no effective treatment.

This horse had difficulty in swallowing and food returned down its nostrils. The cause was a large abscess in the wall of pharynx

Abnormal breathing noises at exercise

Assessment of respiratory sounds at exercise requires a lot of skill and can only be done by experienced veterinarians. Along with abnormal respiratory sounds, there are two uncommon but not problematic rhythmic sounds that may be heard during exercise: 'high blowing' – an expiratory noise at canter caused by vibration of part of the nostrils – and a noise made by geldings at trot caused by air being sucked into the sheath.

Respiratory problems

ASSESSMENT OF RESPIRATORY NOISES: EXAMINATION AT EXERCISE

Examination of the horse at exercise (an important part of the five-stage pre-purchase veterinary exam) is essential to asssess the upper respiratory system adequately. The horse is trotted and cantered to increase the speed of airflow and amplify breathing sounds. Abnormal breathing noises during exercise indicate an obstruction (usually partial) in airflow somewhere in the upper respiratory system. The turbulence created by the obstruction generates a noise.

If possible the exercise test is carried out with the horse being ridden rather than on the lunge as the poll-flexed posture of the ridden horse often accentuates respiratory noises. Riding also makes it is possible to work the horse at a faster speed and also more easily to examine the effect of fatigue.

Causes of abnormal respiratory sounds
Laryngeal hemiplegia (below)
Dorsal displacement of the soft palate (p.82)
Epiglottal entrapment (p.82)
Other functional disorders (p.82)

LARYNGEAL HEMIPLEGIA (Recurrent laryngeal neuropathy (RLN), roaring, whistling)

This is a common condition of Thoroughbreds, warmbloods and Irish Draught horses and their crosses. The condition is rarely seen in horses less than 15.2hh and is especially common in very big horses (50% of horses over 17hh show evidence of this disease).
- In a normal horse during fast breathing the arytenoid cartilages and vocal cords on each side of the larynx are pulled to the side, out of the midline, by contraction of the laryngeal muscles, in order to open the airway and allow air to flow in and out of the lungs without restriction.
- In RLN, due to degeneration of the nerve supply to the left side of the larynx, the laryngeal muscles on that side become partially or totally paralysed and hence the arytenoids and vocal cords are not only *not* pulled to the side, but are sucked across almost to the other side because of the negative pressure created during inspiration. Airflow over these paralysed structures becomes turbulent and generates an abnormal noise.
- The noise is most easily heard at the canter and is an *abnormal inspiratory sound*. A 'roarer' makes a low pitched sound and a 'whistler' a high pitched one.

- Horses with RLN make a low-pitched whinny sound instead of neighing.

In RLN, the obstructing tissues interfere with airflow and hence oxygenation of the blood. The consequences therefore are greatest in sports where there is high oxygen demand, for example racing and eventing. The effect may be minimal in slower speed activities, for example hacking or lower level jumping. The condition is hereditary.

Confirming the diagnosis
Examination of the larynx with an endoscope will reveal the paralysis in most cases. However, recent studies in which horses have been examined endoscopically while galloping on a high-speed treadmill have shown that horses that have moderate grades of paralysis may still be able to function normally when required to work at speed.

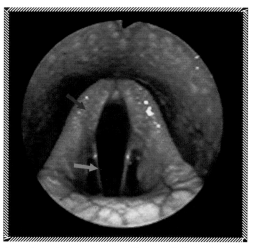

An endoscopic view of a normal larynx, with the arytenoid cartilage (red arrow) and vocal cord (green arrow) symmetrically arranged

What can be done

Many horses performing lower level equestrian activities can work satisfactorily with this condition. If evidence of reduced performance if found, there are two principal surgical methods of treatment:

- **Hobday operation** The tissues to the side of the vocal cords are stripped out and one or both vocal cords removed. Although this will remove the abnormal respiratory noise, the effect on airflow is small. This procedure is reserved for mild cases of RLN.
- **Tie-back operation** A nylon cord is attached to the paralysed left arytenoid cartilage and attached at the other end to the back of the larynx. The cord is tightened so that the paralysed cartilage is pulled permanently open to the side of the airway. Because the larynx can no longer be fully closed during swallowing, some food material may inadvertently escape into the trachea, resulting in about 20 per cent of treated horses developing a persistent cough.

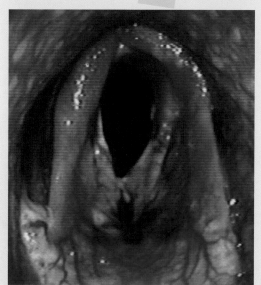

This horse has just undergone tie-back surgery. The left arytenoid cartilage (on the right in this photograph) has been artificially fixed in an open position, and the left vocal cord has been surgically removed

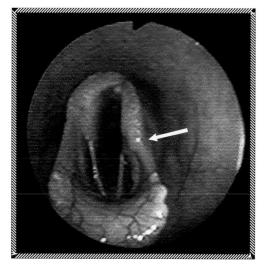

This horse makes an abnormal inspiratory breathing noise when cantering. The endoscopic picture, which was taken while the horse was breathing in, shows the right side of the larynx (on the left) is open normally, but (due to paralysis of the muscles on the left side) the left side is collapsed (arrows). The horse is a roarer

DORSAL DISPLACEMENT OF THE SOFT PALATE (DDSP, gurgling, choking up)

The larynx is normally encircled by the soft palate. In this condition it becomes detached from the soft palate when the horse is working at speed. The free border of the palate then vibrates in front of the larynx, resulting in partial obstruction of the laryngeal opening and a characteristic gurgling sound.

DDSP is seen mostly in horses working at speed. It may also occur in horses working at slower paces in the poll-flexed posture. The laryngeal obstruction is sudden and severe, resulting in an instant onset of an abnormal noise (predominantly expiratory).

At present the cause is unknown but the following may be predisposing factors:
- Unfitness of the horse
- Fatigue towards the end of a race
- Abnormalities the soft palate
- Abnormalities of the epiglottis
- Mouth discomfort (causing breathing through the mouth) due, for example to sharp teeth, bitting discomfort, getting the tongue over the bit, protruding the tongue to one side when ridden
- Excessive flexion of the poll, for example in dressage horses
- During recovery from upper respiratory infections

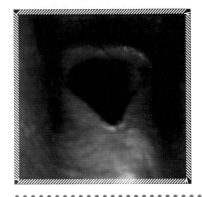

This endoscopic view of the larynx shows the displaced soft palate partially obstructing the laryngeal airway. The flap of tissue vibrates as air flows over it during breathing, creating the typical gurgling noise

EPIGLOTTAL ENTRAPMENT

In this condition a fold of loose tissue, normally sitting under the epiglottis, flips upwards and becomes hooked over the epiglottis. The resultant signs are very variable and include exercise intolerance, an abnormal inspiratory and/or expiratory noise at exercise, intermittent gurgling from secondary soft palate displacement, and coughing when eating. Surgically removing the loose tissue has a high success rate.

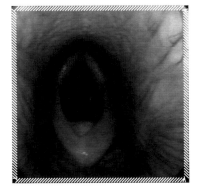

An endoscopic view of a severe case of epiglottal entrapment. A loose flap of tissue has become wrapped around the epiglottis

What can be done

- Young (2-year-old horses) may outgrow the condition. Increasing fitness may also affect a cure.
- Every attempt should be made to remove predisposing factors. For example the teeth should be rasped, a milder bit can be tried, or the position of the bit in the mouth can be altered using an Australian noseband. A tight grackle noseband often helps. A Hackamore bit can be tried. Tying the tongue down to the lower jaw using a 'tongue-tie' may stop it being retracted.
- Various surgical treatments are available; these mostly stiffen the soft palate. Their efficacy is about 60 per cent. More recently, the 'tie-forward' operation, in which the base of the tongue, and hence the larynx, is surgically anchored in a more forward position, has had good success.

OTHER FUNCTIONAL DISORDERS OF THE UPPER AIRWAYS

There are several other uncommon dynamic causes of upper airway obstruction. They are described as dynamic because endoscopic examination at rest reveals a normal respiratory system. However they can be diagnosed by working the horse on a high speed treadmill with a video endoscope in place. They are difficult to treat and may result in retirement of the horse from fast work.

DENTAL PROBLEMS

The teeth

The horse's head is a huge chewing machine. While the 12 incisor teeth at the front of the jaw help him to graze, the 24 cheek teeth occupying most of the head do the real work.

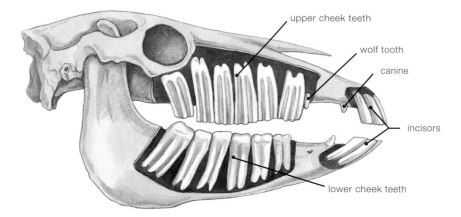

upper cheek teeth
wolf tooth
canine
incisors
lower cheek teeth

A horse spends about 60 per cent of the day eating, and will chew 15–25,000 times when consuming a 5kg (11lb) net of hay, reducing the long stems to very short (2–5mm) lengths before swallowing. This chewing causes enormous wear to the surface of the teeth but equine teeth continue to erupt (2–3mm per year), matching the rate of wear, until horses are about 25 years old. In addition, equine teeth have a very clever self-sharpening mechanism in that the softer dentine component on the surface of the teeth wears at a greater rate than the harder enamel, progressively exposing narrow enamel ridges and ensuring that the surface remains rough (essential for grinding).

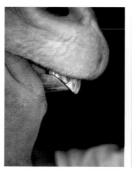 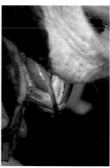

THE EFFECT OF HEAD POSITION ON INCISOR ALIGNMENT

Far left: Head elevated: the relative positions of the upper and lower incisor teeth shows that the lower jaw has retracted. Left: Head lowered to poll-flexed posture: the lower jaw has moved forward. It is important that this movement is not inhibited by the upper and lower teeth jamming against each other

INDICATORS OF DENTAL DISEASE

- **Bit resentment** is by far the most common sign of dental disease. Any horse that shows resistance when ridden should have its mouth examined.

- **Quidding** is defined as expulsion of plugs of partially chewed hay or haylage (occasionally grass but rarely hard feed). True quidding is quite rare and always reflects serious dental pain.

Plugs of hay expelled while chewing. The horse had two infected cheek teeth. Once they were extracted the problem was resolved

- **Food spilling**, often incorrectly called quidding, is simply hard food falling out of the mouth as the horse eats. This may indicate a dental problem or the horse may just be an untidy eater.

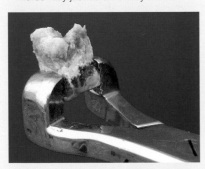

This infected cheek tooth was removed from a quidding horse. The short length of the tooth indicates that it is from an old horse; the normally sharp root pegs have been blunted by the infection

- **Making faces** A horse suffering oral discomfort when eating hay may turn his head on one side, partially protrude his tongue and also hold his mouth partially open.

- **Weight loss** tends only to occur in severe dental disease. Often there is an annual cycle whereby the horse loses weight in the winter when he is relying mostly on hay (the horse is thinnest in early spring), and regains it in the summer when grass, which is more easily masticated, is the principal feed (the horse is fattest in the autumn)

This very thin pony had extensive dental disease, resulting in quidding on both grass and hay

- **Other signs of dental disease**
  - **Swollen cheeks**, due to semi-chewed hay or grass packing inside one or both cheeks.

  - **Long hay stems in the faeces**, caused by poor mastication.

The maximum length of hay stems in the faeces should be 5mm, if properly masticated. Sharp teeth have led this horse to swallow the stems before they have been fully chewed

  - **Halitosis**, usually caused by food trapped around or between teeth and becoming foetid.

- **Sinus infections** caused by an infected root of one of the upper cheek teeth. The horse has a copious, very smelly discharge from one nostril.

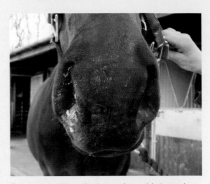

The foul-smelling discharge from this horse's right nostril was caused by sinusitis, which developed secondarily to a fractured upper cheek tooth

  - **Swelling of the facial bones**, especially of part of the jawbone.

  - **A discharging site** on the horse's face (most commonly present on the jawbone) where infection from a tooth root has broken through to the surface.

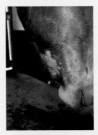

This horse developed a swelling on its lower jawbone (left) which eventually burst and discharged a small amount of pus. A metal probe was introduced into the discharging site and an x-ray taken (below). It revealed that the tract communicated with an infected root on the second cheek tooth

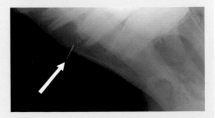

Dental problems

When to check a horse's teeth

From the age of three years all horses' teeth should be checked by a vet or qualified dental technician at least once a year. More frequent checking may be necessary when:

- the horse is in obvious oral discomfort
- the horse is unhappy with bit contact
- the horse is performing high-level ridden work
- before a horse is first broken to ridden
- the shape of the horse's jaw and teeth are such that overgrowths become excessive in less than 12 months
- the horse is suffering from certain dental abnormalities, for example parrot mouth (right) or wave mouth (p.86), or has missing teeth.

FACIAL TOOTH BUMPS

Horses aged 3–5 years develop bumps on their lower jaws. Caused by the adult teeth forming in the jawbone, but not yet erupting upwards into the mouth, these disappear as the horse matures.

INCISOR PROBLEMS

Incisor problems are not common, but include delayed shedding of temporary incisors, extreme wear due to age or windsucking, and fractures. Slant mouth and parrot mouth can cause uneven wear of the teeth.

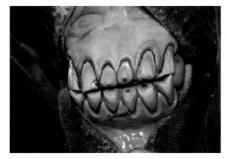

Severely worn incisors on a very old pony

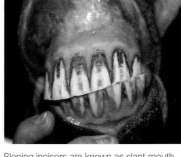

Sloping incisors are known as slant mouth

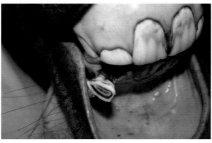

The temporary incisor on this mare was pulled away from the gum. It was removed under sedation and the underlying permanent incisor erupted normally

Despite a severe parrot mouth, this horse could graze normally. His cheek teeth were also out of alignment, causing large hooks, which were reduced with an electric burr

CANINE TEETH PROBLEMS

Canine teeth are present only in male horses. Problems are uncommon. The main ones are: excessive sharpness, build up of tartar, particularly on the lower canines, fractures and abnormal angles of growth. In addition canine teeth may fail to erupt at 4–5 years, a problem that is resolved by incision under local anaesthesia.

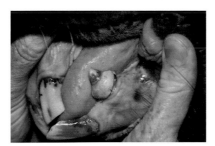

A large accumulation of tartar, which had caused inflamed gums

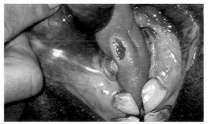

This horse was avoiding the bit because a canine tooth deviating inwards had caused a large ulcer on his tongue. The canine was shortened and the surface smoothed, and the ulcer healed fully in three weeks

WOLF TEETH

Wolf teeth are 'extra' teeth that 40–60 per cent horses have in their upper jaws just in front of the first large cheek tooth (see illustration on p.83); they are very rare in the lower jaw. Although the tooth normally erupts vertically downwards through the gum into the mouth, 'blind' wolf teeth take a more shallow-angled path and never appear. The bump in the gum overlying such a tooth can be felt.

When pressure is applied to a snaffle bit via the reins, the soft tissues of the cheek are pressed inwards against the teeth, impinging exactly where a wolf tooth is situated and potentially causing discomfort. For this reason, wolf teeth are usually removed. This can be done at any age, the younger the better. There is usually a tiny amount of bleeding after extraction but otherwise no adverse effects. The area heals quickly with the horse back in work in 5–10 days.

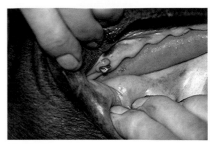

Wolf tooth

CHEEK TEETH PROBLEMS

Cheek teeth problems are very common and could be avoided with good regular dental care. Uneven wear due to the difference in width between the upper and lower jaws results in *sharp points* forming on the outside of the upper teeth and the inside of the lower ones. This is the commonest reason for resentment of the bit.

In addition, the first upper cheek tooth in front and the last lower cheek tooth at the back of the mouth often extend beyond the opposing upper or lower tooth causing uneven growth, or *hooks*, which restrict the normal forward movement of the jawbone when the poll is flexed. These must be removed.

In 2–4 year-old horses one or more of the *short temporary cheek teeth (caps)* may fail to shed cleanly. The partially dislodged tooth may have sharp edges and may trap food underneath causing discomfort. Caps are easily removed.

Excessive wear on the middle of the lower arcade in teenage or older horses results in a curved depression (*wave mouth*, see photo below). It may be necessary to reduce the over-dominant upper teeth to allow the corresponding lower teeth to erupt unopposed.

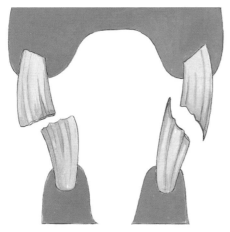

Cheek teeth before rasping (right) and after rasping (left)

A large hook is visible at the front of the first cheek tooth

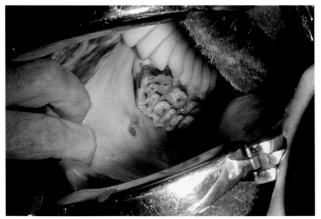

Very sharp outside edges on this horse's cheek teeth have caused ulceration of the inside of the cheek

This jawbone shows that, in life, the horse suffered excessive wear of the back few lower cheek teeth, causing a wave mouth

GAPS AND FRACTURES

Cheek teeth (and incisors) can be affected by *gaps* caused by mal-eruption, retraction of the gum due to infection, and wear. Mal-eruption of the third lower cheek tooth is especially common. It has to push up between two teeth that have already erupted and sometimes cannot fit into the space between them. Consequently, it deviates either inwards or outwards, leaving a gap. Usually this abnormality is present on both sides of the jaw and eventually the teeth will have to be removed.

Because the teeth are conical, the gaps between them widen as the teeth wear. Food trapped in the gaps becomes foetid and causes painful gum disease. Affected horses often quid.

Small 'slab' *fractures* of the cheek teeth are not uncommon but are easily resolved by removal of the fragment, so long as the central cavity of the tooth has not been entered.

The gap left by a *missing tooth* means that the matching tooth on the other jaw will not wear normally and will require regular rasping to prevent overgrowth and difficulty chewing.

This small thin piece of tooth (a 'flake' fracture) was found partially detached from the parent tooth but still attached at gum level. The horse showed discomfort when chewing haylage

MAKING THE BIT MORE COMFORTABLE

Re-shaping the leading edges of the first upper and lower cheek teeth – making a **bit seat** – creates more room for the cheek's soft tissues, which can produce significantly better acceptance of the bit.

CREATING A BIT SEAT

BEFORE	AFTER		BEFORE	AFTER
SIDE VIEW			FRONT VIEW	

TEETH PROBLEMS IN OLDER HORSES

The teeth cease to erupt at around 25 years but continue to wear. The cheek teeth in particular may wear down to the gum leaving a **smooth surface** (smooth mouth). Missing teeth and gaps, with their attendant problems, are more common in older horses. Poor teeth can lead to nutritional deficiencies in older horses, which can be combated through careful attention to the diet, such as feeding chopped forage, specially designed coarse mixes and vegetable oil. Vitamin and mineral supplements are recommended. In addition to this old horses should be rugged in winter to reduce the calorie requirements of keeping warm.

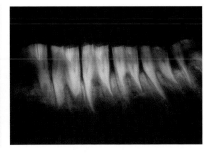

A hay brick is ideal for horses with poor cheek teeth

These comparative x-rays show how long the cheek teeth are in a young adult (left), and how tightly they fit together. The second and third permanent teeth have not yet erupted, and the 'caps' of the juvenile teeth are visible on top of them. The x-ray of the old horse (above) shows teeth shortened by years of grinding, and the gaps that develop between them

DIGESTIVE SYSTEM PROBLEMS

In this section

**The digestive system • Eating and swallowing problems, including choke
Colic • Grass sickness • Diarrhoea • The thin horse • Worms**

The digestive system

The horse's digestive system extends from the mouth to the anus. The abdomen contains four essential components. All are actively contracting most of the time, propelling food towards the anus.

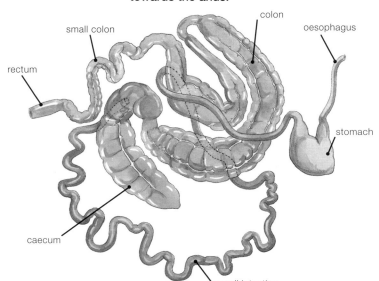

- **The stomach** The equine stomach is small and comprises 10 per cent of the horse's gut volume. Its entrance is controlled by a muscular valve that allows food to pass only one way – a horse cannot belch or vomit. Minimal digestion takes place in the stomach.
- **The small intestine** A thin tube about 20m (65ft) long, in which non-fibrous material is digested.
- **The caecum and colon (the large intestine)** A very large and important part of the equine gut, comprising about 45 per cent of the total volume. Digestion of fibre by microbial fermentation occurs here.
- **The small colon** Its primary function is to absorb water from the very fluid large intestinal contents flowing into it.

EATING AND SWALLOWING PROBLEMS

Eating problems here refer to horses that want to eat but are reluctant to do so because of an oral problem or if they do eat they are clearly unhappy when chewing their food.

Horses may suddenly have difficulty eating because of:

- an acute dental problem, for example a fractured cheek tooth (p.87)
- a foreign body lodged in the mouth, for example a twig or piece of wood trapped across the roof of the mouth between the two rows of cheek teeth (p.84)
- trauma to the face, for example a kick to the facial muscles or a fracture of the jaw
- illness – the horse is suffering from tetanus (p.153) and the jaw muscles are in spasm.

A horse may have difficulty swallowing if:

- it is suffering from some inflammatory condition of the throat, for example strangles (p.72)
- it has paralysis of the pharynx, for example in a fungal infection of the guttural pouches (p.70) or botulism (p.152)
- a foreign body, for example a twig, has become lodged in the throat (p.79)
- it has a functional disorder of the larynx
- it has some disorder of the oesophagus, for example an obstruction (choke, opposite).

CHOKE (Oesophageal obstruction)

The oesophagus is a long, muscular, elastic tube (1–1.5m/1.2–5ft in the average horse) that connects the horse's throat to the stomach. In the neck it is positioned over the windpipe for the first third of its length, and then it moves to the horse's left side until it reaches the entrance to the chest.

The commonest cause of choke by far is the horse eating at a rate faster than the oesophagus can propel the food to the stomach. A significant length of the oesophagus may be impacted with food. Other causes include:

- Large pieces of carrots or apples.
- Unsoaked sugar beet pulp. The pulp swells in the oesophagus when mixed with saliva.
- Horses with poor teeth may inadequately masticate hay and swallow a partially chewed plug that gets stuck.
- Excited horses may swallow hard feed or hay without proper chewing, for example if a horse is given a haynet immediately after racing.
- Rare causes include a mass (for example a tumour) pressing on the oesophagus from the outside and narrowing its internal diameter, or abnormal development of the oesophagus so that a pouch forms in the wall, where food may accumulate.

Clinical signs

A horse with choke may be an alarming sight and is often quite distressed.

- It may arch its neck and make swallowing movements, sometimes accompanied by an audible squeal or grunt.
- Food and saliva may appear at its nostrils.
- It may drool saliva.
- It may extend its neck between swallowing attempts.
- Depending on the cause and site of the obstruction, sometimes a hard cord-like structure (the distended oesophagus) can be felt on the lower left of the neck.
- Some horses show little or no distress and may continue to try to feed.

What to do next

- Don't panic. Many horses cure themselves fairly quickly.
- Put the horse in a loose box with no, or non-edible, bedding, and withhold water.
- Wait for one hour to see if the obstruction clears itself. If the horse becomes more relaxed, swallowing attempts cease and the nasal discharge reduces to almost nothing it is likely that it has recovered.
- If it has not resolved by one hour call for help. The vet will administer drugs to calm the horse and to relax the oesophageal wall, thereby making it easier for the normal contractions to move the food to the stomach.
- Sometimes the vet will need to pass a stomach tube up the horse's nose and down into the oesophagus, under heavy sedation. Warm water is flushed through the tube to clear the obstruction.
- In long-standing cases the horse may inhale saliva and food into the lungs, potentially causing pneumonia. Antibiotics may be given to help prevent this.

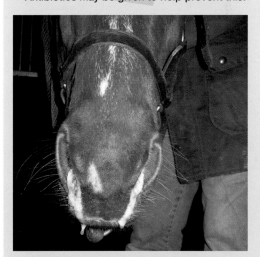

This horse, which had eaten unsoaked sugar beet, was distressed and had copious frothy saliva flowing from its nose. It was also coughing frequently due to inhalation of the saliva. Flushing the oesophagus via a stomach tube relieved the obstruction

Aftercare

- After recovery it is important that food is not immediately offered. Starve the horse for 12–24 hours and then provide a gruel of soaked cubes. Watch to ensure that the horse can swallow this.
- For a further 12 hours feed only soaked cubes, followed by in-hand grazing of soft grass. After a further 12 hours you may re-introduce well-soaked hay.

Preventing choke

Reduce the rate at which a greedy horse eats by placing a salt lick or some smooth stones on top of the feed beforehand. Offer a hungry horse hay before hard feed. If a horse repeatedly chokes on nuts, stop feeding nuts. Ensure that dry sugar beet is inaccessible to the horse, especially if it is inclined to escape from the stable. Have the teeth checked every 6–12 months.

COLIC

While the term 'colic' strictly refers to pain in the colon, in horses it is used to describe the clinical signs seen when they are suffering pain throughout the digestive system. The pain in colic may be intermittent but more usually is continuous, although in any bout of colic the severity may vary from moment to moment.

Does my horse have colic?

Mild or early cases

Ask yourself these questions:

- **Is it restless?** The commonest symptom is restlessness. While adjacent horses are relaxed and munching their hay, the affected horse paces its box. It may also paw the ground. In a few cases the horse may look at its flanks.
- **Is it quiet?** Some horses are unusually quiet.
- **Has it left its food?** A horse with colic stops eating.
- **Is it lying down?** The horse may lie down. It will either lie still or start rolling. Sometimes the horse will crouch as though it is going to get down and roll but at the last minute it changes its mind.
- **Are its droppings regular?** It may pass fewer piles of droppings than normal.
- **Does it want to urinate?** Sometimes the horse may adopt the urination posture but, unlike true urination, the penis is not protruded or the tail lifted.

More severe cases

- In severe colics the horse may sweat, especially behind the elbows and on the flanks.
- Rolling becomes frequent and violent. Injury is possible, especially around the eyes and hips if the bedding is insufficient.
- The horse becomes oblivious to its surroundings.
- In some cases the abdomen is obviously distended.
- The pulse rate rises to above 70 per minute and the pulse becomes weaker.

This pony has colic. If it rolls too close to the sides of the box, it could become cast. It would be safer to allow it to roll out of doors

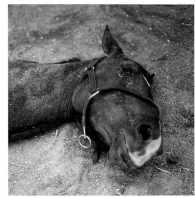

This horse had an obstructed small intestine and was in considerable pain. As it lay on its side it moved it limbs in the sand and it frequently rolled. It was in so much pain it was oblivious to its surroundings. Sand is sticking to the sweat on its neck. It had an emergency operation and 1m (3ft) of intestine was removed

CAUSES OF COLIC

In the majority of cases of **mild colic** an obvious trigger factor is not found. Suggested causes include:

- **A recent dramatic change in diet.**
- **Recent worming.** Transient mild colic sometimes occurs up to 48 hours after worming, especially when treated for tapeworms.
- **Spasm of the intestinal wall**, causing cramp-like pains (spasmodic colic). The causes are unknown but infestation with tapeworm or redworm may be important.
- **Obstruction of the caecum or colon** by food (impaction colic). Impaction colic cases are usually dull, spend a lot of time lying down, rarely roll, and don't pass faeces. There is often a history of the horse eating its bed, poor dental care, or a sudden reduction in the exercise level (especially stabling for 24 hours) for example due to injury, a recent long journey or laminitis.

This horse suffered from low-grade colic for 36 hours. The colon contents, which are normally quite fluid, were impacted and dry. Normally laxatives relieve this type of obstruction, but in this case it was necessary to empty the colon surgically

- **Distension of the stomach** by gorging on unsoaked sugar beet or grass cuttings.

In *severe colics* the fundamental problems are complete obstruction of the gut and, often, death of part of the bowel due to interruption of its blood supply. Fluid accumulates in the area, toxins are released into the bloodstream and eventually the horse goes into shock. *Surgery must be urgently performed*, preferably within six hours of the onset of pain. If a large portion of bowel is involved the horse may become extremely ill very quickly.

The main causes of severe colic are:

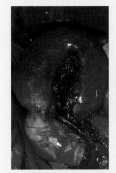

- **Entrapment** of a portion of intestine through an internal opening in the abdomen. The entrapped bowel swells and its blood supply is cut off.

In this case, a length of small intestine was trapped (arrows) in a naturally occurring opening (the epiploic foramen) in the tissue that suspends the bowel, causing severe pain. The entrapped intestine was removed. When opened the removed portion revealed severe congestion and damage (right). Without prompt surgery the horse would have died

- **Torsion** of the bowel along its length.
- **'Telescoping'** of a portion of intestine into the succeeding part (intussusception).
- **Strangulation** of the intestine by a tumour with long stalk (lipoma).

The 'stalk' of this small fatty tumour is wrapped around the small colon in this horse

Conditions that may be confused with colic

- **Laminitis**, mainly because of the pain, and tendency to lie down.
- **Equine rhabdomyolysis syndrome** If 'colic' appears during exercise it is most likely to be ERS (p.60).
- **Foaling** In early labour and immediately after delivery the horse shows colic signs due to uterine contractions.
- **Urinary obstruction** (male horses). This is a rare condition but because horses with colic sometimes adopt the urination posture owners may assume the horse cannot urinate.

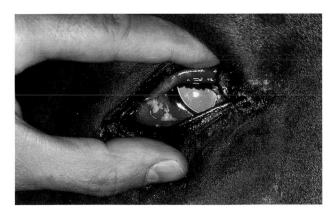

The mucous membrane of the eyes in this very ill horse changed from the normal salmon-pink colour to intensely red. The horse had a twisted intestine and was in shock

What to do next

Summon veterinary help immediately but don't panic. The great majority of colic cases will respond to simple medical treatment.

- If the horse is quiet and not rolling (although it may lie down), provide a generous bed and remove all hazardous objects, such as water buckets.
- If the horse is rolling in the stable, put it somewhere (a manège or level field) where it can roll under supervision without hurting itself. (Although traditionally horses were walked to stop them rolling the current view is that rolling is unlikely to be harmful provided the horse can roll safely and the abdomen is not grossly enlarged.) Alternatively, keep the horse under constant supervision in case it becomes cast. As a last resort, walk it until the vet arrives.
- Don't offer the horse anything to eat or drink, or administer any medication until the vet has examined it.

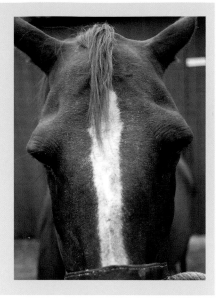

The upper eyelids of this horse are bruised and swollen, due to it rolling overnight in a stable with minimal bedding

What the vet will do

In addition to observing the horse, checking the *pulse, rectal temperature* and *respiratory rate*, the vet will *listen to the intestinal tract* with a stethoscope placed on the flank. In normal horses there is a continuous cacophony of gurgling and bubbling sounds created by the normal mixing and propulsive contractions of the intestines. In horses with colic, gut sounds are most commonly reduced and are only occasionally increased.

The vet will also check the horse's *circulation* and *hydration* status by pinching the skin on the neck (it should snap back into place immediately), observing the *rate at which the jugular vein fills* if temporarily blocked at the bottom of the neck, and looking at the *colour of the mucous membranes* of the eye and mouth. He or she may also perform a *rectal examination* to feel the accessible parts of the horse's digestive system. A rectal examination may reveal loops of intestine distended by fluid or gas, or a mass of faecal material obstructing the colon.

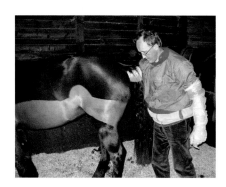

Only the rear half of the abdomen is accessible for rectal palpation. Sequential examinations over several hours may be necessary to detect bowel distension or obstruction

A stomach tube was used to drain this fluid from the abdomen of a horse with severe colic. The horse had an upper small intestinal obstruction. In normal horses little or no fluid is recoverable

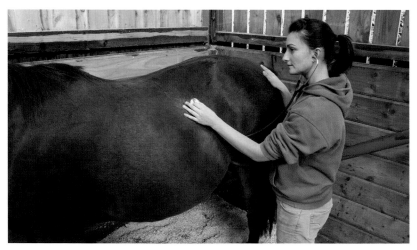

Healthy intestines are continuously contracting, resulting in gurgling sounds, which can be heard through a stethoscope. In colic, contractions usually diminish and there are few audible sounds

Normal clear pale yellow peritoneal fluid (left). Blood-stained slightly cloudy peritoneal fluid (right), recovered from a horse with a small intestinal torsion, suggests the need for urgent life-saving surgery

A stomach tube is used to check for accumulation of *fluid in the stomach*. Fluid pools here when it cannot move past an obstruction downstream.

A sample of the *peritoneal fluid*, which bathes the surface of the intestines, will be collected by inserting a needle through the abdominal wall from the underside. Normally clear and pale yellow, in surgical colics it becomes cloudy and reddish.

Drug treatment
The following may be administered in non-surgical cases:
- Drugs that relax spasm of the bowel. These work very quickly and the horse may be back to normal minutes after injection.
- Drugs that relieve pain.
- Drugs that calm the horse.
- Laxative drugs, usually liquid paraffin (mineral oil) or sodium sulphate. These are used in impaction colic and take a long time (12–24 hours) to work.
- Non-steroidal anti-inflammatory drugs to prevent the development of toxaemia and shock.
- Intravenous fluid therapy to combat shock and dehydration.
- Oral fluids administered by stomach tube to help relieve impaction colic.

SURGICAL TREATMENT

Deciding on surgery
Although early surgery is desirable, where the clinical signs are not clear-cut, it can be difficult to make that decision. The vet may try medical treatment in the first instance or refer the horse for observation at an equine hospital.

Horses that obviously need surgical treatment are usually:
- in severe pain and distress and respond poorly or only briefly to pain-killing drugs
- showing signs of dehydration and poor circulation
- have rectal examination findings that indicate a need for immediate surgery, for example, distended loops of intestine.

What happens during surgery?
Surgery is performed under general anaesthesia. Affected horses are often seriously ill and will require intensive anaesthetic support and intravenous fluids both during and after the surgery. The aims of the surgeon are to:
- determine the precise cause
- remove any portions of bowel that are no longer viable
- relieve obstruction
- relieve distension.

This horse is undergoing colic surgery. The gas-filled small intestine indicates that there is an obstruction downstream

How to prevent colic
The following factors are known to predispose a horse to colic:
- Failure to maintain an adequate worming programme (see p.99).
- Feeding high levels of hard feed. (There is a six-fold increase in risk if a horse is fed more than 5kg/11lb per day compared to horses at grass.) Divide hard feed into as many small feeds as possible, and feed it with a generous amount of high quality forage.
- Recent changes in type of hard feed or forage. Make changes very gradually, mixing old forage with new initially.
- Lack of exercise. Horses that are permanently stabled are at an increased risk.
- Sudden changes in the amount of exercise (increase or decrease) significantly increases risk.
- Restricted access to water.

GRASS SICKNESS

Grass sickness is a disease of the intestinal system of grazing horses, seen usually from late spring to midsummer in horses aged from 2–7 years. Current research suggests that the disease is a form of botulism, caused by horses ingesting *Clostridium botulinum* or its toxin. Some, as yet unknown, conditions cause the organism to multiply on pasture. Cases are more likely to occur if:

- there has been some soil disturbance in the pasture
- the horses have recently changed fields
- the horses have recently been moved to new premises
- the horses have recently been wormed with an ivermectin-type wormer
- the weather is cool and dry
- there have been other cases on the premises before.

The toxin produced by this bacterium damages the nerves controlling the normal propulsive movements of the intestines, resulting in failure of the stomach to empty (it fills with fluid), no audible contractions of the intestines, and hence constipation. The disease occurs in several forms.

Acute grass sickness

The horse shows signs of acute colic. The stomach is tightly distended with a green fluid that can be retrieved with a stomach tube. Swallowing is difficult, and patchy sweating and muscle trembling occur. Many acute cases are assumed to be surgical colics and may be operated on, only to find that there is no correctible problem in the abdomen. There is no treatment, other than pain control. The disease has a rapid course, usually ending in the horse being humanely destroyed, although sometimes it is found dead in the field with a ruptured stomach.

A stomach grossly distended with fluid is characteristic of acute grass sickness. In this case the stomach contents are spontaneously refluxing through a stomach tube

Chronic grass sickness

In chronic grass sickness there is marked weight loss and the horse has an extremely gaunt, tucked up appearance. There is patchy sweating and tremors of the upper muscles of the fore and hind legs. There is dried sticky mucoid material at the nostrils. Very few droppings are passed, and those that are, are hard, dry and dark. The horse has a very poor appetite.

This horse has had chronic grass sickness for three weeks. It has a poor appetite and finds swallowing difficult; it is suffering severe weight loss and a very tucked-up 'greyhound' appearance. No gut sounds are audible and very few faeces are passed

What to do next

- If a suspect case occurs, the other horses in the group should be brought indoors and fed hay until grass sickness is confirmed.
- Most chronic cases will eventually be humanely destroyed. A small proportion (probably less than 25%) may eventually recover but this may take up to a year and it requires a major commitment in time and effort by the owner. Careful nursing is required, including keeping the horse hydrated and especially maintenance of the appetite by offering palatable foods and frequent stimulation of the horse by changing its surroundings and company.

DIARRHOEA

The contents of the horse's digestive system are very fluid in the small intestine but gradually become drier as they move through the large intestine. Horses normally produce approximately 8–12 piles of fully formed droppings per day. If being fed only grass the faeces are slightly looser than when fed hay but they should be fully formed.

Transient self-limiting bouts of mild diarrhoea lasting a few hours without any other signs of illness are common in horses and usually resolve themselves. Diarrhoea caused by disease is more problematic and can be divided into acute cases, with rapid weight loss and dehydration, and chronic cases lasting for weeks or months, in which the horse manages to keep itself normally hydrated although it often becomes thin.

Transient mild diarrhoea

The causes are:

- Excitement, for example when moved to a new premises.
- Fear.
- Travelling. The piles of droppings in the horsebox on arrival are often looser than normal.
- Recent turnout to grass after a long period of stabling.
- Horses being fed silage or haylage made from young grass may develop loose faeces due to a lack of fibre.
- Excessive faecal fluid. Some healthy horses pass normal faeces that are immediately followed by a quantity of green fluid. The amount of fluid may be large and it may result in permanent soiling of the tail. The reason for this phenomenon is unknown and exhaustive investigations are usually unrewarding.

Transient mild diarrhoeas usually pass quickly without treatment, and are not significant. Increasing the fibre content of the diet by feeding straw-based chaff will help where the forage is too low in fibre.

Acute diarrhoea

There are several common causes of acute diarrhoea:
Salmonella infection The source of infection is usually from an environment contaminated by faeces from a carrier horse (or other species). The onset of the disease is precipitated by stress. Initially the horse has a raised temperature, mild colic and is obviously ill. It then develops profuse diarrhoea and becomes very dehydrated. Loss of blood proteins into the digestive system sometimes causes a soft swelling (a plaque of oedema) to develop under the abdomen, and filled legs. Weight loss is marked, the horse is miserable and may die unless treatment is intensive. Humans and other horses may become infected from exposure to an infected horse, contaminated bedding and so on.

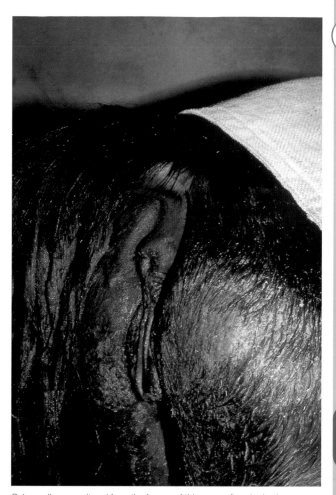

Salmonella was cultured from the faeces of this mare after she had developed profuse smelly diarrhoea and suffered rapid weight loss

Clostridial colitis In this condition *Clostridia* bacteria, normally present in small quantities in the digestive system, suddenly multiply to huge numbers and produce toxins, causing a rapidly fatal diarrhoea that responds very poorly to treatment. Overgrowth of the *Clostridia* is precipitated usually by antibiotic treatment and/or stress such as transport or general anaesthesia. Some very severe cases will die before any significant diarrhoea develops.

Grain overload If a horse gains access to a feed store and gorges itself on hard feed it may develop colic and then diarrhoea. Laminitis is a common sequel.

Toxicity Overdose with anti-inflammatory drugs, or poisoning by acorns or algal-contaminated water may cause acute diarrhoea.

What to do next

- Summon veterinary help immediately.
- Until proven otherwise assume that the condition is infectious for horses and people.
- Move the horse to an isolated stable and severely restrict the number of people in contact with it.
- If at pasture bring indoors, move in-contact horses to another field and monitor them carefully.
- Saturate the bedding, walls and utensils in the vacated stable with disinfectant (for example 'Virkon') and leave in place to be dealt with later.
- Institute barrier nursing of the affected horse by wearing protective clothing, rubber boots and disposable gloves when dealing with it. Place a disinfectant footbath outside the box.
- Wash the horse's hindquarters and tail with warm soapy water, and apply petroleum jelly, to prevent scalding. Provide ample bedding to soak up the excess faecal fluid.
- All removed bedding should be treated with disinfectant or stored in a separate muck heap.

What the vet will do

The vet will ensure that your quarantine arrangements are suitable and may take samples of faeces to determine the cause. Blood tests may be done to establish the degree of dehydration and protein loss into the bowel, and to assist with diagnosis.

In addition:
- Fluid therapy may be started, given by the intravenous, and possibly, the oral route. Large quantities may be required over several days.
- Other therapy, for example antibiotics, anti-inflammatories and intestinal fluid absorbents may be given, depending on the cause.

The mortality rate in severe salmonella diarrhoea exceeds 50 per cent. The faeces of recovered cases will need sampling to ensure freedom from infection.

Chronic diarrhoea

Chronic is defined here as diarrhoea lasting for more than two weeks. The onset is often insidious and sometimes the severity may vary from day to day.

Parasitic colitis (Cyathostomiasis) This condition is most common in horses of 1–5 years old. In late autumn the horse takes in a large number of small redworm larvae from the pasture. These enter the wall of the large intestine and become dormant. In late winter and spring they suddenly become active and emerge from the wall in waves causing an acute colitis. Emergence may be triggered by worming

in the last two weeks or stressful events, such as transport, foaling, or by other diseases.

Often the horse becomes depressed and loses weight initially, then develops diarrhoea. Some horses have an elevated temperature. The diarrhoea may first be intermittent then becomes permanent. Often tiny redworms are seen in faeces. The horse loses a great deal of weight and may develop filling of the hind legs and ventral abdomen due to loss of blood proteins into the damaged gut. Severe cases are difficult to treat and some cases may die in spite of treatment.

Inflammatory bowel disease The cause of this condition is unknown. It occurs in various forms depending on the cellular components of the inflammation. The disease progresses slowly and the appetite is usually normal. Often diarrhoea is preceded by a period of unexplained weight loss. Some cases respond to oral corticosteroid drug therapy but some do not.

'Cow-pat' faeces passed by a horse with chronic inflammatory bowel disease

Peritonitis Infection in the abdominal cavity, usually caused by an internal abscess or bowel leakage, results in peritonitis. The horse usually loses weight and develops diarrhoea, which is rarely profuse. A sample of peritoneal fluid will often be cloudy and discoloured due to the large number of inflammatory cells and proteins present. Some cases respond to treatment but extensive gut perforation may prove fatal.

Peritonitis causes the peritoneal fluid to become cloudy and reddish. (Normal peritoneal fluid is shown on p.93)

Cancer of the digestive system This is usually a lymphoid tumour infiltrating the bowel wall. The horse loses weight, becomes depressed and, at later, in some cases develops diarrhoea. There is no effective treatment at present.

What the vet will do
Determination of the cause can be difficult and can require extensive laboratory investigations. A tiny piece of the rectal wall (rectal biopsy) can be taken for microscopic analysis or the vet may need to take intestinal wall biopsies under general anaesthesia. As the latter is an expensive and potentially hazardous procedure, the vet may try a variety of drug treatments in the first instance. These therapies include:
- anti-inflammatory treatment for inflammatory bowel disease
- anti-parasitic treatments, principally moxidectin
- drugs that slow down gut contractions and suppress bowel secretions such as codeine phosphate.

LIVER DISEASE
Liver disease is not common in the horse. The liver has a huge functional reserve and an extensive amount must be damaged before signs are seen. Liver failure occurs when more than 70 per cent of the liver is diseased.

Clinical signs
The clinical signs of liver disease are very variable depending on the cause, duration and severity of the disease. They include:
- loss of appetite
- a yellow colouration of the mucous membranes of the eyes and mouth known as jaundice. This must be distinguished from the mild jaundice that occurs in many horses that have not eaten for a few days for any reason
- weight loss
- abnormal behaviour (hepatic encephalopathy) including yawning, inco-ordination, tremors, head pressing and compulsive circling
- photosensitisation (see p.139).

Causes of liver disease
The principal causes of liver disease are
- **Ragwort** (*Senecio jacobaea*) poisoning. The living plant is very unpalatable but it may be eaten if present in hay. A significant amount needs to be consumed over a long period of time before signs are seen
- **Mouldy feed** Hard feed which has been allowed to become damp and undisturbed may support fungal growth and the production of toxins which cause liver damage if the feed is eaten
- **Infection** of the bile system
- Miscellaneous other causes

Treatment
Treatment is often unsuccessful because of the usually advanced state of the disease when first noticed. A low protein high carbohydrate diet, vitamin supplements and other supportive therapies are used. Ragwort poisoning rarely responds to treatment.

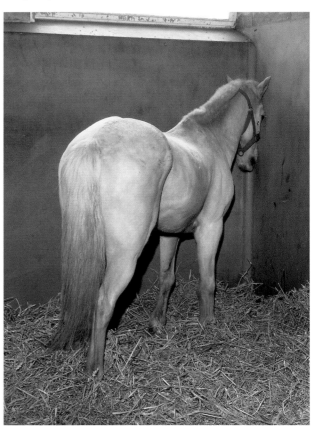

This horse lived on a farm where cattle feed bins had been cleaned out and the contents dumped in the horse's field. The horse consumed the mouldy feed residue and developed liver failure. Here it is showing one of the signs of hepatic encephalopathy – pressing its head against the stable wall.

THE THIN HORSE

In dealing with thin horses it is necessary to establish whether the horse is healthy but malnourished, or has become thin because it is suffering from an illness.

WHY DO HEALTHY HORSES BECOME THIN?

In spite of a normal appetite and the apparent availability of sufficient food, horses may become thin in a variety of situations, for example:

- Underestimation of the feed requirements for the amount of work the horse has to do. A nutritionist should be consulted.
- Overestimation of the nutritional value of what is fed. Chaff products, although bulky, have minimal feed value.
- Reluctance to feed adequate calories because of a fear of making the horse difficult to ride.
- Failure of the horse to compete for food when group fed.
- Loss of appetite. Very fit horses often lose their appetite and it can be difficult to keep weight on them. Solutions include:
  - increasing the calorie density of the diet by changing to a higher specification feed, e.g. from a basic mix to a racehorse mix
  - introducing variety by varying the constituents of each meal
  - allowing access to good grass
  - increasing the number of meals fed but decreasing their size
  - improving the digestibility of forage by feeding higher calorie haylage.
- Some lactating mares lose weight due to the demands of milk production.
- Old horses (>25 years) often have an angular, rather gaunt appearance and will not put on weight in spite of being well fed.

Veterinary causes of wasting in horses

A vet will consider the following when assessing a horse that is not thin for any of the reasons given above.

- Dental disease, usually associated with quidding or hay rejection (p.84).
- Intestinal parasitism, especially small redworms (p.99).
- Chronic peritonitis (p.96).
- Chronic diarrhoea (p.96).
- Other intestinal diseases interfering with digestion and absorption such as bowel cancer or chronic inflammatory bowel disease (pp.96–97).
- Chronic liver disease (p.97) or chronic kidney disease.
- Chronic infection such as an abdominal abscess.
- Chronic pain, such as in longstanding laminitis or severe single-leg lameness.
- Cancer arising in other body tissues, such as the lungs.
- Equine Cushing's disease (p.140).

What the vet will do

- Determine how long the horse been losing weight.
- Ensure that the food and water supply are adequate.
- Determine whether the horse has to compete for food (especially grass or hay) with more dominant horses.
- Establish whether there is any difficulty in eating or masticating.
- Establish whether there are other signs of illness, for example loss of appetite, diarrhoea, excessive drinking, coat changes, filling of the legs, and so on.
- Collect blood for analysis.
- Possibly conduct tests to establish whether the digestive system is normal. The commonest is the glucose absorption test (see diagram below), in which a large dose of glucose is given to the horse by stomach tube. Blood samples are taken before dosing, and then every half hour afterwards for up to four hours. The pre-dosing blood glucose level in a normal horse should double after two hours. If small intestinal disease (for example inflammatory bowel disease) is present the absorption will be poor.

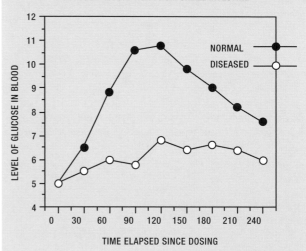

GLUCOSE ABSORPTION FROM SMALL INTESTINE

NORMAL ●
DISEASED ○

LEVEL OF GLUCOSE IN BLOOD

TIME ELAPSED SINCE DOSING

This thin horse had bowel cancer (lymphosarcoma). Very low blood protein (albumin) levels caused the formation of a plaque of oedema on the lower abdomen (arrow)

Worms

Intestinal worms become a problem when some or all of the following are found:

- A lot of young horses (4 years old and under) on a premises. Young animals are more susceptible.
- The pastures are grazed by horses only. Co-grazing by other species 'vacuum cleans' the paddocks of horse worm larvae.
- Droppings are not collected.
- The paddocks are densely stocked and closely grazed.
- Worm control is erratic, or not practised on all horses in a group.
- Inappropriate worming drugs are used.
- Worming drug resistance has developed.

Redworms (Strongyles)

The adult worms live in the large intestine and suck blood, hence the red colour. They lay eggs that pass out in the droppings, develop into infective larvae, which are then ingested by the horse during grazing. These develop into adult worms that lay eggs and so on.
There are two types of redworms:

- **Large redworms** There are three species, the most important of which has a developmental phase in the blood vessels supplying the digestive system. These vessels can become blocked, causing colic. Modern wormers have virtually eradicated these species.
- **Small redworms** (Cyathostomins). There are 51 species of which 5–10 occur commonly. These are only a few millimetres long and just visible to the naked eye. Larvae taken in during grazing develop in the wall of the large intestine and emerge when mature to form adult worms. If ingested in the late autumn some may become inhibited in the wall and then emerge in waves in spring (see 'Chronic diarrhoea', p.96).

The clinical signs of redworm infestation include: colic, diarrhoea, failure to thrive, poor coat and anaemia.

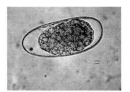

Adult redworms lay microscopic eggs which are passed in the faeces

The worm eggs hatch into tiny larvae, which migrate out from the faecal pat for a distance of up to 30cm (12in). They climb up the grass stems and wait to be eaten. These larvae are very susceptible to hot dry conditions, and survive well in damp cool conditions

Ascarids

Ascarids are parasites of foals and weanlings; older horses become naturally immune. The eggs are taken in while grazing, hatch in the stomach and the larvae travel via the liver and lungs before settling down in the small intestine and developing into adult worms, which may be very large. The adults lay eggs and the cycle continues.

The clinical signs are failure to grow, poor body condition, coughing (due to migration of worms through the lungs), colic due to small intestinal obstruction.

Bots

Bots are reddish grubs that attach to the wall of the stomach and small intestine during winter. They detach in spring and are passed in the faeces, where they pupate and develop into bot flies, which lay their eggs on the horse's legs. The eggs are licked off by the horse and swallowed and develop into grubs.

The clinical signs are annoyance in grazing horses due to bot flies attempting to lay eggs and, rarely, colic, principally caused by the species that attaches to the small intestine.

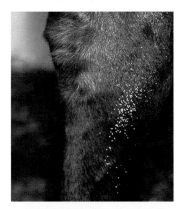

Bot eggs laid on a horse's leg by a bot fly, A horse's stomach, post-mortem, reveals a large number of orange bot-fly grubs

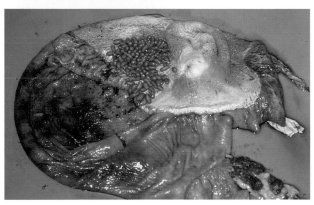

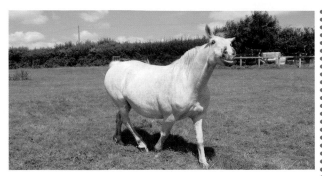

Although they don't bite, the bee-like bot flies cause disturbance to horses as they hover near them to lay their eggs

Tapeworms

These small flat worms live in the small intestine. Eggs are passed in the faeces and ingested by a small mite on the grass. Further development occurs in the mite, which is in turn inadvertently eaten by the grazing horse. Adult tapeworms then develop in the horse.

The clinical signs of tapeworm infection are spasmodic colic (about 20% of spasmodic cases are believed to be tapeworm-associated) and impaction of the lower small intestine, causing colic that requires surgery.

Adult tapeworms passed in the faeces of a horse after tapeworm treatment

Tapeworms attach mostly to the junction between the small intestine (dark colour) and the caecum (pink colour), where they cause thickening and inflammation, potentially impeding the flow of intestinal contents into the caecum (as in this post-mortem specimen). Complete obstruction (ileal impaction) may occur

Pinworms

These worms live in the rectum of horses and cause tail rubbing and anal irritation, but are otherwise harmless. They have an elongated 'tail' and can sometimes be seen in the droppings.

Pinworms in the rectum caused this pony to rub its tail

✓ Diagnosing worm infections

It is often possible to make a diagnosis if the grazing and worming histories are known.

Faecal worm egg counts (WEC) Often erroneously called 'worm counts', these are of limited value in diagnosing whether a horse has a significant worm burden, because:

- the correlation between the number of worm eggs in the faeces and the number of adult worms in the intestine is poor
- tapeworm eggs are not demonstrated by conventional counting techniques
- in the case of small redworms, most of the damage is caused by larvae rather than by egg-laying adult worms. A horse may have a severe small redworm colitis but have a negative faecal WEC.

However WECs are *very useful* in worm control because control relies on ensuring very few eggs are passed onto the pasture (see opposite).

Blood tests A blood test is available that demonstrates the approximate size of the tapeworm burden a horse carries. Blood tests may also give indirect evidence of parasite infection. For example, there may be evidence of anaemia, inflammation and low blood protein levels.

INTESTINAL PARASITE CONTROL

What follows is general advice as equine premises vary hugely and it is important to obtain tailored veterinary advice. What is appropriate for a small stud, for example, may be inappropriate for a large livery yard with a changing horse population.

Redworm control

Because resistance to worming drugs is becoming widespread, it has become necessary to challenge much of the dogma relating to worm control that has been promulgated over the last 20 years.

Key facts

- 20% of the horses carry 80% of the worms. Many horses (around 80–90%) are naturally resistant and produce very few worm eggs.
- Young horses (4 years old or younger) are more susceptible and produce the most worm eggs.
- Control relies on reducing worm uptake from the pasture by:
  - using worming drugs to kill the egg-laying adults in the horse, thereby reducing the number of eggs in the droppings
  - physically removing the eggs by collecting droppings every 1–2 days
  - co-grazing with other species, especially sheep; the worm larvae will be harmlessly destroyed in the other species.

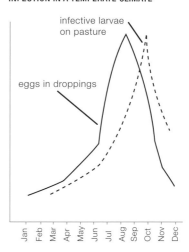

PEAK PERIOD OF POSSIBLE REDWORM INFECTION IN A TEMPERATE CLIMATE

infective larvae on pasture

eggs in droppings

Jan Feb Mar Apr May Jun Jul Aug Sep Oct Nov Dec

Egg output rises as the summer progresses, resulting (after the eggs hatch) in a slightly later worm larvae peak (dotted line) on the grass

DRUG RESISTANCE IN WORMS

- Resistance is a genetic trait coded in the worms' genes.
- Spontaneous natural genetic variation results in the appearance of some resistant strains in an otherwise susceptible population. Resistant strains that survive a drug treatment then become the predominant genetic strain in the next generation.
- Subsequent treatment with the same drug further selects for resistant strains until no susceptible strains are left.
- Resistance to wormers is permanent in a worm population. There is no reversion to susceptibility.

What can be done?

Ensure you give the correct dose. Underestimating the weight (especially of adult horses) and hence under-dosing, is common and under-dosing accentuates the resistance problem. To calculate the dose required, estimate the bodyweight of the horse using a weigh tape or weighbridge. All of the worming drugs have a wide safety margin and if a horse is slightly overdosed it is very unlikely to be harmed.

Use several different drugs during a grazing season. Rotation of drugs, previously advocated, is impractical because of the narrow spectrum of action of the available drugs.

To prevent resistance

- reduce drug usage to reduce exposure of each worm generation
- use alternative methods of control (see Key facts)
- monitor efficacy of treatment by doing WECs on horses before and two weeks after treatment. If the drug is effective the egg count should fall to zero.

THE ROUTE FROM EFFECTIVE TO INEFFECTIVE WORM TREATMENT

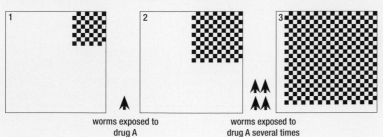

1
2
3

worms exposed to drug A

worms exposed to drug A several times

1. Prior to first exposure, a small percentage of the worm population is naturally resistant to drug A
2. The resistant population selectively survives worming and becomes a higher percentage,
3. Eventually the resistant population becomes dominant and drug A is no longer effective

WORMING METHODS

Interval dosing

This is the traditional approach. The horses are wormed at regular intervals (depending on the drug used) during the high-risk summer grazing period. The aim is to suppress completely egg output in the droppings, thereby reducing worm larval uptake when grazing. After dosing the worm egg count will fall to zero, and then gradually rise again as new adult worms develop and further eggs are laid. Dosing is not necessary during the low-risk winter period or if the horse is stabled for most of the day.

The dosing interval is based on the egg re-appearance time for each drug. These are: Ivermectin 6–8 weeks; Moxidectin 13 weeks; Pyrantel 4–6 weeks.

Interval dosing has been criticised because a lot of the drug is used, horses are treated indiscriminately although many of them have very few eggs in their droppings due to natural resistance and every generation of the worm receives exposure to the drug, favouring the selection of resistant strains.

Targeted strategic dosing (TSD)

This is currently favoured. The aim is to suppress pasture egg contamination at critical times of the year. All horses have WECs performed first and only those with significant adult parasite burdens are treated. This may be only a small minority of the horses tested.

How is TSD done? Faeces are obtained from all horses in the group (see chart) and WECs performed. Only horses with WECs above 150–200 eggs per gram are treated. The drugs to be used are based on veterinary advice. In addition all young horses *must* receive a larvicidal dose of moxidectin in the autumn to remove inhibited larvae.

Targeted dosing will not control tapeworms as tapeworm eggs are not counted in routine WECs.

Benefits of TSD:

- Fewer horses are treated.
- Cost savings in worming drug usage outweigh the costs of the WECs.
- Resistance is avoided or delayed.

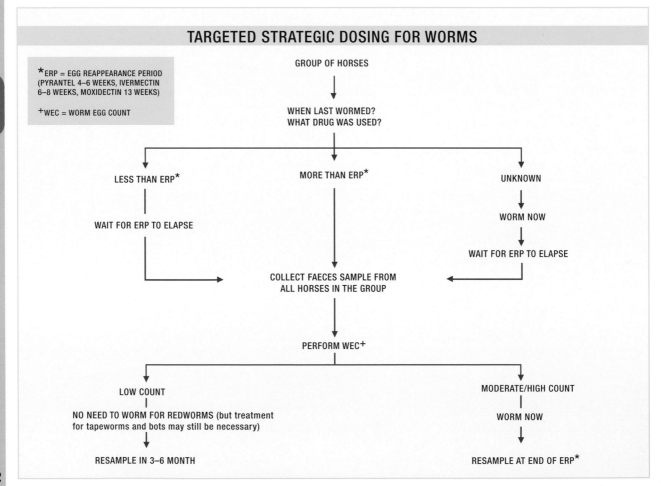

TARGETED STRATEGIC DOSING FOR WORMS

*ERP = EGG REAPPEARANCE PERIOD (PYRANTEL 4–6 WEEKS, IVERMECTIN 6–8 WEEKS, MOXIDECTIN 13 WEEKS)

+WEC = WORM EGG COUNT

GROUP OF HORSES
↓
WHEN LAST WORMED?
WHAT DRUG WAS USED?

LESS THAN ERP* → WAIT FOR ERP TO ELAPSE

MORE THAN ERP*

UNKNOWN → WORM NOW → WAIT FOR ERP TO ELAPSE

COLLECT FAECES SAMPLE FROM ALL HORSES IN THE GROUP
↓
PERFORM WEC+

LOW COUNT
NO NEED TO WORM FOR REDWORMS (but treatment for tapeworms and bots may still be necessary)
↓
RESAMPLE IN 3–6 MONTH

MODERATE/HIGH COUNT
WORM NOW
↓
RESAMPLE AT END OF ERP*

Worming drugs

The following worming drugs are available for treating horses. ('Herbal' wormers have not been scientifically evaluated so they cannot be recommended.)

DRUG	BOTS	REDWORMS	ASCARIDS	TAPEWORMS	PINWORMS
Ivermectin	YES	YES(1)	YES(4)	NO	YES
Moxidectin(8)	YES	YES(2)	YES	NO	YES
Pyrantel	NO	YES(3)	YES	YES(5)	YES
Praziquantel(6)	NO	NO	NO	YES	NO
Fenbendazole	NO	POOR(7)	YES	NO	YES

YES: effective   NO: Not effective or completely ineffective

Notes

1. No activity against inhibited small redworms in the intestinal wall
2. Currently the only drug consistently effective against inhibited small redworms
3. No activity against inhibited larvae, and resistance has been reported
4. Resistance of ascarids to ivermectin has been reported in some countries
5. For tapeworm treatment a double dose must be given
6. This drug is available on its own or combined with ivermectin or moxidectin
7. Redworm resistance is widespread to this drug. I no longer recommend it for equine use
8. Do not use moxidectin in foals under 4 months of age

(For advice on administering a worming paste, see p.155)

Ascarids: The eggs last for years on pasture. Foals and weanlings should be treated from eight weeks (moxidectin cannot be given under four months old).

Bots: Remove the yellow eggs from the coat using a special bot comb. In addition between December and February, kill the bot larvae in the stomach by treating the horse with an ivermectin or moxidectin wormer.

Tapeworms: Twice yearly dosing with either a double dose of pyrantel or a standard dose of praziquantel is recommended. Praziquantel is available either on its own or combined with ivermectin or moxidectin in a single syringe. Praziquantel is the more effective of the two.

This field is the perfect illustration of the value of removing droppings. Regular removal for parasite control brings the added benefit of ensuring more even grazing of the field. Without removal, the grazing area is reduced by 50% after four years continuous occupation by horses.

WOUNDS

Types of wounds

Kicks

Social interactions between horses are often violent, resulting in kicking and biting. Kick wounds are problematic because:

- They are often discovered late because the kick is not usually witnessed. Therefore there may be a delay in treatment, resulting in swelling and the establishment of infection.
- They are usually contaminated.
- The skin is split by blunt trauma, so the wound edges are often devitalised, making them poor sites for suturing (stitching).
- There may possibly be damage to the underlying structures.
- Most kick wounds are on the limbs, where there is minimal spare skin to draw together when suturing.

As a consequence of all of these factors, kick wounds often cannot be sutured.

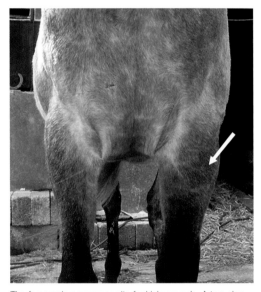

The forearm is a common site for kick wounds. A two-day old wound has become infected. The forearm is swollen (arrow) and the horse is quite lame

Kick injuries: what can happen

- **Kicks to the large muscle masses (rump, thigh or forearm).** These may merely bruise causing a swelling or a haematoma (blood blister), or in addition the skin may be broken causing a wound.
- **Kicks to bone (cannon bones, pastern bone)** These usually split the skin overlying the bone. The bone itself may be damaged, causing a fracture or bruising of the membrane overlying the bone. This bruising often results in the formation of a permanent bony lump.

Sharp edges

Horses may encounter sharp edges in myriad ways, for example in stables, doors, fences, trailers and so on. These wounds often have healthy edges and, depending on their location, the amount of skin lost and the presence of damage to underlying tissues, they may be suitable candidates for suturing. Self-injury wounds occur during exercise, for example overreaches (in which the hindleg strikes the rear of the opposite foreleg, usually in the pastern or tendon regions).

Surgical wounds

Wounds created during a surgical procedure have, in principle, the best chance of healing as they are created under sterile conditions. There is little or no contamination, the wound edges are healthy, they are often sutured and antibiotic therapy may be given before infection can become established in the wound. Surgical wounds 'break down' if they become infected, or movement or post-operative swelling causes excessive tension on the sutures.

This overreach wound occurred in an event horse while jumping. It was sutured very soon after it happened, and healed well

HOW WOUNDS HEAL

The healing process starts within five minutes of a wound occurring. Wound healing can be divided into three phases:

The inflammatory phase

Blood clots in the wound, fluid leaks into the wound cavity and white blood cells migrate into the wound from the surrounding tissues and blood vessels. These cells release enzymes that 'digest' damaged tissue, dead cells, bacteria in the wound, and foreign material. This phase lasts for a variable period (see 'Why is healing delayed?', p.106).

The repair phase

This begins in the first 12 hours but it cannot start until the blood clots, damaged tissue and infection have been eliminated. Failure to eliminate these will delay healing. During the repair phase granulation tissue – a complex mixture of blood vessels, fibrous tissue-forming cells and other components – expands until it bridges the wound. The surface skin cells then migrate from the wound edges over the granulation tissue and the wound begins to heal.

The maturation phase

The healed tissue strengthens and contracts, reducing the overall size of the wound. After one year, scar tissue still has only 80 per cent of the tensile strength of normal skin.

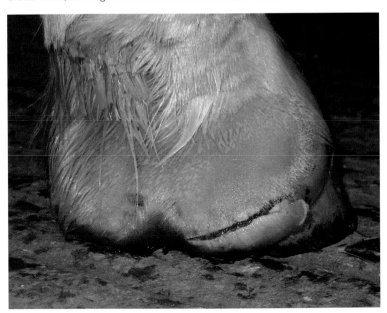

Caused by the horse's leg being caught in a cattle grid, this wound was heavily contaminated and damaged, resulting in delayed healing

Why is healing delayed

Healing is delayed in the following circumstances:

- infection is present
- foreign material (for example hair or soil) is present
- the wound has been allowed to dry out, usually by not being covered. A moist environment in the wound is best for healing
- dead tissue or dead bone is present
- the dressing has not been changed frequently enough

- the horse has been allowed excessive movement
- the horse does not take all of its antibiotic medication
- the horse is malnourished. It is important to ensure that convalescing horses have an adequate protein and calorie intake
- the horse is receiving anti-inflammatory medication or suffers from Equine Cushing's disease (p.140).

PECULIARITIES OF WOUND HEALING

Wounds heal more slowly in horses than in ponies. This is because in ponies the inflammatory phase is more intense and occurs more quickly. Bacteria and debris are cleared more rapidly from the wound and the repair phase starts earlier.

Limb wounds

Most wounds in horses occur on the limbs. Limb wounds heal more slowly than wounds to the trunk because:

- The rate at which skin cells migrate into the wound is ten times slower in the limbs than in the trunk.
- The skin from the knee and hock down has a relatively poor blood supply.

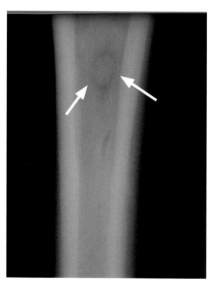

Bone was exposed by a kick wound to this cannon bone. The membrane overlying the exposed bone was damaged, resulting in death of a portion of the bone – visible on this x-ray, taken three weeks after the kick. When this was removed, the wound was able to heal

- If caused by a kick to skin overlying bone, the bone may be damaged. A portion of bone may lose its blood supply and die. Wounds with dead bone will not heal until the dead bone is removed.
- The skin on the lower limbs is tightly applied to the underlying structures. There is therefore a tendency for it to retract when cut, making the wound larger. Equally the healing wound can contract very little.
- Limbs are very mobile. Movement of joints can pull wounds apart.
- Limb wounds are closer to the ground and therefore more susceptible to contamination.
- Limb wounds have a pronounced tendency to develop excessive granulation tissue (*proud flesh*). This expands and rises out of the wound, above the level of the surrounding skin. The inflammation in the wound becomes chronic and wounds with proud flesh may never heal unless it is removed.
- The contraction phase is much slower in the limbs compared to the trunk.

Proud flesh has rapidly developed in this 12-day-old hock wound. It will not heal until this is removed (see p.115)

Wounds

CLASSIFYING WOUNDS

Grazes In these only the hair and the superficial layers of the skin have been lost. The full thickness of the skin has not been breached. These wounds usually heal quickly because if infection occurs it will only be superficial. If a horse with a graze is lame and the area of the wound is swollen, it suggests:
- there has been some bruising of the tissues
- there is a small, perhaps barely visible, penetration of the full thickness of the skin.

Full-thickness wounds are more serious and are more likely to become infected. Puncture wounds may be unnoticed at first. Larger wounds are likely to become contaminated and to expose important underlying structures such as bone and muscle.

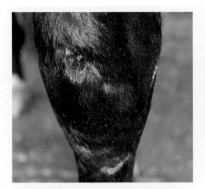

Although they had some bruising and swelling, these grazes were unlikely to become infected. They were treated with an antibiotic spray, which is applied, allowed to dry, then repeated twice to provide a barrier

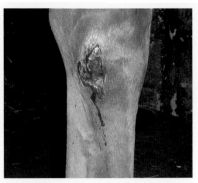

Even if sutured, flexion of the knee will put great tension on the edges of this full thickness wound. The entire limb was bandaged heavily to prevent flexion

Potentially dangerous wounds

The *most dangerous wounds* are those:
- near a joint or tendon sheath
- with damage to and exposure of underlying tissues, especially bone
- with large areas of skin loss
- to the eye or head
- that penetrate the chest or abdominal cavities

- in horses not immunised against tetanus

All these have the potential to develop very serious infections and *must receive urgent veterinary attention*. Infections in joints and tendon sheaths may result in a severe incurable lameness if not treated very quickly. It will be necessary to flush the structure with large quantities of fluid (often under general anaesthesia) to remove the infection, toxins and inflammatory proteins.

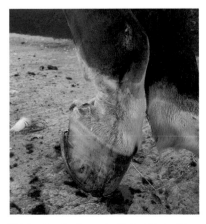

This hunter struck a rock with its fetlock while cantering across moorland. Within 30 minutes it was very lame. Yellow joint fluid is leaking from the fetlock joint. The joint was thoroughly flushed and the horse made a full recovery

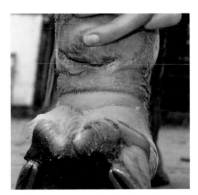

A deep wound very close to the tendon sheath at the back of the pastern

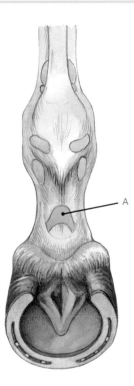

Vulnerable areas at the back of the lower limb where the tendon sheath is protected only by the overlying skin (shaded green). The back of the pastern (A) is very vulnerable to injury (for example an overreach, or a horse striking out through a wire fence)

When you find a wound

ASSESSING THE WOUND

In many cases, assessment of a wound and the decision about how it should be treated are best left to a vet.

Assessment requires good light and the horse must stand still. If it is distressed, sedation may be necessary. As a guide, the key questions to answer are:

- How deep and how big is the wound?
- Is it close to any important structures?
- How contaminated is it?
- Could a foreign body be present?
- Is anything, for example clear yellow viscous joint fluid, discharging from it?
- Do I need to call the vet (see below)?

WHAT NOT TO DO

Don't put anything into a wound that you wouldn't put into your own eye!

- Don't attempt to treat the horse in a muddy field or a dirty stable.
- Don't put into a wound that penetrates the full thickness of the skin anything that may interfere with healing – wound powders, antiseptic sprays, 'healing' lotions are all potential irritants. If something must be placed in the wound hydrogel (see p.112) is best.
- Don't bandage the wound without clipping and cleaning the hair around it.
- Don't use dirty hands, dressings and bandages. Strict cleanliness is essential. Always use a clean bandage, a new sterile wound dressing and a new piece of Gamgee or cotton wool.

SHOULD I CALL THE VET?

The answer is 'Yes' in any of the following cases:

- Full thickness wounds more than 1–2cm (½in) long.
- Full thickness puncture wounds to the forearm and thigh regions, however small. These have a high probability of becoming infected.
- Wounds where a foreign body may be present.
- Wounds classified as dangerous (see 'Classifying wounds', p.107) no matter how small they are.
- Wounds that are very dirty or difficult to assess.
- Wounds where there is a lot of bleeding.
- Wounds where the horse is very lame, even though the wound may be small.
- Minor wounds that fail to heal or have a persistent discharge.
- When the horse is not immunised against tetanus (booster injection in the previous two years).

What to do before the vet arrives

Keep the horse quiet and still if possible. In a stable with a wound in the lower limb, sweep the bedding to the side. Outside, stand the horse on a clean hard surface. Control bleeding, if present (see opposite). The wound can be gently flushed with a hosepipe. If necessary (for example if the horse must be walked through mud or transported to the vet) after cleaning, cover the wound with a light sterile pad, cotton wool, followed by a support bandage.

DEALING WITH A BLEEDING WOUND

Although a bleeding wound is alarming, life-threatening haemorrhage is rare and only occurs if a major artery has been damaged. Blood from an artery spurts in concert with the heartbeat; venous blood flows as a steady stream. In most cases bleeding will cease spontaneously or when light pressure is applied for a short while.

- **Cleanliness is important** In the rush to control the bleeding, don't forget to clean your hands and use clean materials.
- **Haemorrhage is controlled by applying pressure to the wound:**
  - **Pressure with a pad and bandage** Use a non-stick pad (for example Melolin), followed by a piece of cotton wool. Hold this in place by hand (if the wound is on the trunk) or with a bandage. If blood seeps through the pad, place another on top rather than remove the first.
  - **Tourniquet** In general, a tourniquet should only be used in the rare cases where the pressure pad technique has failed. The tourniquet causes a severe limitation of the blood flow to the limb below it, which may cause damage.

    Make a tourniquet by encircling the limb with a bandage just above the wound, inserting a pen or twig under the bandage and twisting until the blood stops flowing. Release it after a maximum interval of 10 minutes to check if the bleeding has stopped. A tourniquet should be used for as short a period as possible.

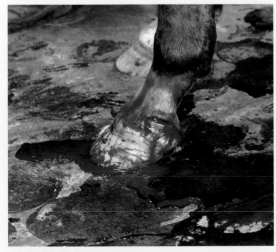

Wounds to the side of the pastern often injure the digital artery, resulting in profuse arterial bleeding

Cleaning a wound

- Always wash your hands first and be aware of the need for absolute cleanliness in your technique and equipment.
- Clip away any overhanging hair around the wound with curved scissors. Make sure none gets into the wound. Filling the wound with hydrogel (see p.112) and flushing it away later will remove any hair that may have dropped in.
- Using previously boiled and cooled water and a very clean bowl (not a dirty stable bucket), gently wash the skin around the wound with surgical scrub (for example Hibiscrub) and cotton wool. Never put a piece of cotton wool that has been used back into the bowl – discard it and use a fresh piece. In general antiseptics (Savlon, Dettol, TCP, Hibiscrub) potentially interfere with healing so if used they should be very dilute.

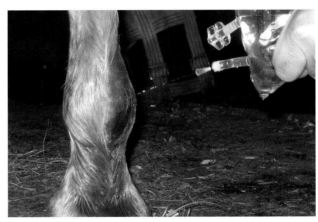

Squeezing a bag of saline that has a hypodermic needle inserted through the top creates a jet of sterile saline

- Then flush the wound itself. Small wounds can be flushed with saline supplied by the vet (see photo above). For larger wounds, gentle flushing with a hosepipe is satisfactory. Start below the wound and work upwards. Avoid washing dirt from the skin around the wound into it.
- Thoroughly flush away any cleansing soap used on the skin around the wound.
- Don't hose a wound for too long – just long enough to get it visibly clean.
- If possible give a final flush with sterile saline to restore the correct salt concentration in the depths of the wound.
- Petroleum jelly can be applied to the skin around the wound to help subsequent cleaning and to protect from scalding by any discharges that may later flow from the wound. If petroleum jelly is used care should be taken to ensure:
  - that the skin around the wound is as dry as possible or the jelly will not adhere to it
  - that none of the jelly enters the wound.

Should the wound be stitched?

If a wound is sutured (stitched) it heals most rapidly with a small scar. As the rate of growth of skin is only 0.5–2mm per day, healing can be very slow in non-sutured wounds. In deciding whether to suture a wound, the vet will consider the following:

- **How long ago did it happen?** Wounds more than about four hours old are generally unsuitable. If there are signs of inflammation, the wound will not normally be sutured
- **Where is the wound?** Wounds to the eyelids, nostrils, face and lips will usually be sutured unless there is substantial skin loss. Large areas of skin loss on the trunk, even with exposure of underlying tissues, will often not be sutured as they usually break down and often heal remarkably well if left open. Wounds to the lower limbs (for example overreach wounds) are often contaminated and have tissue damage. In addition they are often close to very mobile structures such as joints, which tend to pull the wound edges apart during movement. These will often break down if sutured unless the limb can be completely immobilised, for example in a cast.
- **Have underlying tissues been exposed?** Wounds exposing bone will not usually be sutured.
- **Is the wound heavily contaminated?** If the vet cannot be sure that all of the contamination can be removed it may not be sutured.

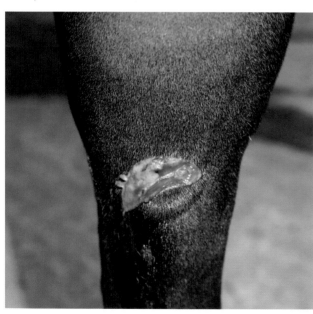

The owner delayed calling the vet to this small hock wound for about 48 hours. The wound edges have swollen and the wound cannot now be sutured

- **Delayed stitching.** Sometimes wounds are sutured 48–72 hours after they occur. This is to allow the body first to clear the wound of debris, dead tissue and so on. This specialised technique, called delayed primary (or secondary) closure, often requires general anaesthesia.

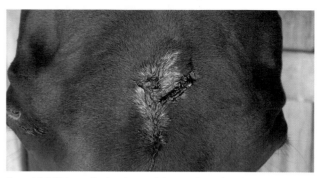

A small full-thickness forehead wound that was later closed with surgical staples. The wound healed well because, on the forehead, there is no movement of or tension on the wound edges, and contamination is usually minimal

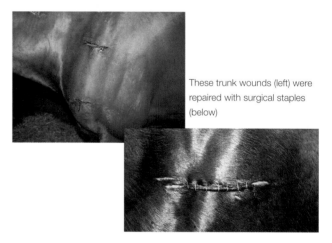

These trunk wounds (left) were repaired with surgical staples (below)

Are antibiotics necessary?

Antibiotics are drugs used to kill bacteria. They are given by mouth, or by injection via the intravenous, intramuscular or subcutaneous routes. The vet chooses the antibiotic based on:

- knowledge of the likely bacteria to be involved
- cost of the antibiotic
- the available routes of administration, for example whether the horse is likely to eat the antibiotic in its food or whether the owner is capable of injecting it.

The vet's decision as to whether or not antibiotics should be given will depend on whether the wound is:

- already showing evidence of infection, for example swollen or discharging pus
- in a site very likely to become infected
- of a size and type that is highly likely to become infected.

FIRST AID KIT

Emergencies happen without warning so a comprehensive first aid kit is necessary in every yard. Keep it away from general equine activity to avoid anyone 'borrowing' its components.

- A clinical thermometer (one of the type used for people is adequate)*
- A jar of petroleum jelly for lubrication of the thermometer
- A plastic bowl
- A supply of sterile non-adherent dressings, for example Melolin*

- A roll of cotton wool or Gamgee*
- Hydrogel (for example Nugel or Intra-site)*
- A poultice dressing (for example Animalintex)*
- A pack of sterile saline solution and a new, sterile, hypodermic needle*
- Bandages (cohesive bandages, such as Vetrap, are best)
- Antibacterial skin cleanser (for example Hibiscrub or Pevidine)*
- Antibiotic spray*
- A pair of curved scissors (15cm/6in long)*

Items marked * are obtainable from the vet

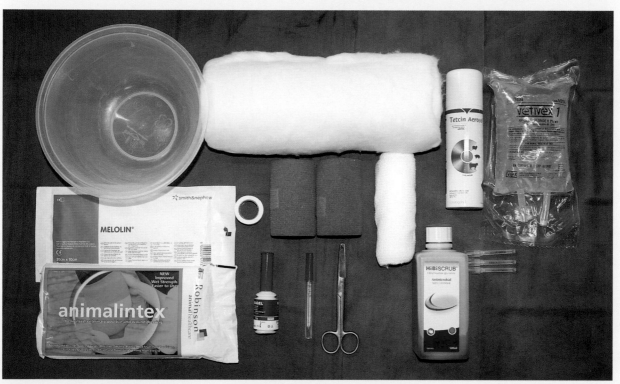

A first aid kit. Pack this in a dedicated box so that it can be taken to events

Dealing with minor wounds

Abrasions If dirty or contaminated on the surface, gently clean these with a weak solution of antiseptic soap, for example Hibiscrub. Blot them dry with tissue paper and leave uncovered. If necessary, apply antibiotic spray.

Small full thickness cuts Clean the wound as described for abrasions and blot dry. Squirt hydrogel into the wound; it may not be retained for long if the wound is discharging or facing downwards. Wound powders and 'healing' or antiseptic gels are best used sparingly and reserved for very small wounds.

Depending on the site, the wound can be left open or dressed. The next day flush it gently to remove the hydrogel. If a minor infection develops the wound will discharge after 24–48 hours. Clean away the discharge with lukewarm water and a weak solution of Hibiscrub, then flush the wound with saline. If a more serious infection develops, the area will swell and become sore, it may discharge, and if the wound is on a leg the horse may become lame. Notify your vet.

Puncture wounds These are caused by thorns, nails and so on penetrating the skin. They are almost impossible to clean because of their size. Notify the vet.

WOUND DRESSINGS

Wounds are dressed by applying a *first layer* directly on the wound (usually a sterile pad just a bit larger than the wound), followed by a *second layer* enclosing the part of the limb involved (cotton wool or Gamgee). The *third layer* is a bandage.

The second and third layers protect the wound from external contamination, support the bandaged structure, limit movement of the wound edges promoting healing and reducing pain. They also control swelling and inhibit proud flesh development by applying pressure to the surface of the wound.

The first layer – dressings and gels

In essence, the commercially available wound dressings are clever ways to stop the secondary layer of cotton wool or Gamgee sticking to the wound surface. The wound is filled with hydrogel followed by a pad.

Types of dressings:

- **Hydrogels** (including Nugel, Vetalintex and Intra-site) have a 95 per cent water content and a huge additional capacity to absorb water. They keep the wound surface moist, promoting optimum healing, and have the capacity to clean the wound of dead material if flushed away at bandage changes.
- **Non-adherent pads** (including sterile thin pads, for example Melolin or Rondopad, and sterile paraffin gauze, tulle, for example Jelonet) are cheap and useful for the early dressing of wounds. They must be covered by an absorbent layer (cotton wool or Gamgee) and changed at least daily. Discharge will move through the dressing into the secondary layer. Paraffin gauze dressings should only be used for the first few days.
- **Absorbent dressings** (for example Allevyn) are thick and have the ability to absorb up to 10 times their own weight. Because of their absorbency, the interval between bandage changes can be longer. They are best used in the later stages of healing.

Two non-adherent pads. With the thin one (Melolin), the shiny non-adherent side is placed against the wound. The thicker pad (Allevyn) is highly absorbent but more expensive

Never poultice a wound. Poultices delay healing, promote proud flesh development and have no role in wound management.

The second layer

Cotton wool is primarily used for the second layer. Gamgee has the advantage of being available in wider rolls, long enough to reach from the top of the cannon bone to the coronet. Wounds should be well padded by using a thick second layer to protect against pressure sores from bandaging.

The third layer

The following are available:
Crepe bandages are cheap cotton non-stretch bandages that can cause excessive pressure and may become bunched causing a rope burn-like effect. They are not recommended.
Conforming bandages (for example K-Band, Co-Form and Knit-Firm) are made of loosely woven cotton. Reasonably cheap, they conform to the surface of the bandaged structure and are very useful.
Cohesive bandages (Vetrap, Equi-Wrap and Wrapz) adhere to themselves only. Although they stretch as they are applied, once in place they have very little give.
Adhesive bandages (Elastoplast, Elasticon and E-band) are sticky on one side. They will stretch and are useful where the bandage must be stuck to the skin to prevent it slipping.
Non-adhesive stretchable bandages (including exercise bandages) are useful as an additional layer on top of cohesive

bandages. They can be washed and re-used but must never be allowed to come in direct contact with wounds.
Adhesive tape (particularly 5cm/2in wide duct tape) can be used to stick a pad directly to the hoof in the case of a coronet wound and as a final layer over the end of a bandage to prevent unravelling. It can be used to cover bandages to protect them from being chewed by the horse. It can also be used to waterproof a dressing, for example on the foot. Silage tape is thicker, very sticky, difficult to use and is not recommended.

From left to right: *Stable bandage* – Not very elastic, tend to slip and not very useful for the first bandage layer. Can be used as a secondary bandage to restrict movement and provide further support. Exercise (elastic) bandages are better. *Crepe bandage* – Non-stretch, likely to cause pressure sores and not recommended for equine wounds. A wide, *conforming bandage* – excellent for use in limb wounds. *Cohesive bandage* – Will stretch by 50 per cent of its length but can cause pressure sores if used incorrectly

A sutured wound on a forearm has been dressed using minimal padding and an adhesive bandage stuck to the skin. The free end has also been secured with sutures through the bandage; duct tape is also very effective for this purpose

Wounds

BANDAGING

Bandages are used to keep dressings in place and to provide support. They should be applied with even pressure, a 50 per cent overlap and without over-stretching. Remember: never bandage a horse's legs without padding underneath; unless used to apply pressure, a bandage should never restrict circulation; the wider the bandage the more likely the pressure underneath is even. (For bandaging a foot wound, see pp.23 and 114.)

BANDAGING A KNEE WOUND

1 Place hydrogel in the wound and *loosely* secure a sterile non-adherent pad (such as 'Melolin') above the knee with micropore tape. The tape is used solely to prevent the pad from moving during the bandaging process.

2 Wrap cotton wool fully around the knee and pick it out over the bony prominences to prevent excess pressure on these (see p.116). Then secure it with an elastic (exercise) bandage. The bandage is applied in a figure of eight pattern so that it forms an overlapping X-shape at the front (illustration) and only fully encircles the limb above and below the knee.

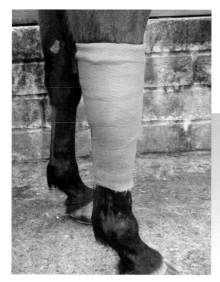

3 Finally, apply a cohesive bandage over the first bandage ensuring it is not too tight at its upper and lower ends. Tuck the ends in to prevent bedding from sticking to the bandage. To avoid the bandage slipping downwards, the space between the lower end of the dressing and the coronet can be filled with an additional layer of padding, again covered by a bandage.

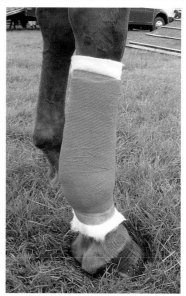

A cannon wound Ensure the padding and bandage extend to just below the fetlock to prevent constriction of the blood vessels at either side of the fetlock (where you can feel the digital pulse). Make the uppermost and lowermost turns of the bandage less tight than the portions overlying the wound itself

BANDAGING A HOCK WOUND

1 Loosely secure the pad over the wound with micropore tape.

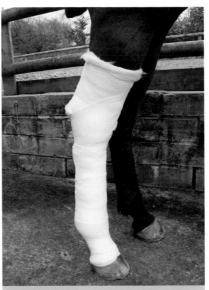

2 Apply cotton wool from mid gaskin to coronet (to prevent the bandage from slipping). Fill the hollows on each side of the Achilles tendon with a soft cotton bandage or tube of cotton wool on each side to reduce pressure of the tendon. Then pick the cotton wool out over the bony prominences (see box p.116)

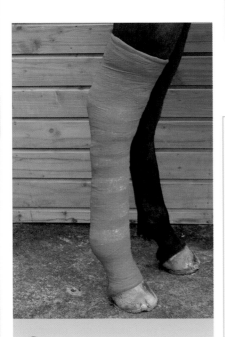

3 Wrap a conforming bandage over the cotton wool, followed by a cohesive bandage. Fold the ends in to prevent bedding sticking to the bandage

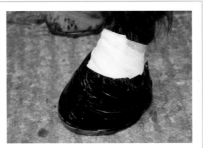

Pastern, heel, bulb and coronet wounds
Bandages on the lower leg can get soiled by bedding and tend to ride up the pastern. It is essential therefore that the bandage is both waterproof and stuck to the hoof wall with duct tape. If necessary continue the tape under the bearing surface of the heels further to secure the bandage. (This wound was a minor coronet injury. For a more significant injury, more padding is required)

BANDAGING MISTAKES

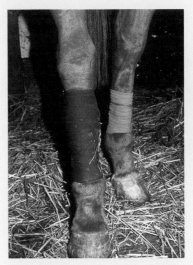

This horse has a wound on the left hind cannon, and a 'support' bandage has been put on the right cannon. The bandages are not padded and both end just above the fetlock. Due to interference with venous and lymphatic drainage, both fetlocks and pasterns are swollen

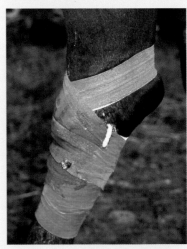

No padding was used in this dressing of a wound on the front of the hock. Pus is overflowing the bandage and the single turn of bandage over the Achilles tendon has caused the point of the hock to swell, leading to a grave risk of a pressure sore on the Achilles tendon

DEALING WITH PROUD FLESH

In a matter of days, granulation tissue can extend across a wound and mushroom outwards as a bumpy pink-coloured mass. Skin cells will not grow 'upwards' over it so the wound fails to heal. Proud flesh will not simply disappear. The following techniques are used to remove it:

- **Excision with a scalpel.** This is the most effective technique and must be done by the vet. No anaesthetic is needed as there are no nerves in the proud flesh, although the horse may be sedated to keep it still. A pressure bandage is used afterwards to control the bleeding.
- **Use of chemicals.** Usually strong caustic substances such as copper sulphate or lead lotion are applied to the proud flesh. Although these

often work well they should only be used in small wounds.

- **Topical corticosteroid cream.** This is best used after the proud flesh has been trimmed away to help avoid regrowth. The cream is applied and the wound bandaged. The drug may interfere with wound healing if used too frequently.
- **Application of pressure.** Pressure bandaging may keep the proud flesh flat and flush with the skin. Care must be taken to avoid bandage pressure sores.

Note that sarcoids can often start growing in a healing wound and may closely resemble proud flesh (see p.126).

Granulation in a hock wound

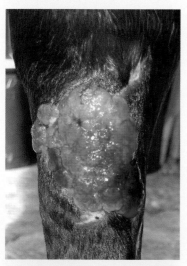

1. This horse sustained a serious hock wound three weeks before this photograph was taken. Suturing was not possible as there was a wide gap between the skin edges, resulting in a large growth of proud flesh. The horse was sedated, the proud flesh cut off and a pressure bandage applied. The horse was put on box rest

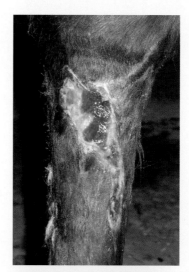

2. The bandage was changed at 5-day intervals and a mild corticosteroid/ antibiotic ointment applied at each change.
After a further three weeks the wound was much reduced in size (primarily by contraction) and the granulation tissue was no longer 'proud'

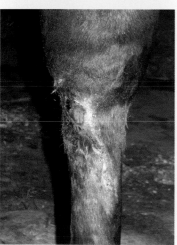

3. The treatment – immobilisation, corticosteroid ointment and pressure bandaging – continued for a further two weeks, by which time healing was nearly complete

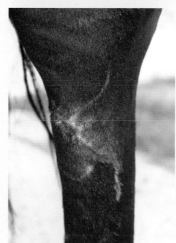

4. Eighteen weeks after the injury, the wound was fully healed with a small scar. There was no residual functional impairment of the hock

Dealing with proud flesh

115

AVOIDING PRESSURE SORES

Horses' legs are very irregularly shaped with many bony bumps covered only by skin. Bandages need to be fairly tight to avoid slippage but consequently there is a risk – when bandages must be used for more than a few days – that pressure sores may develop over the bony bumps. Pressure may cause the skin to split and open, sometimes producing a wound that is impossible to cover with a bandage.

Common sites of pressure sores

Because the *knee and hock* are naturally triangular in cross-section, long term bandaging of these areas can cause sores due to pressure on the points of the triangle. In the knee the points are both sides of the end of the forearm, just above the knee (A and B), and behind it (C). Similar points are problematic on the hock (D and E). The upper surface of the Achilles tendon on the hock (F) is also a common site for pressure sores.

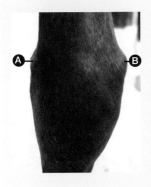
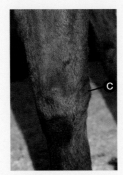
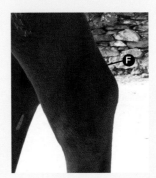
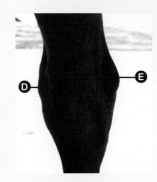

Cross-section of knee

Cross-section of hock

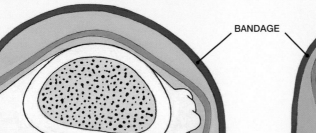
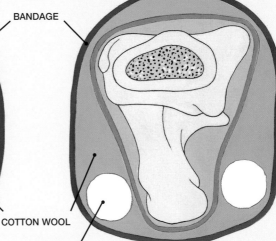

BANDAGE

COTTON WOOL

ROLL OF COTTON BANDAGE

To avoid pressure points the triangles of the knee and hock are converted into circles using cotton wool. The cotton wool is wrapped around the leg and is picked out over the bony prominences until a satisfactory circular shape is achieved.

In addition, in the knee, a 'doughnut' of cotton wool is applied over the bone at the back to lift the bandage off it, and in the hock a roll of cotton bandage (still in its wrapping so it can be reused) is applied on each side of the Achilles tendon to avoid excessive pressure on it.

A bandage is then applide on tope of the cotton wool.

Frequently asked questions

How often should a dressing be changed?
The appearance of the wound and dressing after the first bandage change will assist the vet in determining how frequently a new dressing is required. Wounds that are discharging heavily will need to be re-dressed daily. Once the discharge reduces, the interval can be extended to 3–5 days or sometimes even longer.

This two-day-old pastern wound has been bandaged for 24 hours. When the bandage was removed, heavy exudate was visible in the padding. The dressing needs to be changed at least daily while there is this volume of discharge

Is the bandage comfortable?
The bandage may be too tight: if the horse is uncomfortable on the affected leg and bites at the bandage; if there is filling in the leg above and/or below the bandaged area; if there are pressure sores when the bandage is removed.

How can I stop my horse chewing the bandage?
If it is certain that the bandage is not too tight, try the following:
• application of anti-cribbing cream
• application of a paste made from cayenne pepper and petroleum jelly
• application of the 'bitter spray' used for dog and cat bandages
• attaching a plastic rug bib to the headcollar
• applying a wooden cradle to the horse's neck.

Why does the bandage move?
Consider the following:
• the bandage was applied too loosely
• the horse has been allowed uncontrolled exercise
• the bandage has been applied incorrectly
• the horse has tried to remove the bandage.

Should my horse be on box rest?
Free exercise may not be conducive to rapid healing because the wound edges may move as the horse moves, and dressings slip or become soiled or wet. Wet bandages constrict and become tighter as they dry and should be changed immediately.
   The vet may advise box rest (see p.118) depending on:
• The site of the wound. Limb wounds are best kept fully immobilised but wounds to the trunk and head will not be put under tension if the horse is allowed to move freely.
• The size of the wound.
• The nature of the turnout. Wet muddy fields should be avoided.
• The temperament of the horse. Volatile horses may career around outside which could make wounds break down.

ADVANCED WOUND MANAGEMENT
In large wounds or those occurring in sites where the wound edges are difficult to immobilise, the vet may use a number of techniques to assist wound healing:

Application of a cast Wounds to the lower limbs (from the knee down), especially those in the pastern, may benefit greatly from immobilisation with a cast. In contrast with traditional plaster of Paris casts, which are heavy and soften in contact with water, casts made of synthetic material are light, strong and easy to use.

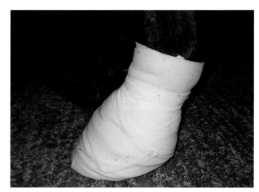

A rigid cast was placed on this severe pastern wound for three weeks

Use of a cold laser Laser treatment has been done for over 20 years to quicken healing. Sadly, experimental studies have failed to demonstrate a benefit.

Skin grafting If the wound is large it may require grafting to speed up healing. The grafts are usually tiny portions of skin (pinch grafts) taken from the neck or flank and implanted in the bed of granulation tissue. Usually only 10–20 per cent survive but this may be sufficient to dramatically increase the healing rate of a wound.

BOX REST

Owners are often worried about how their horse will cope with box rest without any exercise. However, even the most highly-strung horse will adapt, provided some simple management changes are put in place to help it adjust to its new regime.

- **Equine company** Horses really hate solitary confinement. Providing company is the *single most important* way of making box-rested horses more content. Ideally, the confined horse should be able to *see its companion all the time* via a grill or opening between two adjacent boxes.

- **A stable mirror** (stainless steel or acrylic) can significantly reduce separation anxiety.

- **Regular meals** The best feed is chaff to which a handful of nuts or coarse mix is added. A full bucket of chaff twice or three times a day is ideal. Horses recovering from severe wounds or laminitis may need additional feeding: the vet will advise.

- **Access to hay/haylage** Ensure continuous access and reduce eating rates by placing one net inside another or using small mesh nets.

- **Toys** Balls designed to dispense a small quantity of high-fibre cubes when rolled by the horse provide hours of play.

- **Minimal disturbance** If possible, stable the horse away from places of equine activity (stable yards, arenas, and so on). It is more likely to become anxious when adjacent horses are turned out or ridden.

Other important points:

Be careful when mucking out It is strongly recommended that when mucking out the horse is tied up or put into another box. Alternatively, a chain or similar device can be fixed across the doorway.

Remove the shoes Pick out the feet daily to prevent thrush developing.

Sedative drugs given by mouth are occasionally used in the early stages to help the horse to adapt.

Rehabilitation – walking in hand

Walking in hand during rehabilitation helps circulation, which in turn promotes healing. However horses that have been confined for even a short period may be excitable so:

- **Use a bridle** (rather than a head collar) or preferably a Chiffney bit.
- **Use a long lead rope** (e.g. a lunge line) attached to the bit, so you can stand well clear of the horse while remaining in control.
- **Be prepared for an 'explosion'**
- **Consider sedation** for the first few occasions. The vet may supply an oral sedative.
- **Choose a quiet route and time** Avoid obvious 'inflammatory' situations, such as barking dogs.
- **Some horses are safer if ridden rather than walked** This may not be appropriate for certain injuries so please follow the vet's instructions.

Turning Out

Resist the temptation to take the horse out 'for a few mouthfuls of grass' or to turn it out ('to graze quietly'). Even the most stoical horse can explode after a period of confinement, undoing all the benefits of the box rest period in a few minutes. When the horse is finally turned out it is strongly recommend that it is sedated initially. Prepare

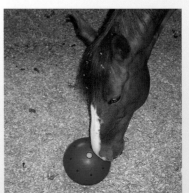

carefully – there should be no horses in the field or adjacent fields to 'wind up' your horse. The horse should be hungry (starve overnight) so that it will put its head down and graze straight away.

A snack-a-ball

SKIN PROBLEMS

Skin essentials

The skin encases the whole body and its efficient functioning is essential for health. It has three layers:

- Hair composed of the protein keratin. Hair helps to regulate body temperature and protect the skin. In autumn (in temperate climates) in response to decreasing ambient temperature and day-length, additional hair is produced by the hair follicles for warmth. The follicles then go into a resting phase until spring when lengthening days stimulate new hair to grow, dislodging the old hair.
- The epidermis is a thin layer of keratin. It waterproofs the skin, prevents evaporation of tissue fluid and acts as a barrier against bacteria entering the body.
- The dermis contains sweat glands, sebaceous glands and blood vessels. The sebaceous glands secrete oil to protect the hair shafts. The blood vessels supply nutrients to the skin and help with temperature regulation, as do the sweat glands.

ASSESSING A SKIN PROBLEM

The key questions to answer are:

- **Is this a seasonal disorder?** Mud fever and rainscald occur in the winter, sunburn and leukocytoclastic vasculitis in the summer.
- **Is the condition itchy?** Itchy skin diseases are almost always caused by parasites or by sweet itch.
- **Is the disease confined to the white areas of the body?** Mud fever and sunlight-activated skin diseases usually only affect white or unpigmented skin.
- **What part of the body is affected?** Ringworm tends to affect the trunk, neck and face whereas mud fever affects the horse's limbs.
- **Are other horses affected?** Ringworm and some parasitic diseases may spread to other horses.
- **Is the affected area painful to touch?** Bacterial skin infections usually cause pain, and if on the limbs, sometimes lameness.

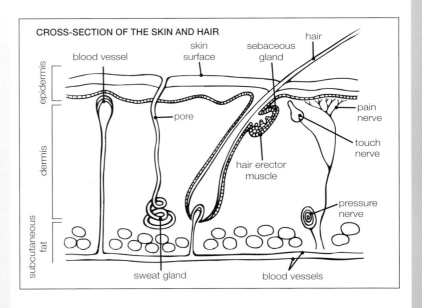

CROSS-SECTION OF THE SKIN AND HAIR

Crusting and scaling disorders

MUD FEVER AND CRACKED HEELS

These are the commonest skin diseases of the horse and are caused by chapping of the skin due to cold wet conditions with subsequent invasion by bacteria and in a minority of cases, the organism *Dermatophilus*.

Clinical signs

- Unpigmented (white) skin is most commonly affected but pigmented skin can be affected too.
- The heel form starts in the skin 'creases' at the back of the pastern and spreads from there. The leg form starts anywhere on the lower legs, often on the front of the cannon bones.
- Weeping crusty sores develop. The exudate turns into scabs that are sometimes hard to lift off. In severe cases the skin may split.
- Sometimes the lower legs may swell. The swollen area may be painful and the horse may be lame.

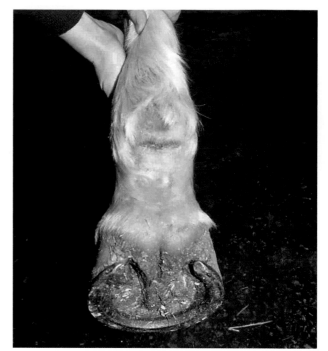

Occasionally the infection begins in the skin crease under the ergot. These cases are especially painful

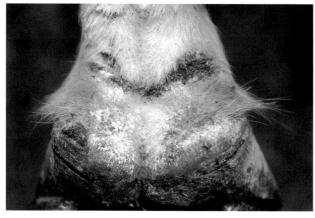

Infection has started in the skin crease at the back of the pastern. If untreated it will spread

What to do next - basic principles

- Clip the area with fine clippers
- Remove the scabs (see 'Treating mud fever', opposite)
- Wash the affected area with antibacterial scrub
- Apply an antibiotic cream
- Repeat until resolved
- Take active measures to prevent recurrence

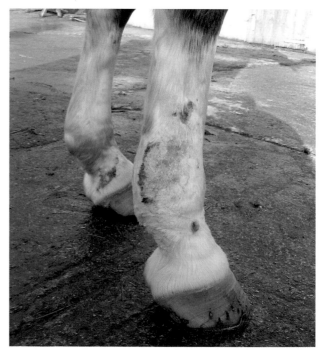

This is a more extensive case, involving both the lower forelimbs (the hair has been clipped)

Skin problems

TREATING MUD FEVER

1 Clip the affected area. In severe cases, sedation may be required.

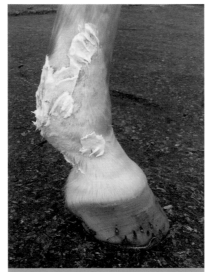

2 Apply a generous coating of aqueous cream or baby oil to the scabs.

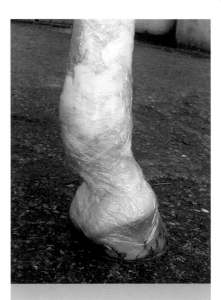

3 Wrap clingfilm loosely on top.

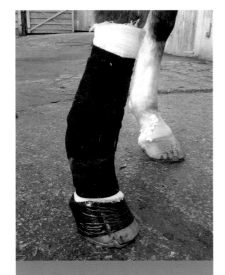

4 Wrap around a few turns of duct tape at ground level to stop the clingfilm from riding up into pastern skin crease. Then apply a pad and stable bandage. Leave this in place for 24 hours, and then wash the limb in surgical scrub and dry thoroughly. An alternative to steps 2–4 is to use a warm poultice (Animalintex) for 24 hours to soften the scabs.

5 Once the scabs have softened, wash the area with an antibacterial scrub, such as Pevidine or Hibiscrub. Wet the legs with hand-hot water, apply the scrub neat and work it in well to loosen any surface debris and scabs. Leave in place for 10 minutes (to allow a more effective bacterial kill), then wash and thoroughly dry the legs with a clean towel.

6 Removing the scabs, exposes raw zones, usually along the skin folds at the back of the pastern. Treat these with an antibiotic ointment obtained from the vet. Follow these three rules: ensure there are no scabs present, dry the raw areas first by gently dabbing with a tissue to improve adherence of the ointment, apply the ointment generously.

Ongoing treatment Antibiotics may be necessary. Riding is not advised until healing is well advanced, but horses may be walked on dry roads.

After the first treatment it is likely that some scabs will re-form overnight but these will be softer and easy to dislodge with antibacterial wash. As before, dab the raw areas with a tissue, and re-apply the antibiotic ointment. In bad cases antiseptic washes *twice* daily for the first few days are recommended. Over the next few days the lesions will gradually heal but it is *essential* that treatment continues until they have completely healed and the affected area is covered by healthy skin.

? What went wrong

If the problem fails to resolve it is likely that one or more of the following apply:

- Attempting to treat the disease without first removing *all* of the scabs.
- Using treatments that are essentially preventative (usually barrier creams, often containing weak antiseptic agents) instead of those that kill the causal bacteria, such as antibiotic creams and antibacterial skin washes.
- Treating only part of the affected area, or stopping treatment before the condition has *completely* resolved.
- Failing to close-clip the affected area. Horse clippers are inappropriate – use fine (dog) clippers or a pair of sharp, curved scissors.
- If in spite of following this advice the horse doesn't improve, seek veterinary help as other conditions can mimic mud fever.

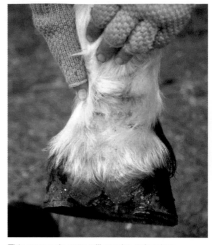

This very early case will require only minor treatment

Preventing mud fever

Although the condition is traditionally associated with mud coating the legs, many horses go through the whole winter in muddy fields without developing any signs. The conclusion is that it is not mud but *constant wetting* of the skin that *is the main cause*. Mud fever is also often rife in yards where the legs are washed frequently, and virtually absent from yards where the legs are almost never washed. It is always better to leave the mud to dry naturally on the legs (leg wraps or bandages applied over the mud will 'wick' away the moisture) and then brush off the next day.

Waterproofing the lower limbs, the heels especially, before exercise or turn out is good practice. Thick creams such as zinc and castor oil cream, 'Sudocrem' or proprietary barrier creams are effective. Udder cream although popular is a bit too thin and hence not very long lasting.

Leaving the lower legs unclipped does little to prevent the problem. Indeed mud fever may be more common in horses with hairier legs, due in part to the longer time these take to dry out and to the difficulty in spotting early lesions.

If the legs must be washed then they must be dried also. Sulphur

powder or 'Keratex Mud Shield' powder sprinkled generously on the heels is very effective (even when sprinkled on wet legs) this is probably due to the fact that they have a marked drying effect.

Get into the habit of running your fingers upwards against the direction of the hair at the back of the pastern every few days to detect the very small scabs indicating an early problem. If treated immediately these small lesions will respond very quickly.

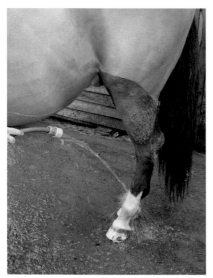

Avoid routine washing of muddy legs unless strictly necessary. Mud fever is not caused by mud but by constant wetting,

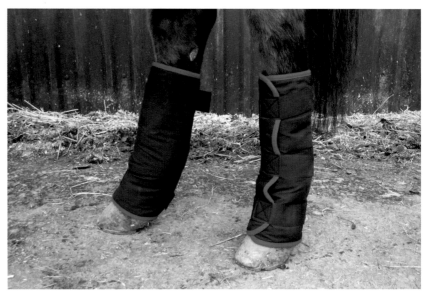

Leg wraps applied directly to wet, muddy legs will both dry and warm them, and prevent mud fever. The next day the dried mud can be brushed out

SUMMER MUD FEVER (Leukocytoclastic vasculitis)

Very similar in appearance to mud fever, this condition occurs in hot dry conditions. It is believed to be an interaction between sunlight and blood vessels in the skin, although it is not true photosensitisation. The same horses are affected year after year.

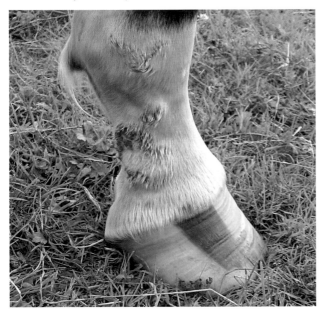

Leukocytoclastic vasculitis starts as thick, tenacious scabs on the outside of the pastern and lower leg in the summer months

Preventing summer mud fever

Protect the white lower limbs by one of the following:
* keeping the horse indoors during the day in a sunlight-free stable

Clinical signs

* Only the white skin of the legs only is affected, especially on the outside of the pastern. Other areas of white skin on the body are normal.
* The skin is reddened and reddish thick crusty, wart-like scabs form, sometimes in a ring or horseshoe shape.
* The scabs are very hard to remove.
* The affected area is painful.

What to do next

Do not mistake this condition for classical mud fever.
* Bring the horse indoors and protect it from sunlight. It may be turned out at dusk and brought in very early in the morning.
* Remove the scabs (see 'Mud fever', p.121).
* Apply an antibiotic ointment that also contains a corticosteroid as an anti-inflammatory.
* It may be necessary to give the horse a long course of oral corticosteroid tablets.

* applying high-protection factor (at least factor 30) waterproof sun block daily to the white parts of the limbs
* applying stable bandages from the coronet to below the knee or hock
* using gaiter-type boots designed to be worn for mud fever prevention. These must extend from the coronet to below the knee/hock.

BACTERIAL FOLLICULITIS

In this condition, the hair follicles become infected with skin bacteria. Predisposing factors are dirty tack and saddlecloths, and also friction from tack, for example on the side of the neck due to contact with the reins.

Clinical signs

* Rapid development of multiple, very small, painful swellings in the skin.
* Affected areas are mainly the neck, chest and back, sometimes also the legs.
* The first sign is often areas of erect hairs.
* The lesions are more easily felt than seen.
* A small crusty scab forms at each infected site.
* Some lesions may merge leading to pustules (acne).
* Occasional cases are itchy.

What to do next

* Avoid all tack and rug contact with the affected areas until recovered.
* Wet the affected skin with hand-hot water, shampoo with an antibacterial scrub and dislodge the scabs. Leave the scrub in contact for 10 minutes, and then rinse. Dry the area with a clean towel. Repeat twice daily for the first few days.
* Antibiotics may be prescribed by the vet. Usually a long course (two weeks or more) is required.
* Sterilise all tack, saddlecloths and grooming tools. Ensure this equipment is not shared.
* Prevent recurrence with good stable hygiene and regular cleaning of tack and saddlecloth. Treat lesions early to prevent spread.

RINGWORM

This is a common fungal skin infection – it is not caused by a worm and often the lesions are not circular. They may occur anywhere but are most commonly seen in the head, girth and saddle areas. They start as a slightly raised area of skin. Depending on the strain of ringworm, some then shed the hair leaving a flaky bald area or form a scab, which when peeled off leaves a moist raw red patch. Ringworm is usually not itchy.

The disease is highly infectious and will spread through a yard if precautions are not taken. The infection may also spread to humans. The incubation period is up to 30 days. Young (<4 years) horses are more susceptible to the disease, and slower to recover.

HOW DOES RINGWORM SPREAD?

Infection results from:

- Direct contact with infected horses. Often a new arrival is the first to show signs of infection.
- Contact with hair shed by an infected horse. The infection may become endemic on a premises with outbreaks every year as the spores live for years.
- Contact with buildings and fencing previously used by cattle.

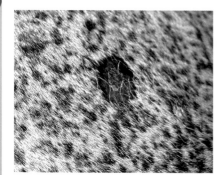

An early ringworm lesion. The base is raw and a central scaly portion of dead upper skin layers is about to lift off

What to do next

Treat the horse as described below and also:

- Isolate the affected or suspect horses from contact with others. Warn personnel of the risk of human infection. Wear gloves or wash hands when dealing with affected horses. Wear an overall when handling affected horses.
- The vet may take hair samples to confirm the infection.
- Ensure affected horses have their own tack, headcollars, boots and grooming tools. To prevent contamination, if possible rugs should not be worn and the horse should not be groomed. If the head or saddle area are affected, the horse should not be ridden until the infection is cured.
- **Do not clip** as this will contaminate the clippers and spread the infection.

Treatment

Although a self-cure will occur in 1–4 months, affected horses should be treated promptly to prevent spread and contamination of the stable environment. The following treatments are used:

- Topical antifungal sprays and shampoos, which rapidly render the horse non-infectious. Scrub the lesions first with a coarse brush. The whole horse is treated on the first one or two occasions, and thereafter just the lesions.
- In-feed griseofulvin is widely used but its effectiveness is not certain. It is poor at preventing spread but may be the only possible treatment for unhandled horses. It should not be used in pregnant mares, and there are handling precautions for users.
- Once a fine layer of hair is visible growing through the lesions they are no longer infectious.

Treat all equipment, including rider's boots with an antifungal agent. Bleach is suitable for tools, and rugs may be immersed in a disinfectant such as 'Virkon'. Use a mild anti-fungal on leather tack to prevent damage to the leather. If possible bedding should be removed and the stable pressure-washed and scrubbed with disinfectant. Pay particular attention to areas where horses rub, for example door frames.

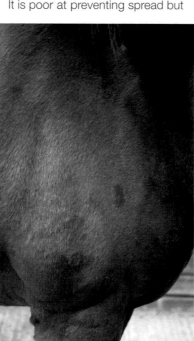

Ringworm is widespread on the shoulder of this horse. The lesions have lost hair. The horse has been treated and a light re-growth is occurring

RAINSCALD

This condition occurs in wet weather in horses out-wintered at grass. It is caused by *Dermatophilus*, an organism that thrives in wet, cold skin. The problem is worst in fine-coated horses, such as Thoroughbreds, and debilitated horses. Mountain and moorland breeds with thick waterproof winter coats are rarely affected.

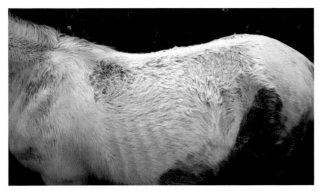

This out-wintered horse has developed extensive rainscald on its neck and back

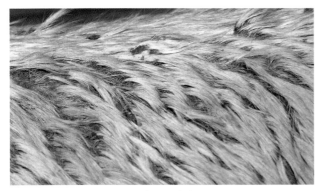

A close up view shows the matted, crusty hair

The scabs can be easily lifted off, revealing tufts of hair bound together by crusty material

Clinical signs

- The shoulders, back and rump are affected. Also the face due to wetting by rain as the horse stands with its head over the stable door.
- Thick scabs form, causing matting of the hair growing through them.
- Under the scabs the skin is red and inflamed.
- Horses wearing turnout rugs may develop localised rainscald in areas where the rug is no longer waterproof.

What to do next

Bring the horse indoors until healing is advanced. Mild cases may resolve without any treatment other than keeping the coat dry. If treatment is required:

- Wet the coat with hot water and apply neat antibacterial scrub.
- Work the scrub vigorously into the skin with a plastic curry comb to loosen the scabs.
- Leave the scrub in place for 10 minutes and then rinse off. Dry the area with a clean towel.
- Repeat once or twice daily until the condition has completely resolved.
- In severe cases the vet may give antibiotics. Once recovered the horse may be turned out wearing a good quality turnout rug.

Prevent recurrence by providing out-wintered fine-coated horses with a turnout rug, which should be removed regularly to check for problems. Treat small areas early to prevent spread. Provide shelter.

Warts and tumours

Warts and skin tumours are common in horses and should be assessed carefully at an early stage to ensure prompt treatment.

SARCOIDS

Sarcoids are the commonest tumour of the horse. They can occur at any age although most appear between two and ten years. The cause is believed to be a cattle wart virus but the way the virus induces the tumours is unknown. *Flies may play a key role in transmission, so fly control is vital to prevent spread.*

Sarcoids are found:
- In areas where the skin is thin, has little or no hair, and has a tendency to sweat. This includes the groin, the head and around the eyes. These are also areas where flies feed.
- Rarely on the upper trunk, back and neck, unless the skin has been traumatised. The trauma may be slight, for example, bridle rubs on the face or rein rubs on the neck.
- On the limbs, often at the sites of wounds where they may be mistaken for proud flesh.

Buying sarcoid-affected horses

Because in principle they are treatable, it may be unreasonable to fail a horse with sarcoids at a pre-purchase

KEY FACTS ABOUT SARCOIDS

- Some horses and breeds (Lipizzaner) are naturally resistant and will never develop sarcoids.
- Sarcoids should never be underestimated. They have the potential to grow and spread, and be resistant to treatment. Every year many horses are humanely destroyed because of uncontrollable sarcoids.
- A horse may have only a few to over a hundred sarcoids.
- Some sarcoids remain quiescent for years, whereas others may grow, multiply and ulcerate.
- A few horses self-cure but these are very uncommon.
- Treatment must be intensive. Treatment failure often prompts the sarcoid to re-grow in a more aggressive (and more difficult to treat) fashion.
- Even when successfully treated, new sarcoids may appear on a treated horse at any time.
- **The earlier treatment is started the more effective it is.** It has been stated that *'The fewer sarcoids a horse has, the fewer it will get'.*

veterinary examination. The vet's advice will depend on the number, size, type and location of the sarcoids, and whether previous attempts at treatment have been made.

However, if they are detected at a pre-purchase examination, insurance companies will normally exclude sarcoids from cover.

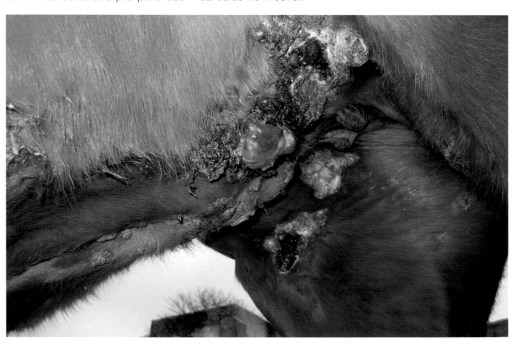

This horse has very extensive sarcoid formation, principally fibroblastic. Treatment has been attempted before and the sarcoids have re-grown. Successful treatment at this stage is unlikely

THERE ARE FIVE MAIN TYPES OF SARCOID, AND A RARE SIXTH VERY AGGRESSIVE (MALEVOLENT) TYPE.

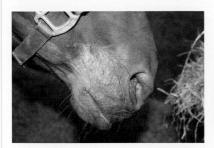

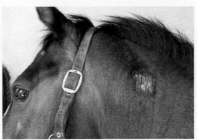

Type 1 Occult: these are often very subtle in their early stages and may be (as in this case) just a hairless area with a slightly roughened surface. They are often circular and can look like ringworm

Type 2 Verrucose: these have a roughened, warty appearance and occur especially inside the elbow and on the groin. In this horse the sarcoid has probably developed due to trauma to the site, perhaps as little as a fly bite

Type 3 Nodular: usually covered by normal skin, these hard nodules occur especially in the groin. There may be multiple sarcoids or, as in this horse, just one. Sometimes the skin overlying the sarcoid ulcerates

Type 4 Fibroblastic: the pink fleshy appearance of this sarcoid is typical. These are especially aggressive and fast-growing sarcoids. Treatment failure of sarcoid types 1–3 often results in the development of this type at the treatment site

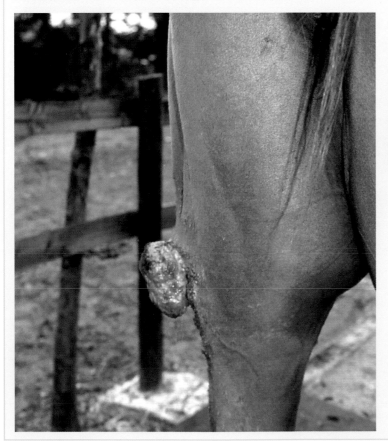

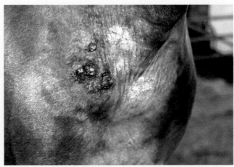

Type 5 Mixed: often several types will occur on one horse. In this horse there is mixture of occult and fibroblastic sarcoids

Warts and tumours

127

What to do next

Consult your vet **as soon as** you suspect your horse may have a sarcoid. The vet will determine the most appropriate treatment. The options are:

- **Do nothing** Very flat, occult lesions may be left untreated but must be watched carefully to ensure they are not transforming into another type.
- **Surgical excision** This is a good option for some nodular sarcoids but there is high rate of re-growth with other types.
- **Application of rubber ligature** This is best reserved for nodular sarcoids with little or no skin involvement. It is sometimes combined with injecting a cytotoxic drug into the sarcoid.
- **Freezing with liquid nitrogen** This is only moderately effective and there is a high rate of re-growth. It is only appropriate for very shallow tumours.

- **Injection of the human BCG vaccine** The vaccine is injected into the sarcoid and is very effective in sarcoids around the eyes but there is a risk of side effects.
- **Injection of anti-cancer drugs** This is effective in some cases but the drugs are difficult to obtain, require multiple treatments and there are safety risks to personnel.
- **Use of cytotoxic creams** Currently this is the best method, provided the appropriate strength of cream is used and treatment protocol is observed.
- **Radiation therapy** This is very effective but also very expensive. It is usually reserved for small sarcoids present around the eyes or over the joints where collateral damage to the adjacent structures (almost inevitable to a degree with the other treatment methods) is undesirable.

GRASS WARTS

Grass warts are a fairly common virus infection of yearlings, although they may occur in older horses if they were not exposed at a young age.

Confirming the diagnosis

- Multiple warts mostly around the muzzle. They also occur in the groin region in both male and female horses.
- Occasionally single isolated warts are found, especially in the groin region.
- They may be mistaken for sarcoids.

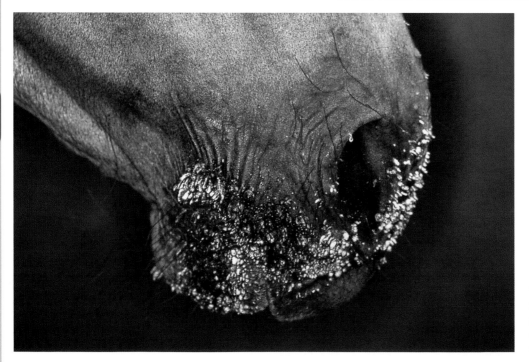

Warts were present on this yearling's muzzle for about three months before disappearing without treatment

What to do next

No treatment is necessary as spontaneous recovery is the norm. Many so-called cures may have been 'effective' because the horse will recover anyway.
- Seek veterinary advice if 'warts' are found in the groin as they are more likely to be sarcoids.

Healing may be accelerated:
- by collecting a few warts for the preparation of a vaccine, which is then injected into the horse
- by gently scarifying a few warts with sandpaper to stimulate an immune response

The horse will become immune to the virus and self-cure after 3–4 months. Small permanent pink scars may form at the site of attachment of healed warts.

AURAL PLAQUES

The wart virus can also cause warts inside the ears. These usually appear as flat white plaques, but in some horses they may be ragged wart-like structures that in some cases protrude from the ears. Some aural plaques regress spontaneously; some may persist for life. As they cause no clinical problems, no treatment is necessary. Treatment usually results in a very head-shy horse.

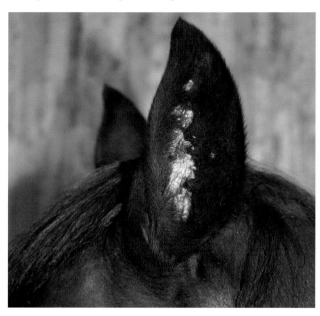

Most aural plaques are flat. In this horse they are more proliferative. No treatment was necessary

MELANOMAS

Melanomas are found almost exclusively in grey horses. Eighty per cent of greys over 15 years old will have melanomas.

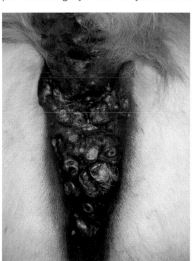

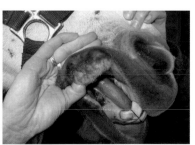

Far left: There is a very large cluster of melanomas around the anus and vulva in this mare. Some are ulcerated and it is likely that the mare will have difficulty passing faeces in the future. The ulcers healed following treatment with cimetidine, but its effect on the size of the tumours was small

Left top: This mare had a cluster of melanomas on the upper lips on both sides

Left bottom: The small melanoma inside the lower eyelid of this horse was successfully removed surgically

Warts and tumours

Confirming the diagnosis

Melanomas are circular (usually) slow-growing masses with normal overlying (black) skin found mostly under the tail, around the vulva or anus. They may also develop around the eyes and ears, on the sheath, the neck and rarely in the limbs. Another common site is in the parotid salivary gland behind the jawbone, where they are covered by normal grey hair. Here, if large, they may interfere with neck flexion and even cause respiratory difficulties. The tumours rarely cause a problem directly but as they grow they may:

• ulcerate, smell and attract flies and hence maggots
• cause obstruction of the anus when passing droppings, or of the vulva interfering with breeding and foaling.

Melanomas rarely become malignant but may spread locally, including invading the spinal cord from the vulva/anus resulting in hindlimb lameness and inco-ordination (p.148).

What to do next

Some veterinarians are reluctant to treat melanomas because there are (rare) reports of rapid aggressive re-growth at the site of surgical removal. Small melanomas may be left untreated but carefully observed for growth. Large clusters, especially around the anus/vulva may be problematic. Surgical removal or freezing of small tumours is effective with a low recurrence rate. Larger tumours are much more problematic. Treatments include:

• **Surgical removal** of the bulk of the tumour followed by freezing of the remaining part.
• **Injection of anti-cancer drugs** These drugs are difficult to obtain and hazardous to use.
• **Administering cimetidine** by mouth for 3 months or more. This drug is said to be effective in shrinking the tumour by 50 per cent in some cases, but in others it has no effect. It is impossible to predict which cases will respond, but it is worth trying.
• If there is ulceration and a smell, frequent washing in surgical scrub will help. 'Frontline' spray will control maggots.

SQUAMOUS CELL CARCINOMA

This is an uncommon tumour affecting three principal sites: the eyelids and conjunctiva (especially the third eyelid), in males, the penis and in females the area around the vulva, the nasal passages, sinuses and guttural pouches. It shows either as a reddish proliferative form or as an ulcerative type where the affected area is progressively eroded.

Treatment The tumour may be locally invasive or in some cases malignant spread may occur. Surgical treatment, chemotherapy and radiation therapy have been used successfully but malignant spread carries a very poor prognosis.

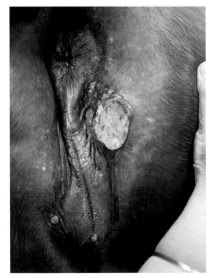

A squamous cell carcinoma adjacent to the vulva in an elderly mare,

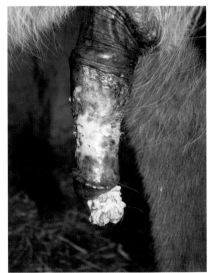

The squamous cell carcinoma on the penis of this horse was successfully treated by amputation of the end of the penis

Itchy skin conditions

Itchiness is a common symptom in the horse. The cause is usually determined by considering the season and the parts of the horse that are affected. The skin also needs to be carefully inspected.

CAUSES OF ITCHING

Key questions to answer are:

- **What is the time of year?** Louse infestations occur usually from January to April, leg mites are a problem the whole year round, sweet itch is a problem mostly from March to October and harvest mites occur in the autumn.
- **What part is the horse rubbing?** Leg mites affect the legs, sweet itch the face, mane, topline and tail, lice mostly the chest, neck and flanks.
- **Is the horse kept outdoors?** Sweet itch only occurs in horses kept out of doors for all or part of the day.

SWEET ITCH

Sweet itch is extremely common and one of the most difficult skin conditions to control. The disease is caused by an allergic skin reaction to midge saliva introduced when the midges bite. Most cases are seen from March to October and remission usually occurs in the winter. All breeds from are affected. There is evidence that susceptibility is inherited.

It is inadvisable to buy an affected horse unless you are prepared to make a major commitment in time, effort and expense to control the problem. Should the horse prove unsuitable for your requirements, it may be difficult to resell.

Clinical signs

- The horse is at grass for all or part of the day.
- The problem can start at an early age, even as a foal. Older cases may occur when the horse is moved somewhere where midges are more common.
- Rubbing usually starts on the mane and tail and then spreads to the face, topline and rump. The area is rubbed bald, the skin may break and weep serum or even blood.
- Occasionally severe cases will also rub their legs, chest and belly.
- Rugs may be damaged due to rubbing on fence posts and so on.
- If the horse has nothing to rub on (for example if the paddock is surrounded by an electric fence), it may roll frequently, or when it is brought indoors, rub frantically on the stable walls.
- Long-standing cases develop corrugation and thickening of the skin of the dock and base of the mane.

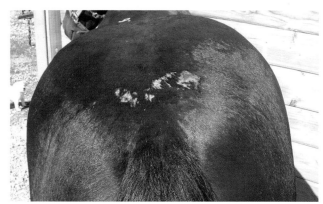

As rubbing continues the skin over the rump and on the dock becomes broken (above). Very severe irritation will cause major self trauma. This horse (below) needed urgent treatment with corticosteroids to suppress the irritation

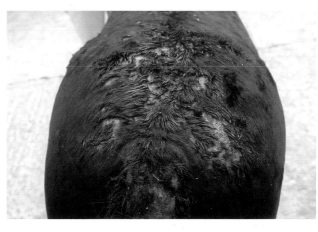

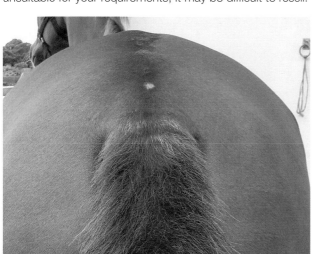

Early or mild cases of sweet itch show slight roughening of the tail hairs with obvious signs of rubbing,

Early rubbing of the neck causes hair loss and thinning of the mane

Long-standing cases show permanent thickening and corrugation of the neck skin

What to do next

Control relies upon the following, often in combination:
- **Preventing the midges from landing on the horse with a physical barrier or applying an insect repellent.**
- **Killing the midges with an insecticide before they have had a chance to bite.**
- **Keeping the horse indoors when midges are active.**

Insecticides

A second-best approach is to apply an insecticide to the susceptible areas of the body. Benzyl benzoate is the ingredient of most proprietary sweet itch preparations. It is best mixed with an equal volume of liquid paraffin.

Insecticides containing pyrethroid compounds are moderately useful but the concentration must be increased from that recommended for fly control and they must be applied every day. 'Switch', a concentrated pyrethroid insecticide applied weekly to the topline, is only moderately effective. Fipronil dog flea spray applied weekly

has also been reported to be effective but is expensive.

There are a huge number of proprietary anti-sweet itch skin lotions and creams. Most are combinations of repellents and insecticides and must be applied generously (on the face and dock, and extending about 30cm/12in either side of the spine) and at least daily. They are rarely as effective as a sweet itch rug.

Insecticides are much more effective if the mane is hogged and the dock is trimmed or pulled short, and they must never be applied to inflamed skin. In general pure fly repellents,

highly concentrated insecticide, available for application as a pour-on to the topline, is only moderately effective

Sweet itch rugs

Undoubtedly the best control method is a purpose-made sweet itch rug that covers the head, neck, belly and dock. This *must be used all the time*, including when the horse is indoors.

Sweet itch rugs should not be used if the horse is already rubbing, as it will ruin the rug in a matter of days. Obtain the rug and then arrange for the vet to administer a short-acting corticosteroid or antihistamine treatment to eliminate the clinical signs before rugging. If in spite of rugging the horse is *still itching* it suggests one of the following:
- the rug was first used while the horse had active disease. Sweet itch may take a long time to subside and initial drug treatment is usually advisable
- not enough of the body is covered or the mesh size is too large, i.e. it is not a purpose-made sweet itch rug.

A purpose-made fabric (not mesh) sweet itch rug covers the body, belly neck, and as much of the head as possible. This pony rubbed its face and ears. Rubbing ceased when a repellent/insecticide cream was applied to these areas every two days

especially if based on essential oils (citronella, tea tree and so on) are useless as they are far too short-lived. Repellents containing DEET are more effective but they need to be applied twice daily at least.

Stabling
Keeping the horse indoors during the peak periods of midge activity (dawn until 10am, and 3pm until after dusk) is useful. However, during still, humid weather midges may be active all day. Hang net curtains over doors and windows and use a strong fan to discourage midges entering stables.

Other approaches
Environment Sweet itch-susceptible horses are best kept in exposed windy fields well away from damp sheltered areas where midges breed.

Feed supplements The myriad dietary supplements available may aid control but will never be sufficient on their own:
- Garlic is popular but no true repellent activity has been demonstrated in research studies in people
- Recent research in Canada indicates that feeding linseed (cooked linseed or feed-grade linseed oil) reduces the irritation resulting from midge bites.

Homeopathic remedies have in general been ineffective.

Veterinary treatments Drug treatment, principally using corticosteroids and antihistamines, are reserved for:
- when short-term treatment is necessary to eliminate clinical signs while other methods are organised,
- where the owner is not able or willing to use other approaches.

Corticosteroids are extremely useful and will suppress clinical signs effectively. However long-term corticosteroid treatment carries a risk of inducing laminitis and should only be used as a last resort. Antihistamines are only moderately effective and must be given in large doses.

Desensitisation This is an immunological approach to control. The aim is to induce blocking antibodies that prevent the sweet itch inflammatory response. Unfortunately, the treatment is expensive, requires multiple injections, has mixed results and takes a long time to work. It is not recommended at present. New immunological approaches are being developed.

LICE
Lice infestations occur in the winter, mostly from January to April while the coat is long. They are rare in fine-coated horses. Heavier burdens are found in debilitated animals.

Clinical signs
- The horse will rub and bite accessible areas of skin, chiefly the neck, chest, flanks and hindquarters.
- There is thinning of the coat (the long outer hairs are lost) and in severe infestations, damage to the skin.
- Lice are visible to the naked eye as dark grey objects about 3mm long. The best time to look is immediately after removing a rug. The creamy eggs (nits) are attached to the base of the hair.

Rubbing of the shoulder area due to louse infestation has caused hair loss and skin damage

What to do next
Lice are host specific so there is no risk of transmission to humans. Treat all horses in the group.
- Apply insecticide, either use:
  - the concentrated pyrethroid insecticide marketed for sweet itch ('Switch'). When poured along the topline, it is very effective and because of its persistent action only needs one application. Test treat a small area first, as these products can cause skin irritation in a few horses
  - a water-based pyrethroid spray. These are effective but must be repeated after two weeks. Spraying may be undesirable in cold weather.
Powders that claim to 'repel' lice do not work. A louse powder that did contain effective insecticides is no longer on the market.

LEG MITES

These microscopic mites (*Chorioptes*) prefer heavy breeds of horses with dense feathering, although horses with fine coats can also develop the infestation. The source is usually a symptomless carrier horse.

Clinical signs

- Itchiness, restlessness, biting at the legs and stamping of the feet are the main signs. Some horses show only increased flakiness of the skin of the legs without itching.
- Self-trauma may cause skin flaking and scaliness, and serum may weep causing crust formation and matting of the hair.
- Long-standing cases develop corrugation of the skin and typically, thick accretions behind the upper cannon region and knees.

What to do next

The vet may collect scrapings for microscopic examination to confirm that mites are present.

- Clip the lower legs and remove the scabs by softening and washing as for mud fever (p.121). Clip on a bare floor and collect and burn the clipped hair and debris.
- The vet will supply an insecticidal dressing for the legs. Sometimes the drug doramectin is administered by injection and repeated after a two-week interval, although this product is not licensed for use in horses.
- Remove all bedding and pressure-wash the stable to prevent re-infection.
- Skin corrugations and thickened scab-like accretions can be improved by rubbing in aqueous cream daily until softened.

A long-standing case of leg mites (the feathering has been removed by clipping) that has caused thickening of the skin, crusting, and raw areas due to the horse biting the affected area

OTHER CAUSES OF ITCHING

Non-specific tail rubbing Some horses rub their tails without any apparent reason and continue to do so in spite of exhaustive investigations. The cause may be boredom. *Pinworms* (see p.100) may also cause tail rubbing and occasional horses with *ringworm* may find the lesions itchy.

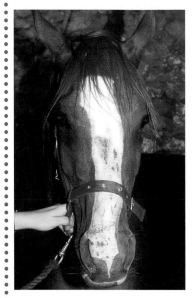

Harvest mites *(Trombicula)* are a rare cause of itching and self-trauma of the legs and muzzle in horses grazing chalky soil in the autumn. Typically clusters of specks of serum resembling pollen grains are found on the muzzle. Topical insecticides are curative.

This pony's face was intensely itchy due to harvest mite infestation

Sarcoptic mange is another rare cause of intense itching, hair loss and self-trauma. The face and trunk are mainly affected. Injectable doramectin, repeated after two weeks, will eradicate the mites.

Although *forage mites* do not feed on horses, heavy infestations in feed or bedding may result in the mites coming on to horses' legs and causing irritation.

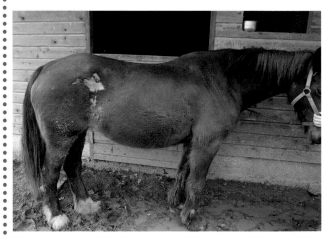

This pony was one of three in the same herd that developed intense irritation and self-trauma due to sarcoptic mange

Skin problems

Lumps, nodules and wheals

ASSESSING LUMPS, NODULES AND WHEALS

The key questions to answer are:

- **Are they painful to touch?** Saddle sores and girth galls are often painful, whereas nodular skin disease and urticarial plaques are not.

- **How quickly did they appear?** Urticarial plaques appear over a 24-hour period, whereas nodular skin disease gradually develops over a few weeks.

- **Has something changed in the horse's environment?** Has there been a recent dietary or bedding change, or a recent use of a topical skin preparation that might have triggered the urticaria?

- **Are biting flies (for example horse flies) active?**

- **Where are the lesions?** Contact allergies to bedding will occur along the flanks and underneath the belly.

NODULAR SKIN DISEASE (Collagenolytic granulomas)

This common disease is thought to be allergic in nature. Insect bites may be the main cause although some cases have no insect contact. It occurs mainly in the spring and summer, mostly in horses 8 to 15 years old. It is commonest in bays and chestnuts.

- Single or multiple firm painless nodules develop along the neck, shoulders and saddle area. The saddle area is the commonest site.
- They are 5–10mm in size, occasionally up to 20mm.
- The overlying hair is normal.
- Some have a small scab on top; when this is removed, a small, calcified plug can be expressed.
- They rarely cause a significant problem although nodules in contact with weight-bearing areas of the saddle may enlarge due to the pressure.

Treatment Some nodules will spontaneously disappear. Corticosteroid treatment is very effective, if given early enough; older calcified lesions may respond poorly. The drug is administered in tablets, or by injection, usually into the nodules. Surgical removal is also possible and may be the only effective treatment for long-standing nodules.

Where direct injection of a corticosteroid is used a special pressure injector is needed due to the density of the nodules

A fairly severe case of nodular skin disease

INSECT BITE REACTIONS

Bites from horseflies and stable flies may trigger an allergic reaction, resulting in a large wheal at the biting site. Treatment is not usually necessary as the wheal will usually disappear after 24 hours.

To prevent fly bites:

- in grazing horses, use a special fly rug

A purpose-made fly-rug

- in stabled horses, spray the stable walls with a suitable insecticide to kill the flies or use an electronic fly-killer with a blue strip light.

URTICARIA (Nettle rash)

Urticaria can make a dramatic appearance, with a horse developing clusters of wheals on its body overnight. Although an alarming sight, the horse is rarely bothered by these wheals.

CAUSES OF URTICARIA

- Topical applications, including fly repellents and shampoos
- Contact allergies to bedding or grasses
- True nettle stings
- Drug treatments such as antibiotics, anti-inflammatory and worming drugs
- Allergies to feed, especially cereals
- Allergies to feed supplements such as garlic
- Localised heat and pressure, for example under the saddle.

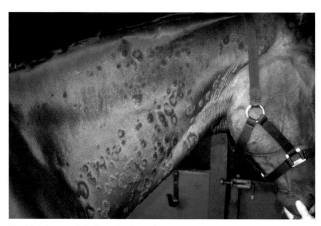

Feed intolerance is believed to have been the cause of this very extensive urticarial reaction

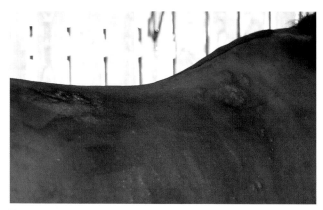

Upon removal of the saddle, this horse developed urticarial reactions at all of the pressure points. This pressure- or heat-related urticaria is uncommon

Clinical signs

- Variable sized wheals appear in the skin anywhere on the body. If contact related they will appear where the offending substance has touched the horse's body (if bedding, the wheals will be on the belly). Very extensive lesions can occur in a matter of hours, and the head can become quite swollen. Some wheals are doughnut-shaped with a shallow centre.
- The wheals are usually painless but sometimes itchy.
- Nettle stings can cause multiple small bumps on the limbs and marked lameness. If several limbs are stung the horse may appear unco-ordinated, and may become frenzied.
- If present for a few days some of the wheals may enlarge, coalesce and weep serum.
- Some horses suffer from recurrent attacks.

What to do next

Unless the cause is known, withhold all hard feed, feed additives and topical shampoos, fly sprays, and so on. If the horse is receiving medication consult the vet before withdrawing it. Feed only hay or grass until the horse is cured. Cardboard or paper bedding is preferred as it is non-allergenic.

- Some cases will self-cure in a few days. Nettle stings will resolve in a few hours without treatment.
- If there is no improvement in the condition after 48 hours, call the vet. Most cases will respond rapidly to corticosteroid treatment.
- If the triggering factor is unknown, once the horse is recovered the suspect substances can be re-introduced one at a time and the response noted for confirmation.
- Blood tests are available which claim to be able to pinpoint the allergen but they are very unreliable.
- Horses allergic to the ingredients of hard feeds can receive adequate nutrition from high quality forage, alfalfa and vegetable oil. Consult a nutritionist to ensure the diet is balanced.
- Obstinate or recurrent cases may need to receive prolonged low-dose treatment with corticosteroids to keep the disease at bay.

Skin problems

Injuries caused by tack

Tack injuries usually occur because the tack does not fit properly. It is sensible to have it checked regularly by a skilled saddler.

Saddle sores

Wheals may appear an hour after removal of the saddle after a long ride. They usually occur just to one side of the withers at a site under the point of attachment of the stirrup leathers and result from the blood supply rapidly returning to an area deprived of blood due to abnormal focal pressure. Eventually a scabby area will develop or patches of white hair. Raised scabby areas of skin may be tender to touch. The hair may be rubbed off underneath the rear of the saddle. If the pommel is close to the spine, damage to the skin over the point of the withers will occur.

CAUSES OF SADDLE SORES

Saddle sores are generally caused by an ill-fitting saddle. Even a saddle that fitted perfectly when purchased may become uncomfortable because the horse changes shape or the flocking has compressed. Possible saddle problems:
- too large or too small for the horse
- a broken tree
- uneven flocking
- large accretions of dried sweat.

High withers. Horses with very little muscle on either side of the withers are extraordinarily difficult to fit for a saddle even in skilled hands.

Riders that ride unevenly (perhaps due to a bad back).

What to do next
- Do not ride the horse until the lesion has resolved.
- Have an experienced saddle fitter check the horse and the saddle *together*.
- The rider's balance when mounted should be checked.

The saddler may:
- Recommend the use of a special full or partial numnah to improve the fit of the saddle or relieve pressure
- Re-flock the saddle to help weight distribution
- Advise the purchase of a new saddle.

A temporary measure to control pressure wheals is to loosen the girth slowly, one hole every five minutes, after a ride.

Injuries caused by the girth

A girth gall is a localised sore area in the girth area behind the elbow. The causes are:
- poor fitting of the girth
- pinching of the skin under the girth
- dirty girths, or applying the girth to dirty skin
- having the girth too tight.

Nylon girths or string girths may irritate fine-skinned horses.

Initially the skin is sore, the hair is slightly raised and the horse resents touching of the area. If the problem is not rectified eventually the affected area becomes thickened, raw, scabby or corrugated.

Treatment Apply an antiseptic and anti-inflammatory cream to the affected area. Do not put a girth on the horse until the area has healed. Long-standing large lesions may have to be surgically removed.

When girthing up:
- before fully tightening the girth, lift each foreleg up and forward in turn to stretch the skin under it
- use a clean cotton or neoprene girth sleeve to pad the girth
- use a wider, softer girth.

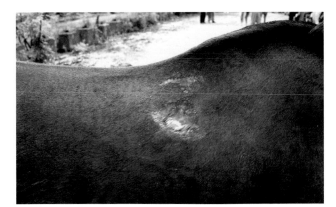

A sore back is almost inevitable in this very high withered horse, which has minimal muscle on either side of the withers. The horse will require very skilled saddle fitting

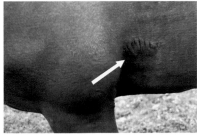

This sore area was found in the girth area of an endurance horse the day after a long ride. The skin may have been pinched by the girth or there may have been another unnoticed focal pressure

Injuries caused by boots

Boot rubs develop on each side of the back of the fetlock, starting as raw areas that eventually develop a scab. Tendon boots with a rigid protective strip (at the back overlying the tendons) can if fitted too low or if too large for the horse cause a pressure lesion in the back of the pastern. The pastern flexes when galloping and the end of the rigid strip in the boot is forced against the pastern skin.

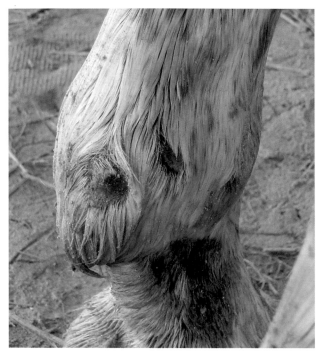

The pressure of the boot, probably aggravated by sand rubbing the skin, caused these lesions in an endurance horse competing in the desert. The area near the back of the fetlock is the commonest site for boot rubs

Injuries caused by the bit

Hard-pulling horses, excessively severe bits or over-vigorous use of the reins may cause ulceration and splitting of the lips at the corner of the mouth, and bruising and slitting of the bars. Bits acting on the nose or on the underside of the jaw (for example hackamores) may cause pressure damage to the skin overlying these areas. Curb chains may also damage the area on which they act.

Pressure from the noseband portion of a long-shanked hackamore bit caused a sore to develop on this horse's nose

Treatment If possible the horse's mouth should be rested until healing is complete. Human haemorrhoid creams, which are designed to adhere to moist surfaces, may aid the healing process.

Make every effort to determine the reason why a horse is hard-pulling:

- Check the horse's teeth, and the condition, fit and design of the bit.
- Schooling of the horse and rider may be required.
- Creating a 'bit seat' (see p.87) may improve bitting comfort for the horse.
- Changing the design or tightness of the noseband may help the situation.
- A hackamore may be more acceptable to the horse.
- Changing to a non-jointed, rigid or flexible, or thicker bit may help.
  - Combination' bits, where the force of the reins is applied simultaneously to the poll, mouth, jaw and nose may require significantly less effort from the rider and hence cause less damage to the horse.

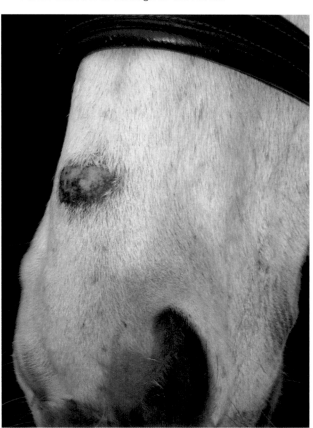

Other skin problems

SUNBURN AND PHOTOSENSITISATION

Sunburn is a common condition that affects the unpigmented skin of the face, which becomes reddened, weeping and crusty. Keep the horse out of the sun and apply a soothing antibacterial and anti-inflammatory ointment to the affected area until it has healed. Prevent a recurrence by only allowing the horse to graze at night, fitting a face mask or applying a high factor sun block.

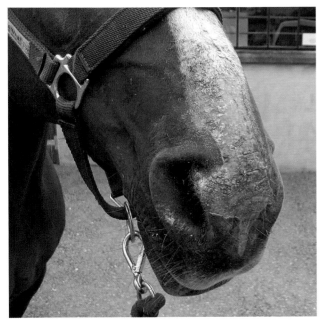

Extensive sunburn of the pink (unpigmented) area of this horse's face has caused marked weeping and crusting

CAUSES OF PHOTOSENSITATION

- Primary photosensitisation occurs when the horse eats a plant (classically St John's wort) that contains a substance, which when distributed to the skin in the bloodstream, reacts with sunlight in the unpigmented areas of the body.
- Secondary photosensitisation results from severe liver disease. Chlorophyll, the green pigment of plants, is normally converted in the horse's gut to phylloerythrin, which is detoxified by the liver. Where a horse is suffering extensive liver disease the amount detoxified is low, resulting in phylloerythrin accumulation in the skin. In unpigmented skin, this reacts with sunlight causing an inflammatory response.

Photosensitisation is an uncommon condition caused by sunlight interacting with chemicals in the skin (see below). In primary photosensitisation the horse is otherwise well, but the pink skin of the muzzle and areas of white hair on the body and the limbs become reddened, sore and weeping. There is a sharp cut-off at the boundary of the unpigmented skin.

Cases of secondary photosensitisation also show other signs of liver disease such as weight loss, depression, oedema, jaundice and neurological signs. Blood tests usually confirm liver disease. In severe cases the skin may be painful, cracked and may separate from the surrounding normal skin. If the coronets are affected the hoof may start to detach.

Treatment Bring the horse indoors until it has healed. If the muzzle is very sore feed hay loose.
- Check whether the horse has access to St John's wort (*Hypericum*).
- If liver disease is suspected, the vet will perform blood tests for confirmation. The prognosis is very poor in liver-related photosensitisation because there is usually extensive and irreparable liver damage.

A full-face mask completely covers this pony's unpigmented face and muzzle

Other skin problems

ABNORMAL HAIR GROWTH (Equine Cushing's disease)

Equine Cushing's disease is a very common disorder of older (>15 years) horses and ponies. The cause is abnormal pituitary gland activity, which in a minority of cases is caused by a true pituitary tumour.

 ## Clinical signs

Hirsutism, or failure to shed the winter coat, is the commonest sign of this disease, with the growth of abnormally long (sometimes curly) hair. Initially the horse acquires a partial summer coat but retains winter-length hairs on the neck, shoulders and trunk. Eventually no summer coat is acquired.

Other signs include:
- patchy sweating and a matted smelly coat
- secondary heavy parasite infestations with redworms and tapeworms
- poor wound healing and an increased susceptibility to infections
- laminitis of moderate severity, often occurring in older horses with no history of laminitis and in the absence of the usual nutritional trigger factors. It responds poorly to treatment unless specific anti-Cushing treatment is also given
- abnormal fat distribution. There is a plaque of fat over the rump but the ribs may be clearly visible
- bulging of the fat pads over the eyes
- the horse is lethargic
- a pot bellied, sway-backed appearance
- excessive drinking and urine production in some cases.

The vet may perform blood tests to confirm the condition.

Photographed in early June, the pony on the right has acquired a normal summer coat. The pony on the left has Cushing's disease. Contrary to popular belief a curly coat is not common in this condition

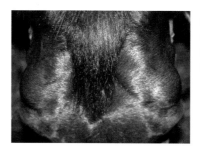

Bulging of the fat pads over the eyes is typical of Cushing's disease, although not all cases show this sign

 ## What to do next

If abnormal hair coat is the only sign, no action (other than clipping in the summer months) may be required.
- Parasite control must be rigorous.
- The nutritional management should be as for conventional laminitics (p.134).
- Once laminitis or excessive drinking develops, drug treatment should be started. Several drugs are available but the best a present is probably pergolide. With an effective dose the hair will shed almost normally. It may prolong life by 2–3 years but must be used continuously.

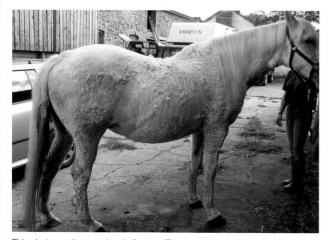

This photograph was taken in August. The horse has failed to shed its winter coat and has Cushing's disease

Above left: This pony developed the coat that is typical of Cushing's disease. It also had laminitis, which responded poorly to conventional treatment
Above right: Following treatment with pergolide the coat became normal (photographed in March) and the laminitis resolved

EYE PROBLEMS

In this section

Eye essentials • Assessing the abnormal eye • Tear staining of the face
Conjunctivitis • Injury to the cornea • Equine recurrent uveitis • Cataracts

Eye essentials

Eye disease is common in horses, perhaps because their large open eyes are very susceptible to external trauma. Treatment is more likely to be successful if started early.

THE STRUCTURE OF THE EYE

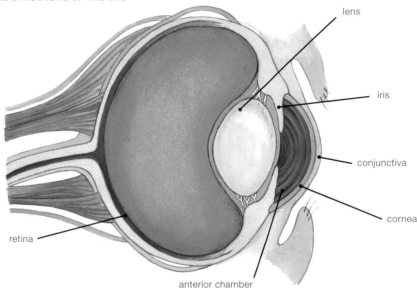

lens

iris

conjunctiva

cornea

retina

anterior chamber

ASSESSING THE ABNORMAL EYE

The key questions to answer are:

- **Is the affected eye fully open?** Compare it with the other eye. If a horse is keeping an eye partially or completely closed it indicates eye pain.
- **Is the surface of the eye bright and completely clear?** Many eye diseases cause cloudiness of the cornea.
- **Do the eyelids appear swollen or show the presence of any nodules on or around them?** Conjunctivitis or injury to the eyelids may cause them to swell.
- **Is the pink conjunctiva swollen and prominent?** It should only be visible at the inner corner of the eye.
- **Is the pupil size the same in both eyes?**

- **Is there mucus or a discharge at the corner of the eye or along the edge of the lower lid?** Eye infections will often cause a pus-like discharge.
- **Is there any tear-staining (indicating tear overflow) of the skin below the eye?** Tear overflow indicates excess tear production due to either irritation, pain, or blockage of the tear duct.
- **Is the third eyelid in its normal position in the inside corner of the eye and against the eyeball?** The edge of the third eyelid should be a sharp clean edge. Tumours and foreign bodies may cause distortion or lift of this edge.

What will the vet do

To examine the eye the vet may:

- Sedate the horse to allow detailed examination.
- Perform a nerve block of the nerve supply to the muscles of the upper lid. Because these muscles are very strong, if the eye is painful it can be very difficult to open the eye adequately to examine it. The nerve block in effect temporarily 'paralyses' the lid muscles allowing the upper lid to be pushed up out of the way.
- Shine a bright light into the eye to closely inspect its external and some of its internal structure.
- Use local anaesthetic so that the horse does not resent detailed examination of a painful eye.
- Use an ophthalmoscope (essentially an illuminated magnifying glass with a adjustable focal length allowing

detailed examination of different depths in the eye) to inspect all internal structures of the eye.

- Check for any blockage of the tear ducts using green flourescein drops (see photo below).
- Check for damage or ulceration of the cornea using flourescein. The dye will stick to an area of corneal damage (unless it is very shallow).
- In complicated cases, other illuminating and magnifying devices may be used.
- In an eye infection, the vet may take swabs or scrapings from the surface of the eye to find the causal organism.
- The vet will also check the general health of the horse in order to determine if the eye problem is part of a more generalised problem.

TEAR-STAINING OF THE FACE

Tear staining of the face below one or both eyes reflects:

- Tear production in excess of the capacity of the naso-lacrimal duct to conduct it away from the eye. This usually reflects a diseased eye or conjunctiva, most commonly conjunctivitis.
- Obstruction of the openings of the naso-lacrimal duct, or alteration of their position (for example by eyelid swelling or deformity, or conjunctival swelling or previous lid trauma) such that they are no longer close to the tear 'lake'.
- Obstruction of the naso-lacrimal duct somewhere along its length by:
  - a plug of mucus
  - external pressure on the duct as it courses through the head, for example in sinusitis
  - complete absence of one or both openings of the ducts in the nostrils. This occurs as a congenital defect and should be suspected if older foals and yearlings appear to have recurrent conjunctivitis.

A simple way to check whether there is a tear duct obstruction is for the vet to instil into the eye the harmless green dye flourescein. If the duct is clear the dye should travel along it to appear at each nostril within 30 minutes. The time to appear should be the same in both eyes.

Clearing an obstruction within the tear duct

The easiest way to do this is for the vet to sedate the horse and then pass a fine tube a short distance up the nasal opening of the duct. Sterile saline is then flushed through the tube in a reverse direction to normal tear flow, so that saline flows from the eyelid openings of the duct.

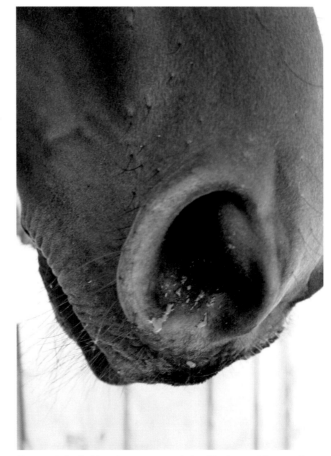

Flourescein instilled into the eye appeared after 15 minutes at the nostril, indicating that the naso-lacrimal duct is unblocked

CONJUNCTIVITIS

Conjunctivitis is the commonest eye disorder of the horse. The causes are:

- Trauma to the eye (the commonest cause) by grass stems, twigs and so on. Usually only one eye is affected. Secondary bacterial infection may occur.
- Foreign material getting into the eye, for example dust or grass seeds from hay. Usually one eye only.
- A primary virus or bacterial infection, for example equine herpes virus or equine viral arteritis virus. Both eyes are affected in this case.
- Fly worry in summer (one or both eyes). Flies may cause:
  - irritation of the eye, resulting in the horse rubbing the eye against the inside of a foreleg. The rubbing action irritates the eye
  - transmission of infection from one eye (or horse) to another via their feeding activities around eyes.
- Allergic conjunctivitis, usually caused by exposure to aerosol sprays, for example fly sprays.

Secondary conjunctivitis is caused by:

- Inversion of the (usually lower) lid such that the eyelashes are directed inward against the eye (entropion). This is seen in newborn foals especially if premature or weak. One or both eyes may be affected.

There is a muco-pus discharge from the eye, with overflow of tears, in this conjunctivitis case

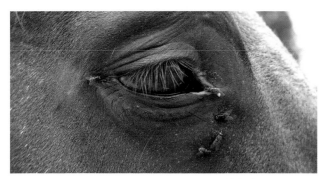

Flies are attracted to a discharging eye and will spread infection from horse to horse

- A tumour of the eye or the eyelids.
- Lacerations to the eyelids with poor apposition of the cut surfaces when healed.
- Obstruction of the naso-lacrimal (tear) duct.

Conjunctivitis may also be present in association with more serious eye diseases such as corneal ulceration

Clinical signs

- There is usually a discharge from the eye. This may be mucus, pus, tear overflow or all of these.
- The eyelids are partially closed.
- The eyelids are sometimes swollen. The conjunctiva may be swollen and reddened, and may protrude from under the lids.
- The surface of the eye may be cloudy (corneal oedema) if the conjunctivitis is part of a more complex eye problem.

What to do next

- Call your vet as soon as possible.
- Simple primary conjunctivitis is usually treated with antibiotic eye drops or ointment several times a day (see 'Treating a horse's eye', p.145). In addition corticosteroids may be used.
- Before medicating, gently wipe away any discharge accumulating around the eye.
- Protect the horse from sunlight and flies by stabling

 during daylight or using a fly mask. Fly fringes are not adequate.

Unless good fly control is practised, conjunctivitis cases recover poorly due to repeated re-infection

In uncomplicated bacterial conjunctivitis the response to treatment should be rapid. Notify the vet if there has not been an obvious improvement in three days or the condition appears to be worsening.

Failure to improve may indicate:

- the medication is not being properly applied (common) i.e. insufficient is being placed in the eye or the application is not repeated with sufficient frequency
- the organism is resistant to the medication used
- the diagnosis is incorrect.

INJURY TO THE CORNEA

The causes of corneal damage include trauma from grazing in tall grass, head-rubbing, fighting, whips, ropes, dust, foreign bodies in the eye, and protruding objects in the stable or fencing (hedges, barbed wire). Primary bacterial and viral corneal infections occur also. Infection of the eye is common after corneal trauma, and inhibits healing. If the traumatic injury damages deeper than the superficial layers of the cornea the lesion is called an *ulcer*.

To detect the presence of ulcers flourescein drops are placed in the eye. The dye doesn't stick to the surface of a healthy eye, but will bind to the cornea (revealing the damaged area as a bright green zone) if the inner layers are exposed.

Clinical signs

- The eye is invariably painful and the lids will be held partially or fully closed.
- There is excess tear production, possibly in conjunction with muco-pus discharge if secondary infection occurs.
- The surface of the eye usually becomes cloudy, either immediately adjacent to the ulcer or more diffusely.
- The horse will resent handling of the eye.
- The pupil in the centre may be constricted or normal size.

The surface of the cornea is cloudy (corneal oedema)

Flourescein dye reveals an oval ulcer on this cornea

What to do next

Ulceration of the cornea is a serious condition. Summon veterinary help immediately. The vet will thoroughly examine the eye, possibly collect samples or swabs, and commence treatment with:

- **Antibiotics** Broad-spectrum antibiotics are used until the causal organism is known. Initially the antibiotic must be applied to the eye every two hours.
- **Anti-fungal agents** may be used.
- The vet may remove lose material from around the ulcer (debridement).
- Enzymes released by white blood cells (accumulating in the eye as a result of infection/inflammation) can further damage the cornea, so drugs may be placed in the eye to block their action.

On-going treatment

The healing of the ulcer must be monitored by regular veterinary checks. In long-standing or non-responsive cases additional treatments may be used:

- the eyelids, or the third eyelid, may be temporarily sutured across the surface of the eye to protect the healing ulcer from their movement
- a contact lens may be fitted for a similar effect.

Horses on long-term eye treatment often become reluctant to receive eye medication. A plastic in-dwelling tube inserted in the eyelid of this horse allows the owner to treat the eye by injecting medicine into the tube

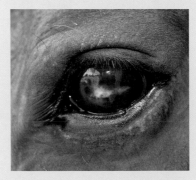

This horse has recovered from a corneal ulcer. There is large scar on the front of the eye

TREATING A HORSE'S EYE

A horse with a painful eye rapidly becomes averse to the application of cream or drops, and may become very difficult to treat. The problem is compounded by the fact that eye treatments have to be applied very frequently, sometimes every few hours. It is essential therefore to use good restraint and a good technique. Use a new tube of medication or drops for each eye.

1 Gently wipe away any accumulated mucous or discharge in the corner of the eye with cotton wool. Have an assistant stand on the opposite side of the horse, holding its head still by placing a hand on the nose and another underneath.

2 Place the fingers as close to the eyelid margins as possible and then part them.

3 Press the eyeball gently back into the socket. The third eyelid comes across, creating a space in front of it. Note: if an ulcer is present, the eyeball should not be pressed.

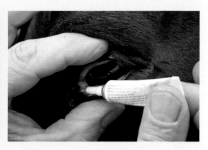

4 Introduce the medication into the space and then hold the lids closed for a minute to allow the drug to spread across the eye

EQUINE RECURRENT UVEITIS (ERU, periodic ophthalmia, moon blindness)

In this condition the iris and its associated structures (known as the uveal tract) become inflamed and damaged. The cause is believed to be an autoimmune reaction by the horse against its own uveal tract in one eye. The reaction may be triggered by bacterial infection of the eye (principally by *Leptospira* bacteria) or other unknown causes.

To prevent excessive damage to the eye, immune responses in the eye are naturally tightly controlled. In ERU it is believed that this control mechanism is faulty. It is thought that ERU may be a group of diseases with a single set of symptoms.

In this early case of ERU, white blood cells have accumulated in the anterior chamber of the eye

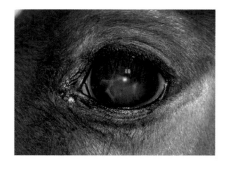

 Clinical signs

A range of signs and severities are seen, although invariably the eye is painful and partially closed.
- There is excessive tear production.
- The conjunctiva is reddened.
- The surface of the eye is clear or slightly dull.
- The iris (pupil) is constricted and looks 'muddy'.
- There may accumulation of white blood cells in the anterior chamber.

With effective treatment, the condition lasts about 7–10 days.

Recovered cases may show residual damage, such as:
- cataracts
- adhesions between the iris and the lens behind it
- loss of coloration of the iris

A key feature of ERU is its tendency to recur at an unpredictable interval (from weeks to years), eventually resulting in a shrunken eye, cataracts and blindness. For this reason if signs of a previous attack of ERU are detected at a pre-purchase examination, the vet may discourage purchase of the horse.

What to do next

ERU is an emergency. The horse must be treated without delay to prevent lasting damage to the eye.
- Atropine drops will be given into the eye to dilate the pupil.
- The vet will use aggressive anti-inflammatory therapy, both directly into the eye (drops, ointment or subconjunctival injection) and also by mouth or injection. Initially the drops are given every hour for 4-6 treatments (or until improved), then every 6-12 hours
- During treatment keep the horse in a darkened box.
- Treatment is continued for two weeks after apparent recovery.

Long-term prognosis

There is every chance that the condition will recur but an unpredictable interval, so the owner must be constantly vigilant for the early signs so that treatment can commence as early as possible. Although blindness is not inevitable, many cases develop significant permanent damage to the eye.

CATARACTS

A normal eye lens is completely clear, like glass. A cataract is an opacity of the lens or its capsule. The causes are:
- **Congenital** (present at birth), but often not recognised until older.
- **Hereditary** (very rare).
- **Senile** Cataracts are common in horses over 20 years of age but rarely affect vision.
- **Secondary** to some other disease process in the eye, for example ERU, see p.145.

Many cataracts cause little or no detectable effects on vision. Some may progress over time but the timescale during which this happens is impossible to predict. In a pre-purchase examination the vet will check carefully for other signs of eye damage, indicating that the horse has suffered from ERU.

What to do next

Treatment is not normally contemplated unless a significant effect on vision can be demonstrated. Many horses can live normal productive lives even while blind in one eye.
- The only effective treatment is surgical removal of the lens. This is rarely successful if there are associated signs of ERU. The best candidates for treatment are young foals with congenital cataracts.

TUMOURS IN AND AROUND THE EYE

The eye and the surrounding lids are common sites for tumours – sarcoids, melanomas and squamous cell carcinomas – in the horse. In these sites they can be very difficult to treat due to the risk of damage to the lids or the eye itself.

These very extensive sarcoids around the eye were successfully treated by injecting BCG vaccine directly into them

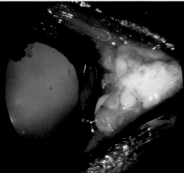

A typical squamous cell carcinoma

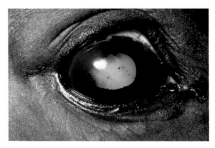

Several attacks of ERU have left this horse with a very abnormal eye. There is a large cataract, and damage to the iris

ABNORMAL BEHAVIOUR

Stable vices and colic (p.90) are the most common causes of abnormal behaviour in the horse. This section deals with the less common causes, of which the two most frequent are headshaking and wobbler syndrome. Abnormal behaviour may occur because of some abnormality in the brain or spinal cord, or it may result from an abnormality outside of these regions. For example, a recumbent horse may be unable to rise simply due to the pain caused by arthritis in its hindlimbs.

HEADSHAKING

Headshaking is one of the most difficult conditions to control and it is rarely possible to achieve a permanent cure. Horses that headshake have *facial pain* and the shaking is an involuntary response to some trigger factor stimulating the sensory nerves of the skin of the face (including the ears and muzzle), the eyes, the teeth, sinuses and nasal cavity. The horse shows an *exaggerated response* to an otherwise very mild stimulus, for example a pollen grain or particle of dust landing in the nasal cavity.

Usually there is a sudden onset of the behaviour. It can occur at a young age, even before breaking.

KEY FEATURES OF HEADSHAKING

- **Seasonality** Most headshakers show signs only at particular times of the year, usually spring and summer. This can be explained by the occurrence of trigger factors, such as pollen, dust, warmth, cold and wind. There is often complete remission in the winter.
- **Intermittency** Most headshakers show signs under a particular set of circumstances, such as exercise, light, sunshine, wind, rain, on particular parts of a hack (for example in shade or when exposed to pollen or insects).
- **Severity** Some cases are very mild and the movement of the head is slight and almost imperceptible. The horse is not unduly distressed and the rider may ignore it. At the other extreme some cases are very distressed and may be uncontrollable. Any attempt to restrain the horse or even to make it go forward is extremely resented. It may rub its face so badly that it bleeds.

What does it look like?

Various combinations of clinical signs are seen, these include:

- Involuntary up/down twitching of the head. Usually there is a quick upward flick of the head with a slower down movement. Some cases shake from side to side.
- Snorting, high blowing and sneezing.
- The horse acts like it has a fly up its nose.
- Nostril clamping at exercise.
- Striking at the face with the forelegs during exercise.
- Rubbing the nose on the ground when stationary and while moving.
- Abnormal behaviour, such as stopping, refusing to go forwards, loss of impulsion, rearing. Some horses can override the stimulus if distracted by, for example, being asked to jump.
- Stumbling, caused by attempting to rub the nose on a limb or on the ground.
- Some horses may show intense irritation, even in the stable. In other cases the horse may be too dangerous to ride.

What to do next

The vet will examine the horse clinically, at exercise and at rest. The aim is to find an obvious trigger factor, for example dental or guttural pouch disease (p.70). The nasal cavities and upper airways may be examined endoscopically. The effect of various interventions, for example a nose net, will be tested.

Although some cases self-cure, many respond poorly to treatment and may be unrideable during the headshaking season. The condition is not known to be hereditary. The following treatments are used:

Nose net This is the most consistently successful treatment, resulting in a complete or partial improvement in 60 per cent of horses. It is believed to act by providing a counter stimulant to the muzzle, by filtering particulate matter from the air, or by altering blood flow through the nostrils. The horse's 'whiskers' should be kept trimmed short if a net is worn.

Ear covers These can be used in combination with a nose net.

Fly fringe Fitted to the noseband, this may provide a counter stimulant.

Eye covers (blinkers) – if the horse responds to local anaesthetic drops in the eyes.

Drug treatment A variety of drugs have been tried with variable success. Some cases show no response at all.

Other considerations

- **Pre-purchase examination** As there is often complete remission in the winter, a headshaker may inadvertently be purchased, following a standard pre-purchase examination. It is safest to obtain a written warranty from the seller stating that the horse has never shown signs of headshaking.

Insurance As many cases are unrideable, a claim under 'Permanent Loss of Use' insurance may be successful.

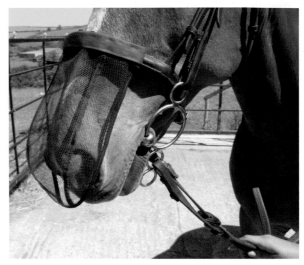

Competing while wearing a nose net is permitted in certain disciplines, such as dressage

INCO-ORDINATION

Inco-ordination is uncommon in horses. Often there is some disease process that is interfering with the ability of sensory nerves to relay information regarding position and posture from sensors in the limbs and inner ear to the horse's brain. Unless this information is correct and complete, the horse cannot initiate co-ordinated movement. In addition, damage to the signal-processing centre in the brain may be present. Often there is also interference in the nerve stimuli travelling from the brain to the muscles, resulting in irregular movement and muscle weakness.

The commonest cause of inco-ordination in horses is wobbler syndrome.

Due to arthritis of the lower neck joints, this 18-year-old horse developed wobbler syndrome. Unusually, it had difficulty in standing; here it is supporting itself by leaning against the stable partition

Wobbler syndrome (Cervical vertebral malformation)

This condition has two forms. The *juvenile form* occurs in rapidly growing horses of less than four years old, especially Thoroughbreds. The vertebrae in the upper part of the neck develop abnormally, resulting in pressure on the spinal cord as it travels down the neck through the centre of the vertebrae. There is often some traumatic event (for example a fall, or rearing over backwards) that initiates the inco-ordination, despite the vertebral malformation preceding the trauma.

The other form is seen in mostly *older horses* (15 years or more) and is caused by arthritis of the lower neck joints. The new bone that is laid down around these joints as part of the arthritic disease process presses on the spinal cord interfering with its function.

Clinical signs

- The severity varies. Some horses are only very mildly affected, others may be unable to stand.
- The horse is usually bright, alert and eating normally.
- It is obviously unco-ordinated, especially if asked to turn sharply.
- It drags the hind (occasionally fore) toes.
- The hindlimbs are weak and the horse can readily be pulled to one side if the tail is pulled sideways as the horse walks (the tail-pull test).
- If the horse is made to canter, a 'bunny-hopping' gait is seen.
- The hindlimbs are usually the worst affected. Occasionally there are forelimb signs.
- The limbs move stiffly, with reduced flexion.
- Some reflexes may be abnormal.
- Often there is no obvious neck pain.

What to do next

- The vet will perform a neurological examination to attempt to localise the problem. The effect of blindfolding the horse (to remove any visual compensation it may be using) and asking it to walk up and down a hill, step sideways, and so on will be checkedduring this examination.
- An x-ray of the neck maybe taken. Myelography, in which the compression of the spinal cord is demonstrated by injecting an x-ray-dense chemical into the spinal canal, is also very useful but requires general anaesthesia.
- Treatment is difficult and many affected horses are humanely destroyed. Surgical fusion of the vertebrae is performed in specialist centres with moderate success. The degree of improvement seen depends on the duration and severity of the disease. Horses with the juvenile form treated early show the most improvement. Some residual inco-ordination may remain, rendering the horse unsuitable for riding, although breeding may be possible.

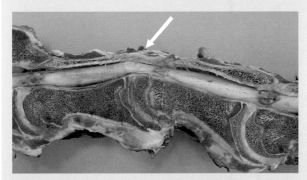

This post-mortem specimen, prepared from the neck of a wobbler, clearly shows that the spinal cord has been 'pinched' by the abnormally angled vertebra

A Thoroughbred yearling with wobbler syndrome. It was able to walk but fell over if made to trot

Other causes of inco-ordination

EHV infection (p.72) Certain strains of the virus cause neurological signs. EHV virus is the second most common cause of inco-ordination. There is usually a recent history of elevated temperatures, respiratory signs or abortion in in-contact horses, and more than one in the group may show inco-ordination. The onset is sudden and horses may progress rapidly to recumbency (12–24 hours after onset). Weakness of the hindlimbs and urine dribbling are typical. The condition is usually diagnosed via blood tests. Affected animals should be isolated and the yard quarantined. Mildly affected horses may respond to corticosteroid treatment, but if recumbent for more than 24 hours the prognosis for recovery is poor.

Trauma to the vertebrae causing fractures and consequently damage to the spinal cord – usually as a result of an accident.

Liver disease Horses with extensive liver damage (usually caused by ragwort poisoning) may become inco-ordinated but there is also dullness, loss of appetite, weight loss and characteristic abnormalities on blood testing (p.97).

RECUMBENCY

A recumbent horse is unable or unwilling to rise from a lying (on its side or sitting up) position.

Severe laminitis caused this Clydesdale horse to spend most of the day lying down. When asked to rise, it adopted the classical stance of the laminitic horse (see photo p.34)

This horse fell at a steeplechase fence and was unable to rise. It had fractured a vertebra in its lumbar spine, causing hindlimb paralysis

KEY QUESTIONS TO ANSWER WITH SUDDEN RECUMBENCY

- **When was the horse last seen standing?**
- **Is the horse trying to rise?**
- **Are there any visible injuries indicating an accident has occurred?** For example skin abrasions.
- **Are there any environmental clues indicating an injury may have occurred?** For example a broken fence.
- **Can the horse keep itself in the sitting up (sternal) position?** Inability to do so makes the prognosis for recovery less good.
- **Are the limbs positioned normally?** A limb in an abnormal position may indicate a fracture or dislocation.
- **Is the horse bright and eating?** If yes (unless the horse is very thin), the cause is likely to be related to the musculoskeletal system. If the horse is quiet and depressed, the cause is probably an illness elsewhere.
- **Is the horse very thin?** Weakness and a lack of muscle strength may prevent a horse from rising.
- **Is the horse showing any other sign of illness?** For example, rolling may indicate colic (p.90).

Causes of recumbency

Musculoskeletal problems Severe laminitis (p.34) or a sole abscess (p.19) in more than one foot may make a horse very reluctant to stand. Old horses with arthritis in the hind limbs will often have difficulty rising due to pain. Usually, you will have noticed that they are stiff, slow moving and possibly reluctant to have their feet picked up. If they lie down close to a fence or in soft or sloping ground they may find it too difficult to rise.

Any severe injury to a limb may make it impossible or too painful for the horse to rise. An upper limb long bone fracture if underneath the horse may discourage it from rising. If the horse is rolled over most will then stand up. Major trauma to the vertebrae (for example a fractured spine causing damage to the spinal cord) or pelvis due to falling or colliding, may also cause recumbency.

Colic Sometimes horses with colic (especially colonic impactions) may be found lying down, often flat out. There may, at least initially, be little or no additional typical signs of colic. They can usually be persuaded to rise, however, and the vet can confirm the horse is suffering from colic.

EHV infection (see p.72 and left).

Other severe diseases for example peritonitis, toxaemia, tetanus or botulism. Almost invariably, the horse will have already been obviously ill the day before recumbency occurred.

This old horse was finding it increasingly difficult to rise due to arthritis in both hocks. Eventually it was found unable to rise (the muddy patch nearby shows it has been struggling) and was humanely destroyed

Heavy milk production in a lactating mare combined with stress (the mare and foal escaped into an adjacent field and were chased for a long time before being caught) can cause the blood calcium level to fall, resulting in muscle weakness and an inability to stand. After an intravenous calcium injection this mare rapidly recovered

What to do next

- Call the vet. He or she will examine the horse and may take blood samples if EHV infection is suspected.
- Prevent further injury by ensuring a deep soft bed.
- Under veterinary instruction gently try to persuade the horse to rise.
- Sometimes, if musculoskeletal pain is suspected, the vet may administer a pain-killing or anti-inflammatory injection, and the horse is persuaded to rise once it has taken effect.
- A specific diagnosis is essential if the prognosis for recovery is to be estimated.
- Horses that are recumbent and are making no attempts to rise, are not eating or drinking after more than 48 hours carry a poor prognosis.

COLLAPSING

Collapsing is unusual in horses, but when it happens it may be very dramatic and dangerous for the owner if they are nearby or riding the horse at the time. Possible causes of collapsing are:

- **Narcolepsy** (Excessive daytime sleep syndrome) The horse appears to drop off to sleep. The head and neck are lowered close to the ground, the fetlocks buckle and the horse crumples to its knees. Most wake up immediately and stand up. Some become recumbent for a few minutes, rarely up to 15–20 minutes. Attacks may be triggered by:
  - tacking up
  - grooming or plaiting
  - leading the horse out of the stable
  - stroking the head and neck
  - feeding (after the first few mouthfuls)
  - some may collapse while being ridden

Episodes may occur daily, or one every few months. The causes are unknown. It is postulated that many affected horses are *sleep-deprived* due to:
  - insecurity in a herd situation (fear of bullying, loss of a

herd mate the horse is bonded with) or a lone horse insecure in its environment,
  - disease in the spine or limbs making the horse reluctant to lie down, due to pain in lying down or getting up,
  - heavy pregnancy reducing the mare's ability to lie down,
  - uncomfortable stables, hard floors, insufficient bedding, lack of space.

Management changes or provision of painkilling drugs may resolve many of these problems. Horses that collapse when being ridden are unsafe to ride.

- **Syncope** An acute fall in blood pressure may cause a horse to faint. It can occur when the head is raised, the horse is receiving dental treatment or when the girth is being tightened.

The mechanism by which the phenomenon occurs is unknown but the effect is transient. The horse recovers immediately and there are no after-effects apart from abrasions to the limbs if the horse fell onto concrete.

- **Heart disease** Collapse may occur in certain cardiac disorders, especially those that interfere with the electric impulses controlling the heart. However, early fatigue when exercised is a more common sign. There is no treatment.

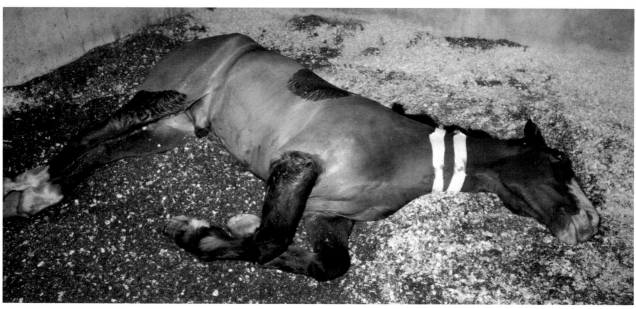

This botulism case was very weak

WEAKNESS

Weakness is a very general symptom and often occurs in the later stages of starvation, poisoning (especially lead poisoning), some debilitating diseases (especially those causing marked weight loss) and chronic grass sickness (p.94).

Botulism

A specific weakness syndrome seen in horses is botulism, which can effect any age of horse. The commonest cause is ingestion of the toxin of *Clostridium botulinum* in baled silage (usually of poor quality) or haylage about 10–14 days before the onset of signs.

Clinical signs

The toxin blocks transmission of nerve impulses to muscles causing a flaccid paralysis. Signs include:

- progressive loss of muscle strength, weakness, stumbling
- loss of strength in the tongue, slow mastication. The tongue hangs out and the horse drools saliva. If the tongue is pulled out of the mouth the horse is unable to return it to the mouth
- the horse plays with water and is unable to drink
- there is urinary and faecal incontinence
- eventually the horse becomes recumbent.

Treatment

The only treatment available is the injection of hyper-immune serum from vaccinated horses. This is difficult to obtain and also is very expensive. In addition general nursing care and nutritional support is essential. In adult horses if the onset of the disease is slow the prognosis for recovery is better, although complete recovery will take weeks to months. Where the disease progresses rapidly, the response to treatment is poorer. Many affected cases will die. A vaccine is used in some countries and is very effective.

TETANUS

Horses are especially susceptible to tetanus. The organism *Clostridium tetani* is widespread in the environment and is also found in horse faeces. Once in the body it produces a neurotoxin that interferes with nerve function causing muscle spasm.

The horse becomes infected via:

- wounds, especially puncture wounds to the foot and the coronet,
- surgical wounds, for example castration,
- the navel in newborn foals.

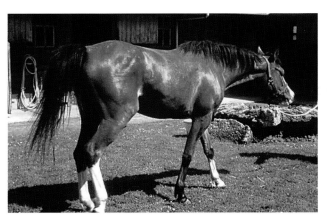

A classical tetanus case, with the tail held extended, the nostrils flared and a stiff gait

Clinical signs

The incubation period is seven days to a month. The signs of tetanus are:

- A sudden onset of a stiff gait leading to generalised muscles spasm.
- The horse walks with difficulty.
- The horse continues to eat but cannot chew properly.
- The head is extended, the nostrils are flared and the ears are erect.
- The limbs are placed in a 'sawhorse' stance.
- The third eyelid flicks across the eye when the face is tapped with a finger.
- The signs are worsened by any stimulation, for example a handclap.
- Severely affected horses become recumbent with the legs rigidly extended.

Treatment is intensive because recovery takes up to six weeks. The horse must be kept quiet in a darkened box with minimal stimulation. Continual sedation is necessary in the first few weeks. Adequate bedding is necessary in case the horse becomes recumbent. Antibiotics and tetanus anti-toxin are given to combat the infection. Long-term fluid and nutritional support are necessary.

Outcome If the horse can drink the prognosis is good. Horses that survive more than seven days have a fair chance of recovery. In recumbent cases the mortality rate is around 80 per cent.

Prevention Recovery from the disease does not confer protection. Vaccination is necessary. *Tetanus vaccination is essential for all horses* because the organism is widespread and horses are especially susceptible. The vaccine course comprises two injections at a 4–6 week interval, followed by booster vaccination every 2–3 years (depending on the vaccine).

USEFUL TECHNIQUES

Using a twitch

Using a twitch on the upper lip is a quick and often very effective way to briefly restrain a horse that objects to some potentially unpleasant event, for example mane pulling, clipping the head, injections or minor dental treatment.

Research has shown that the physiological effect of a twitch is very similar to acupuncture in that pain-relieving and calming beta-endorphins are released into the bloodstream. However, rising beta-endorphin levels may eventually cause a twitched horse to 'explode' by violently striking out with a foreleg or leaping forward, about 25–30 minutes after a twitch is applied (much earlier in some horses). An imminent explosion is signalled by heavy breathing, sweating and a rising heart rate. If these signs are seen the procedure should be finished immediately and the twitch removed. For this reason, sedation is often a better choice for painful or lengthy procedures – don't use a twitch when sedation would be better.

It is important that the twitch loop is the correct size. One and a half hands' breadth is about right

The twitch must be applied tightly

- Make the twitch from a soft rope or three strands of baling string plaited together. The twitch loop should be one and a half hands' breadth.
- Place the loop over your strongest hand, and firmly grasp as much as possible of the nose with the same hand. It is helpful if at the same time another person is applying downward pressure to the poll via the headcollar.
- Pass the twitch loop up the nose as far up as it will go.
- *Slowly* tighten the loop. Rapid tightening may cause a horse to snatch its head away.
- Often the horse will slightly open its mouth when the twitch is just tight enough.

Be safe

- Nobody should stand in front of a twitched horse.
- Carry out the necessary treatment or procedure as quickly as possible.
- Remove the twitch immediately if the horse shows signs of explosion.

Avoid these common mistakes

- A rope that is not thick enough, potentially causing damage to the horse.
- A loop that is too large, requiring too many turns of the handle before it tightens.
- A loop that is too small, making it difficult to slide it over the hand that is grasping the nose.
- Positioning the loop to low on the nose, or applying it too loosely, so that it falls off if the horse struggles.

Taking a horse's temperature

The normal rectal temperature is 38°C (100.4°F). It is not uncommon to find normal horses with temperatures as low as 37°C (98.6°F). A temperature up to 38.5°C (101.3°F) is possibly abnormal and needs to be re-taken a few hours later to check if it is rising. If the temperature is 39°C (102.2°F) or above it is definitely abnormal. Electronic thermometers are easiest to use because the digital display is easily read. With a mercury thermometer, shake it down so that the mercury column is below the marked scale before use.

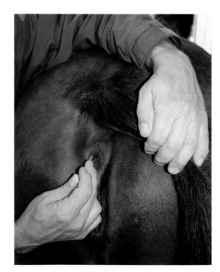

Keep the tail away from the hand holding the thermometer

- Stand the horse with its right side against a wall.
- Lubricate the thermometer with petroleum jelly.
- Lifting the tail with the left hand, introduce the thermometer into the rectum, angling it against the rectal wall, until your fingers are close to the anal opening. Keep the tail elevated until the temperature has been taken.
- Wait a *full* minute or until the digital thermometer bleeps, then remove it and read the temperature.

Taking a horse's pulse

The pulse may be elevated in pain (for example in horses with colic or severe lameness) and in infection. The normal pulse rate is 30–40 beats per minute. However, it is very volatile and a falsely elevated reading may be obtained if the horse is nervous, excited, hot, or recently exercised.

- Put your left hand on the horse's nose, and the fingertips of your right hand on the lower end of the horse's jawbone.
- Move the fingers along to feel the facial artery, which can be rolled under the fingertips.
- Resting your fingertips *lightly* on the artery, count the pulse for 15–20 seconds.
- Multiply the count to give the pulse rate per minute.

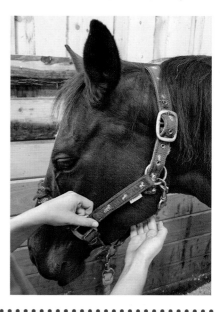

Taking the pulse from the facial artery

Administering paste medication

- **Make sure the horse has no food in its mouth**.
- Back it into a corner and stand on its right-hand side (assuming you are right-handed), with the medication in your right hand and facing the same way as the horse.
- Holding the noseband of headcollar with your left hand, introduce your left thumb into the corner of the mouth. This will usually cause the horse to open its mouth.
- Place the tube of paste into the horse's mouth, push it well back and expel the contents.
- Hold the horse's mouth closed for a few minutes.

If the horse resents administration:
- Add it to a large feed – so long as the horse's appetite is normal. Most pastes are quite palatable.
- Use a bridle. It will give more control and the bit will not interfere with the administration.
- Use a twitch.
- Use a special worming bit with perforated mouthpiece connected to a tube to which the worm paste syringe is attached.

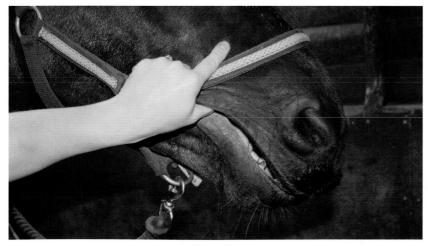

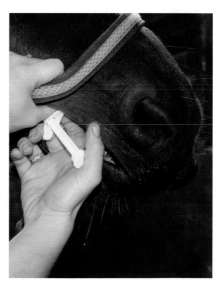

Above: Most horses will slightly open their mouths when a thumb is pushed into the corner.

Right: Push the paste as far into the mouth as possible

Giving in-feed medication

In-feed medication is designed to be eaten all at once. If the horse has a poor appetite or tends to eat very slowly then it may not be appropriate.

- **Prepare the feed**
  - Make the feed as palatable as possible. Mollassed coarse mixes and sugar beet pulp seem to be the best. Nuts are unsuitable.
  - Give a reasonably large amount to dilute the taste. Chaff can be used to add bulk.
  - Exercise great care where *competition horses* are being fed. Inadvertent use of an incorrect feed bowl might result in another horse taking in a small quantity of drug and subsequently failing a dope test.
- **Improve the flavour**
  - In-feed medication can sometimes by disguised by adding flavouring to the feed, for example molasses/treacle, apple juice or apple puree, carrot juice or grated carrot.
- **Make the drug easier to mix**
  - Crush tablets, for example, between two dessertspoons or in a coffee grinder.

If you are able to administer an injection, your vet will tell you where to inject

- **Dampen the feed first**
  - If the feed is dampened *before* adding the drug, much less will stick to the walls of the feed bowl when it is mixed.
  - Mix the feed with a spoon or stick, so that the drug does not get on your hands.
- **Supervise eating**
  - Make sure the feed bowl cannot be tipped over while eating. Sometimes it is better to hold the bowl while the horse eats.
  - Check that it has all been eaten.
- **Contact the vet if the horse refuses all or part of the feed**
  - Some drugs are available in an alternative paste form.
  - A home-made paste can be made by mixing the drug with some sticky viscous substance, for example seedless jam or an instant dessert product. The mixture is then given through a wide-mouthed syringe (available from vets).

Giving injections

Administering drugs by the *intravenous* route should only be done by vets and qualified veterinary nurses under veterinary supervision. Occasionally the vet will place an intravenous catheter in a horse's vein to allow drug administration by the owner or trainer. In these circumstances, the vet will provide the horse's carer with full training.

If a horse needs a course of *intramuscular* injections it may be possible for experienced owners

The food should be damped **before** adding the medication

to administer them. The vet will demonstrate the technique and show you where to inject.

- **Restrain the horse** It is essential that *another* person holds the horse, preferably alongside a wall so it cannot move away.
- **Fill the syringe** Good sterile technique is essential at all times. A new needle and preferably a new syringe are used each time.
  - The needle must never be touched or come into contact with anything other than the top of the bottle and the injection site
  - Shake the bottle *vigorously* and clean the top with a piece of cotton wool soaked with surgical spirit
  - With the needle attached to the syringe, invert the bottle and inject air (roughly equivalent to half the volume of liquid to be withdrawn) into the bottle
  - Withdraw the desired dose into the syringe. Expel any bubbles back into the bottle
- **Clean the injection site** Swab it with surgical spirit.
- **Give the injection**
  - Detach the needle from the syringe and hold it parallel to the skin. Firmly tap the injection site recommended by the vet with the heel of your hand a few times. Rotate your hand and firmly plunge the needle into the skin. The skin is thick and more force is required than you would expect
  - If blood emerges from the needle, remove the needle and use another site close-by
  - Attach the syringe to the need and suck back to check for blood. If blood is seen *do not inject* but use another site
  - Inject the drug reasonably quickly, making sure that the needle and syringe are tightly attached
  - Withdraw the needle and the syringe and immediately apply the needle cap

- Massage the injection site to promote dispersal of the injection in the muscle.

Needle-shy horses If a horse resents injections it is best to apply a twitch before you start.

Disposing of needles and syringes
Keep used syringes and needles in a safe place and give them to the vet for disposal at his or her next visit.

Tilting the bottle slightly aids expelling air from the syringe at the end

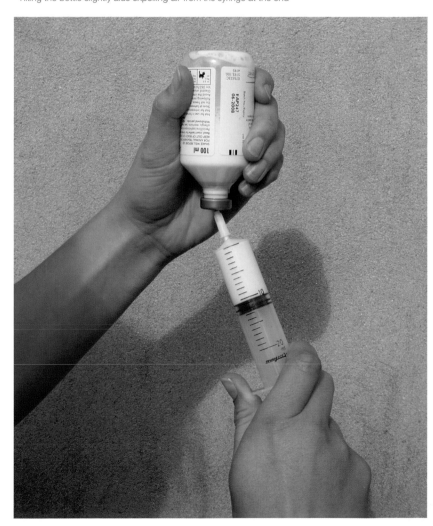

Further information

VETERINARY PRODUCTS

Some of the products mentioned in this book are available under a different name in the USA. NUE = No US equivalent.

UK	USA
Adequan	Adequan
Allevyn	Hydrasorb Foam Dressing
Aqueous cream	NUE, Baby oil can be used
Animalintex	Animalintex
Dettol	NUE
Elastoplast, E-Band	Elastikon
Frontline	Frontline
Gamgee	Combine Roll
Hibiscrub	Nolvasan Scrub
Keratex Mud Shield Powder	NUE, Sulfur powder can be used
K-Band, Knit firm	NUE
Melolin, Rondopad	Telfa pad
NuGel, IntraSite, Vetalintex	Curafil Gel
Pevidine	Betadine
Savlon	Nolvasan Solution
VetRap, EquiWrap	VetRap, EquiWrap

BIOGRAPHICAL NOTE

Kieran O'Brien is a senior clinician at a busy specialist equine veterinary practice, which brings him into daily contact with exactly the sort of horse owners at whom this book is aimed. He previously taught at Bristol University, and officiates at many international equestrian events for the International Equestrian Federation (FEI).

Acknowledgements

I am very grateful to my long-suffering clients who patiently and generously allowed me to take photographs of their horses, often at a stressful time. Veterinarians Tim Brazil, Rod Fisher, Richard Hill, Chris Johansson, and Jo Woodman read earlier drafts of sections of the text and made many helpful comments. I owe a particular debt to Gary Gray, our remedial farrier, who read several chapters and has frequently shared with me his huge knowledge of foot problems in horses. My colleagues at EqWest Equine Veterinary Clinic, Tavistock kindly allowed access to some case records. The persons named below kindly supplied some of the illustrations, often at very short notice.

PHOTOGRAPHIC CREDITS

All photographs by the author, except:

S. Barakzai, p.65 bottom left
J. Boswell, pp.40, 41 (x-rays)
K.Chandler, pp.149 bottom, 150
Prof P. Clegg, p.116 (illustration, adapted)
Prof P. Dixon, p.87 (x-rays)
Dr C. Hahn, p.149 top
Dr M. Hillyer, pp.144 top left, 145 bottom, 146 bottom left, 152

Intervet, p.74
J.G. Lane, pp.70 right top and bottom, 81 right, 82 both
Dr A.G. Matthews, p.146 bottom
A. Nelson, p.17 left
Dr F. Taylor, p.153
Vet Cell Ltd., p.50
The late A.I. Wright, pp.99 left top and bottom, 124 right, 125 centre

Index